A PRACTITIONER'S GUIDE TO THE FSA REGULATION OF DESIGNATED INVESTMENT BUSINESS

A PRACTITIONER'S GUIDE TO THE FSA REGULATION OF DESIGNATED INVESTMENT BUSINESS

Consultant Editor
Tim Cornick
Macfarlanes

Third Edition

City & Financial Publishing

City & Financial Publishing
8 Westminster Court, Hipley Street
Old Woking
Surrey GU22 9LG
United Kingdom
Tel: 00 44 (0)1483 720707 Fax: 00 44 (0)1483 727928
Web: www.cityandfinancial.com

This book has been compiled from the contributions of the named authors. The views expressed herein do not necessarily reflect the views of their respective firms. Further, since this book is intended as a general guide only, its application to specific situations will depend upon the particular circumstances involved and it should not be relied upon as a substitute for obtaining appropriate professional advice.

The law is stated as at 1 December 2007. Whilst all reasonable care has been taken in the preparation of this book, City & Financial Publishing and the authors do not accept responsibility for any errors it may contain or for any loss sustained by any person placing reliance on its contents.

ISBN 978 1905 121 267
© 2008 City & Financial Publishing and the named authors.

British Library Cataloguing-in-Publication Data. A catalogue record for this book is available from the British Library.

Typeset by Cambrian Typesetting, Camberley and printed and bound in Great Britain by Biddles Limited, King's Lynn.

Biographies

Tim Cornick joined Macfarlanes as a partner in 1995 having been a partner at another City law firm since 1988.

Since 1983 he has had substantial involvement in legal matters on behalf of investment funds, investment managers, custodians and trustees. Those areas, plus financial services regulatory/compliance matters and related securities work form the bulk of his practice, with a strong emphasis on investment management and collective investment schemes in the UK and offshore.

He is a partner in Macfarlanes' Investment Funds and Financial Services Group which deals with all legal aspects of investment management including a wide variety of open and closed-ended investment vehicles, in the UK and elsewhere, together with the full range of financial services-related work.

He is a regular conference speaker and article writer, lead editor of *Collective Investment Schemes Law & Practice* (Sweet & Maxwell), Consultant Editor of *The International Guide to Marketing Investment Funds* (Finance & Investment Research), and of *A Practitioner's Guide to FSA Regulation of Designated Investment Business* (City & Financial). He also serves on the Law Society's sub-committee on collective investment schemes and on the Legal Advisory Group of the Investment Management Association.

Michael Wainwright is a partner at Eversheds specialising in retail financial services law. He advises on the development of new financial products, joint ventures and marketing agency appointments, life assurance and unit trust fund mergers and company acquisitions and disposals. His recent work includes advising Cofunds on its strategic relationship with Legal & General; MetLife on the establishment of a new life assurance business in the UK; and Paternoster on the launch of a new insurance company to insure the liabilities of occupational pension schemes. He is a regular speaker at industry conferences and in-house seminars.

David Bickley is an assistant in the Financial Services Group at Eversheds. He joined Eversheds in 2006 and specialises in financial services law, advising a wide variety of clients on regulatory and perimeter issues. He has been closely involved in Eversheds' work assisting clients to prepare their systems and documentation for the implementation of the Markets in Financial Instruments Directive.

Daniel Tunkel is a partner in the Financial Markets Group of SJ Berwin LLP. Daniel specialises in financial services transactions with a particular focus on investment fund formation and promotion. Daniel has published a number of articles in the legal and industry press and is a regular speaker at conferences dealing with both of these areas as well as other aspects of financial services regulation.

Daniel's recent experience includes the formation and promotion of a variety of venture capital, private equity and real estate vehicles; advising on the promotion of investment funds to institutional and retail investors, both in the UK and worldwide; and assisting a number of overseas (principally US) investment firms to establish their UK and European operations.

Arun Srivastava is a partner in Baker & McKenzie's Financial Services Group. He spent a year on secondment to the FSA between April 1999 and April 2000. He advises regulated firms and other parties on a broad range of financial services regulatory issues, money laundering requirements and regulatory enforcement matters.

Sandra Zivcic is an associate in Baker & McKenzie's Financial Services Group. Prior to joining Baker & McKenzie, Sandra was a senior associate in the Financial Services Group of Mallesons Stephen Jaques in Australia specialising in financial services regulation. Before joining Mallesons, Sandra worked for ASIC, Australia's financial services regulator, and was deeply involved in the preparations for Australia's reform of its financial services and markets regulatory system.

James Perry is a partner and co-head of the Financial Institutions Group at Ashurst in London. James specialises in corporate transactional and regulatory matters particularly within the financial services sector.

James has advised financial institutions including Skandia, Royal & Sun Alliance, Credit Agricole, Société Générale and others on commercial transactions, and regularly advises on insurance regulation. He has also been involved in much of the firm's outsourcing work for financial institutions. James edited the firm's book entitled *The Financial Services and Markets Act: A Practical Legal Guide.*

Glynn Barwick is a counsel in the corporate department at Ashurst in London. He has wide experience advising clients on a range of non-contentious regulatory matters under the Financial Services and Markets Act 2000 and the Financial Services Authority's Rules, including investment managers, investment banks, brokers and insurance companies. Glynn also advises on custody, market abuse and money laundering issues. He was previously a member of the Legal Unit of the Bank of England.

Dick Frase is a partner in Dechert LLP's Financial Services Group. He has extensive experience of the legal and regulatory aspects of the UK financial services industry, both in-house and in private practice. He qualified in 1981 with Allen & Overy, and was a partner at Denton Hall, now Denton Wilde Sapte, from 1988 to 1992. During this period he was seconded to the Securities and Futures Authority, where he advised on policy and legal matters, and carried out extensive work on the redesign of the SFA conduct of business rules. In the mid-90s he worked for MeesPierson, now Fortis Bank, and sat as an arbitrator with the London Metal Exchange and Securities and Futures Authority. From 1995–1998 he was head of litigation at the Personal Investment Authority, which subsequently merged to form the Financial Services Authority. He left the Financial Services Authority to join Dechert in 1998.

Kirstene Baillie is a partner at Field Fisher Waterhouse and a financial services specialist. The focus of her practice is advising financial services institutions on a wide range of retail and institutional investment funds, insurance and pension products – and related financial services regulatory issues.

Kirstene leads a top three funds practice, as recorded in the UK Funds Industry Review and Directory. She is best known for her advice on UK authorised funds, and she advised the FSA on the structure and governance of UK authorised funds prior to the FSA preparing its New Collective Investment Schemes Sourcebook.

Her practice has evolved with the globalisation of the fund management businesses, to cover a wide range of international funds and products, including alternative investment funds and property funds. Also she advises a wide range of clients on UK financial services regulation, including FSMA perimeter issues, insurance and pension products, conduct of business issues and the impact of the implementation of EU Directives.

Kirstene is vice chair of the Investment Funds Committee of the International Bar Association, and participates in the Financial Services Section of the Association's LPD Council.

Contents

Biographies   **v**

1 The Principal Provisions   **1**
Tim Cornick
Partner
Macfarlanes

1.1   Introduction   1
1.2   FSMA Part II – Regulated and prohibited activities   1
1.3   FSMA 2000 Part IV – Permission to carry on
      regulated activities   8

2 Specified Investments   **17**
Michael Wainwright
Partner
David Bickley
Assistant Solicitor
Eversheds LLP

2.1   Overview   17
2.2   Deposits   19
2.3   Electronic money   22
2.4   Insurance   22
2.5   Transferable securities   23
2.6   Collective investments   26
2.7   Rights under Pension Schemes   31
2.8   Derivative instruments   32
2.9   Lloyd's underwriting interests   34
2.10   Funeral plan contracts   34
2.11   Residential mortgages, equity release and Islamic
       finance   35
2.12   Rights to or interests in investments   38
2.13   Overlap between different types of specified
       investments   38

3 Regulated Activities **41**

Michael Wainwright
Partner
David Bickley
Assistant Solicitor
Eversheds LLP

3.1	Introduction	41
3.2	Accepting deposits (Article 5)	42
3.3	Issuing electronic money (Article 9B)	43
3.4	Providing insurance (Article 10)	44
3.5	Dealing as principal (Article 14)	45
3.6	Dealing as agent (Article 21)	48
3.7	Arranging deals in investments (Article 25)	49
3.8	Arranging mortgages (Article 25A)	52
3.9	Arranging regulated home reversion plans (Article 25B)	54
3.10	Arranging regulated home purchase plans (Article 25C)	55
3.11	Operating a multilateral trading facility (Article 25D)	55
3.12	Advising on investments (Article 53)	56
3.13	Advising on mortgages (Article 53A)	57
3.14	Advising on regulated home reversion plans (Article 53B)	58
3.15	Advising on regulated home purchase plans (Article 53C)	58
3.16	Providing basic advice on stakeholder products (Article 52B)	59
3.17	Managing investments (Article 37)	60
3.18	Administration of insurance (Article 39A)	60
3.19	Custody services (Article 40)	61
3.20	Sending dematerialised instructions (Article 45)	63
3.21	Providing collective investments (Article 51)	64
3.22	Providing a pension scheme (Article 52)	65
3.23	Lloyd's (Articles 56–58)	65
3.24	Funeral plans (Article 59)	66
3.25	Regulated mortgage contracts (Article 61)	66
3.26	Regulated home reversion plans (Article 63B)	67
3.27	Regulated home purchase plans (Article 63F)	68
3.28	Agreeing to carry on regulated activities (Article 64)	68
3.29	General exclusions	69
3.30	Certain exclusions not available to MiFID and IMD firms	81
3.31	Designated investment business	82

4 Further Orders   85
Daniel Tunkel
Partner
Financial Services Group
SJ Berwin LLP

4.1   Introduction   85
4.2   The Financial Services and Markets Act 2000
        (Professions) (Non-Exempt Activities) Order 2001
        (the "Professions Order")   86
4.3   Financial Services and Markets Act 2000 (Carrying
        on Regulated Activities by Way of Business) Order
        2000 (the "Business Order")   102
4.4   The Financial Services and Markets Act 2000
        (Appointed Representatives) Regulations 2001 (the
        "AR Regulations")   111

**5 Scope and General Application of Conduct of Business
Rules**   117
Arun Srivastava
Partner
Sandra Zivcic
Associate
Baker & McKenzie LLP

5.1   Introduction   117
5.2   COBS Chapter 1 – application and general provisions   121
5.3   COBS Chapter 2 – conduct of business obligations   136
5.4   Conclusion   149

6 Getting New Customers   151
Arun Srivastava
Partner
Baker & McKenzie LLP

6.1   Introduction   151
6.2   Prior history and MiFID implementation   153
6.3   COBS   156
6.4   Retail clients   159
6.5   Professional client   159
6.6   Eligible counterparty   164
6.7   Policies, procedures and records   167

6.8	Transitional provisions	169
6.9	Consequences of client categorisation	170
6.10	Regulatory protections – eligible counterparties	170
6.11	Consequences of incorrect categorisation	171
6.12	Conclusion	173

7   Servicing Clients   **175**
James Perry
Partner
Glynn Barwick
Counsel
Ashurst LLP

7.1	Introduction	175
7.2	Dealing with clients	176
7.3	Information for clients	192

8   The Client Asset Regime   **201**
Dick Frase
Partner
Dechert LLP

8.1	Overview	201
8.2	The non-MiFID rules – introduction	203
8.3	The non-MiFID custody rules	204
8.4	Collateral	217
8.5	The non-MiFID client money regime	220
8.6	The MiFID custody rules	236
8.7	The MiFID client money rules	245
8.8	Records, accounts, reconciliations and defaults	251
8.9	Distribution of client money on a default	252
8.10	The mandate rules	252

9   Specialist Regimes   **255**
Kirstene Baillie
Partner
Head of Financial Services and Funds Group
Field Fisher Waterhouse LLP

9.1	Introduction	255
9.2	Why is there a special regime for collective investment schemes and trusts?	256
9.3	What is a collective investment scheme?	257

9.4	What are the different types of schemes?	259
9.5	Who operates a collective investment scheme?	262
9.6	What is "scheme management activity"?	263
9.7	What modifications apply to the COBS rules for operators?	264
9.8	Are there any additional rules for unregulated schemes?	267
9.9	If unregulated schemes are not subject to the COLL Sourcebook, what provisions govern them and what information is to be given about these?	267
9.10	What is a depositary?	271
9.11	What modifications apply to trustee firms who are depositaries?	272
9.12	What are trustee firms?	273
9.13	What special rules apply to trustee firms that are not depositaries?	274
9.14	When must a trustee firm obtain proper advice?	276
9.15	What regulation applies to an occupational pension scheme firm?	277
9.16	How is corporate finance business regulated?	279
9.17	What COBS rules apply for corporate finance business which is MiFID business?	280
9.18	What COBS rules apply for corporate finance business which is non-MiFID business?	281
9.19	What is energy market activity and oil market activity?	282
9.20	What rules apply for corporate energy market activity and all market activity which is non-MiFID business?	283
9.21	What rules apply to energy market activity and oil market activity which is MiFID business?	284
9.22	Are there any special provisions for stock lending?	285
Index		**287**

Chapter 1

The Principal Provisions

Tim Cornick

Partner
Macfarlanes

1.1 Introduction

This Guide outlines the regulatory structure established by the Financial Services and Markets Act 2000 ("FSMA 2000") as it affects firms carrying on "regulated activity". Broadly, this Guide covers all of those areas which constituted "investment business" under the Financial Services Act 1986 ("FS Act 1986"). It does not examine in detail the FSMA 2000 regime as it relates to deposit taking, insurance business, mortgage lending and administration, or Lloyd's, nor is it particularly concerned with corporate finance activities. Similarly, there is not space here for a detailed examination of the regime for financial promotion, although the outlines are traced in this Chapter and Chapter 6 of this Guide. These matters are covered by other Guides in this series.

The FSMA 2000 came fully into force on 30 November 2001. It is a substantial piece of legislation but it is nevertheless supplemented by a very large amount of delegated legislation and by the Financial Services Authority's ("FSA's") Handbook.

With effect from 1 November 2007 the Handbook was amended in order to implement the Markets in Financial Instruments Directive ("MiFID"). This Guide reflects those amendments.

1.2 FSMA Part II – Regulated and prohibited activities

1.2.1 Section 19 – The general prohibition

This lies at the heart of the regulatory regime and much of the material in the FSMA 2000, the delegated legislation, and the Handbook flows from it, directly or indirectly.

1

"No person may carry on regulated activity in the United Kingdom, or purport to do so, unless he is – (a) an authorised person; or (b) an exempt person."

The approach is, of course, to ensure that any person carrying on activities that relate to investments should be under an obligation to do so in accordance with the detailed rules and regulations which make up the bulk of the new regime. It is those detailed rules which together are designed to achieve the FSA's statutory regulatory objectives of market confidence, public awareness, the protection of consumers, and the reduction of financial crime.

An "authorised person" is a person who is authorised for the purposes of the FSMA 2000 (Section 31(2)). In the vast majority of cases authorisation is embodied in a permission granted to the person in question under Part IV of the FSMA 2000. The obtaining of a "Part IV permission" is discussed below.

An "exempt person" is entitled to carry on regulated activity without a Part IV permission. The main place to look for exemptions is in the Financial Services and Markets Act 2000 (Exemption) Order 2001 (SI 2001/1201) (the "Exemption Order") made under Section 38. Contravention of the general prohibition is a criminal offence punishable with imprisonment for up to two years, or a fine, or both (Section 23). Falsely claiming to be authorised or exempt is also a criminal offence (Section 24).

1.2.2   Section 20 – Requirement for permission

Clearly, not all firms will carry on the same kind of regulated activity and it is not the policy of the FSMA 2000 to give blanket authorisation to all firms to carry on all activities. Instead the firm may only carry on the activities specified in its Part IV permission. This circumscribes what a firm can do and also triggers the application of the relevant parts of the Conduct of Business Sourcebook ("COBS") which will then govern the day-to-day activities in the firm.

A firm which carries on regulated activity outside its Part IV permission does not commit a criminal offence but may incur regulatory sanctions and/or civil liability.

1.2.3 Section 22 – Regulated activities

The terms of Sections 19 and 20 obviously beg the question, what is "regulated activity"? Section 22 addresses this although the detail lies elsewhere. Note that activity is not "regulated activity" unless it is "carried on by way of business". That test is sufficiently important that an Order has been made under Section 419 FSMA 2000 setting out circumstances in which a person is or is not to be regarded as carrying on a regulated activity by way of business. This is examined in Chapter 4 of this Guide.

Section 22(2) gives effect to Schedule 2 to the FSMA 2000 which outlines the sort of activities which may constitute regulated activity but it is illustrative only because the definitive statement of what constitutes regulated activity lies in the Financial Services and Markets Act 2000 (Regulated Activities) Order 2001 (SI 2001/544) made under Section 22. This is examined in greater detail in Chapters 2 and 3 of this Guide.

1.2.4 Section 21 – Financial promotion

With a view to protecting consumers from securities fraud, the law has for many years imposed controls on how investments may be offered to the public. The principal source of rules on this subject is now Section 21 FSMA 2000 and the regime for "Financial Promotion".

The full picture is provided by Section 21 itself and by Section 397 which deals with misleading statements and practices, plus the Financial Services and Markets Act 2000 (Financial Promotion) Order 2005 (SI 2005/1529) (the "Financial Promotion Order") made under Section 21 and Chapter 4 of the COBS.

Section 21 is in essence a prohibition on promotional activity:

> "A person must not, in the course of business, communicate an invitation or inducement to engage in investment activity."

The term "communicate" is deliberately wide as it was a policy objective to make the FSMA 2000 "media neutral".

Subsection 21(8) defines "engaging in investment activity" as entering or offering to enter into an agreement the making or performance of which by either party constitutes a controlled activity or exercising any rights conferred by controlled investment to acquire, dispose of, underwrite or convert a controlled investment. Subsections (9) and (10) expand on "controlled activity" and "controlled investment".

Note that a communication that originates outside the UK will be caught by the regime if it is capable of having an effect in the UK.

Contravention of Section 21 is a criminal offence and agreements entered into as a result of a breach of the Section are unenforceable. A third party will be entitled to recover any money or property transferred, as well as compensation for any loss suffered.

The most important exemption is in Section 21(2) which disapplies the prohibition if the person communicating the financial promotion is an authorised person or if the content of the communication is approved by an authorised person. It follows that it is a defence for a person facing a charge under Section 21 to show that he believed on reasonable grounds that the content of the communication was prepared or approved by an authorised person, or that the accused person took all reasonable precautions and exercised all due diligence to avoid committing the offence.

The FSMA 2000 regime abolishes the distinction between investment advertising and cold calling, but it brings in a new distinction between "real time" communication and "non-real time" communication. This is set out in the Financial Promotion Order (*see* 1.2.5 below), but in brief:

(a)   a real time communication means one made in the course of a personal visit, telephone conversation or other interactive dialogue;
(b)   a non-real time communication means everything else and so includes letters, e-mails and communications in any form of publication, including on a website.

Within real time communications, the new regime also distinguishes "solicited" and "unsolicited".

A solicited communication is one which is initiated by the recipient or takes place in response to an express request from the recipient. Everything else is unsolicited. The importance of the distinction is that not all of the exemptions set out in the Financial Promotion Order apply to all kinds of communications.

The new regime also introduces the concept of "indications". These are "health warnings" and certain exemptions will not be available unless the person communicating the financial promotion includes the prescribed indications.

1.2.5 *The Financial Promotion Order*

The Financial Promotion Order sets out exemptions from the basic prohibition on financial promotions which appears in Section 21. Importantly, the exemptions are available to both authorised and unauthorised persons.

Significantly, in the normal course an authorised person must comply with the requirements of Chapter 4 of COBS when communicating a financial promotion. These include contents requirements and record-keeping obligations. Where an authorised person communicates a financial promotion which is exempt within the Financial Promotion Order, however, the requirements of COBS are largely disapplied apart from general principles such as the requirement that communications must be clear, fair and not misleading.

In addition, "indications" must be given with an adequate "degree of prominence" which means that they must be portrayed in a way that can be easily understood and in a manner which is best calculated to bring the matter in question to the attention of the recipient. This implies an end to the common practice of putting risk warnings etc. in the small print at the foot of an advertisement.

The Financial Promotion Order provides a number of exemptions available in relation to all controlled activities, then further exemptions which are available only to specific kinds of activity. The generally available exemptions apply to:

(a)   certain communications to overseas recipients;
(b)   communications from customers and potential customers;

(c) certain activities by way of follow up to solicited real time communications;

(d) certain introductions;

(e) communications by exempt persons;

(f) generic promotions which do not identify the party offering the investment or the service;

(g) communications caused to be made or directed by unauthorised persons;

(h) communications by parties which act as "mere conduits" where the content of the communications is devised by another person, and the communicator has no material input, including electronic commerce communications;

(i) communications to investment professionals (authorised persons, exempt persons and other persons whose ordinary activities involve them carrying on controlled activities to which the communication relates); and

(j) communications by journalists.

Part VI of the Order then provides a host of further exemptions in relation to certain controlled activities. These include:

- one-off communications fulfilling certain conditions;
- a number of exemptions for overseas communicators;
- communications by governments and central banks;
- communications by industrial and provident societies;
- communications by nationals of European Economic Area ("EEA") states;
- communications by certain financial markets;
- certain communications among participants in a joint enterprise;
- certain communications among participants in recognised collective investment schemes;
- certain communications in relation to bearer instruments;
- certain communications to and among members and creditors of bodies corporate and open-ended investment companies;
- communications among bodies corporate in the same group;
- certain offers of credit to companies;
- communications by persons whose business it is to place promotional material or to disseminate information;
- certain communications to certified high net worth individuals, high net worth companies or other bodies;

- sophisticated investors or associations of high net worth or sophisticated investors;
- communications to a "common interest group" of a company;
- communications among settlors, trustees and personal representatives or between beneficiaries under a trust, will or intestacy;
- certain communications by members of professions;
- communications in relation to certain employee share schemes;
- communications made for the purposes of or in connection with a sale of goods or a supply of services; or
- in relation to transactions under which 50 per cent or more of the voting capital of the body corporate will change hands;
- various communications in relation to the takeover of certain unlisted companies; and
- certain communications relating to the listing of shares on stock markets.

The exemptions are detailed and many of them have very precise conditions attaching to them.

1.2.6 Conduct of Business Sourcebook

Chapter 4 of the COBS imposes further obligations on regulated firms when issuing financial promotions. The main purpose is to drive home the general obligation to treat customers fairly and to communicate in a way which is fair, clear and not misleading. COBS not only applies to communications directed into the UK, but also in a number of cases to communications made by UK authorised persons to persons outside the UK (the EEA territorial scope rule).

Significantly, Chapter 4 is disapplied in relation to financial promotions only to eligible counterparties.

Where Chapter 4 does apply it imposes obligations on firms to ensure that a financial promotion is clearly identifiable as such and that a firm communicating or approving a financial promotion has systems and controls in place to comply with the rules in Chapter 4. This systems and controls requirement is set out in Chapters 3 and 4 of the Senior Management Arrangements, Systems and Controls Sourcebook ("SYSC").

COBS Chapter 4 goes on to set down the record-keeping requirements and rules on the form and content of promotions.

1.3 FSMA 2000 Part IV – Permission to carry on regulated activities

1.3.1 Applications under Part IV

Section 40 FSMA 2000 states that an application to carry on one or more regulated activities may be made to the FSA by:

(a) an individual;
(b) a body corporate;
(c) a partnership; or
(d) an unincorporated association.

A permission granted by the FSA to an application made under Section 40 is referred to as a "Part IV permission".

In certain circumstances, an application for permission under Section 40 is not appropriate. For example, a firm which has already obtained a Part IV permission would not make a further application under Section 40 if it wished to conduct an additional regulated activity but would need to vary its existing permission in accordance with Section 44 FSMA 2000.

In addition, an EEA firm which is able to use its passporting rights under MiFID or the Second Banking Coordination Directive would not make an application for permission under Section 40 in order to establish a branch in the UK or provide services in the UK but would need to follow the procedures applicable under those Directives.

1.3.2 The application procedure

The formal procedures for applying for Part IV permission are described in the FSA's Guidance on its website under the heading "Doing Business with the FSA". Applicants are able to "build their own" application pack appropriate for their type of firm. The application pack will generally contain the following documents:

(a) Checklist and declaration: this contains a declaration checklist referring to the contents of the entire application pack. Before signing, the applicant must have completed the checklist for the application pack and read the declaration;

(b) Core Details: this form identifies core information about the applicant such as the date of incorporation, legal status and group structure. The form also identifies the proposed regulated activities, specified investments and the category of client;

(c) Form A: details of all persons performing a controlled function (such as directors, investment managers or advisers).

After receiving the application pack, the FSA will begin its formal process of consideration. At an early stage, the FSA will determine whether an application is complex or non-complex. If the application is complex, the FSA is likely to request additional information and meet the applicant's management team and visit its premises before determining the application. If the application is non-complex, it is possible that a visit to the premises will not be necessary. The FSA stresses that the application process is "interactive" and that applicants are encouraged to discuss an application with the FSA's corporate authorisation department about their plans and applications. Where an application is complex, applicants are encouraged to meet with the FSA prior to submitting an application.

1.3.3 The Threshold Conditions

Section 41(2) states that, in giving or varying permission, or imposing or varying any requirement, the FSA must ensure that the person concerned will "satisfy, and continue to satisfy, the Threshold Conditions in relation to all of the regulated activities for which he has or will have permission".

The Threshold Conditions are set out in Schedule 6 to the FSMA 2000. In addition, the FSA has set out guidance on the Threshold Conditions in the Threshold Conditions Sourcebook contained in the High Level Standards section of the FSA Handbook. When assessing an application for authorisation, the FSA will assess that application against the Threshold Conditions.

The following paragraphs set out the various Threshold Conditions.

1.3.3.1 Legal status

(a) If the regulated activity concerned is the effecting or carrying out of contracts of insurance, the authorised person must be a body corporate, a registered friendly society or a member of Lloyd's.

(b) If the person concerned appears to the FSA to be seeking to carry on, or to be carrying on, a regulated activity constituting accepting deposits, it must be:

(i)   a body corporate; or
(ii)   a partnership.

This Threshold Condition further restricts the requirements on legal status set out in Section 40(1) in relation to effecting and carrying out contracts of insurance and accepting deposits. These restrictions are as a result of the provisions of the Banking Consolidation Directive and the First Non-Life Directive.

1.3.3.2 Location of offices

(a) If the person concerned is a body corporate constituted under the law of any part of the UK:

(i)   its head office; and
(ii)   if it has a registered office, that office,

must be in the UK.

(b) If the person concerned has its head office in the UK but is not a body corporate, it must carry on business in the UK.

This condition implements the requirements of Article 6 of the Post BCCI Directive and extends this condition to firms which are outside the scope of the Single Market Directive and the UCITS Directive.

"Head office" is not defined, although the FSA has stated that the key issue in identifying the head office of a firm is the location of its central management and control, that is, the location of the directors and other senior management, who make decisions relating to the firm's central direction, and the material management decisions of the firm on a day-to-day basis and the location of the central administrative functions of the firm.

1.3.3.3   *Close links*

(a)   If the person concerned ("A") has close links with another person ("CL") the FSA must be satisfied:

    (i)   that those links are not likely to prevent the FSA's effective supervision of A; and

    (ii)   if it appears to the FSA that CL is subject to the laws, regulations or administrative provisions of a territory which is not an EEA state ("the foreign provisions"), that neither the foreign provisions, nor any deficiency in their enforcement, would prevent the Authority's effective supervision of A.

(b)   A has close links with CL if:

    (i)   CL is a parent undertaking of A;

    (ii)   CL is a subsidiary undertaking of A;

    (iii) CL is a parent undertaking of a subsidiary undertaking of A;

    (iv) CL is a subsidiary undertaking of a parent undertaking of A;

    (v)   CL owns or controls 20 per cent or more of the voting rights or capital of A; or

    (vi) A owns or controls 20 per cent or more of the voting rights or capital of CL.

(c)   "Subsidiary undertaking" includes all of the instances mentioned in Article 1(1) and (2) of the Seventh Company Law Directive in which an entity may be a subsidiary of an undertaking.

In summary, Threshold Condition 3 requires that the FSA is satisfied that the close links that a firm has will not prevent effective supervision. The factors which the FSA will take into account include, among other things, the following:

(a)   it is likely that the FSA will receive adequate information from the firm, and those persons with whom the firm has close links, to enable it to determine whether the firm is complying with the requirements and standards under the regulatory system; this will include confirmation of whether the firm is ready, willing and organised to comply with FSA Principle 11 which relates to dealing with the regulator in an open and cooperative way;

(b) the structure and geographical spread of the firm, the group to which it belongs and other persons with whom the firm has close links, might hinder the provision of adequate and reliable flows of information to the FSA; factors which may hinder these flows include the fact that there may be branches or connected companies in territories which supervise companies to a different standard or territories with laws which restrict the free flow of information, although the FSA will consider the "totality of information available from all sources";

(c) the firm and the group to which it belongs are, or will be, subject to supervision on a consolidated basis (consolidated supervision) (e.g., if a financial resources requirement is determined for the group as a whole); and

(d) it is possible to assess with confidence the overall financial position of the group at any particular time; factors which may make this difficult include lack of audited consolidated accounts for a group, if companies in the same group as the firm have different financial years and accounting dates and if they do not share common auditors.

1.3.3.4 *Adequate resources*

The resources of the person concerned must, in the opinion of the FSA, be adequate in relation to the regulated activities that he seeks to carry on, or carries on.

In reaching that opinion, the Authority may:

(a) Take into account the person's membership of a group and any effect which that membership may have.

(b) Have regard to:

   (i) the provision he makes and, if he is a member of a group, which other members of the group make in respect of liabilities (including contingent and future liabilities); and

   (ii) the means by which he manages and, if he is a member of a group, which other members of the group manage the incidence of risk in connection with his business.

Threshold Condition 4 requires the FSA to ensure that a firm has adequate resources in relation to the specific regulated activity or activities which it seeks to carry on. The FSA interprets the term "adequate" as meaning "sufficient in terms of quantity, quality and availability" and "resources" as including "all financial resources, non-financial resources and means of managing its resources" such as capital, provisions against liabilities, holdings of or access to cash and other liquid assets, human resources and effective means by which to manage risks.

The FSA has set out its requirements with regard to systems and controls in the High Level section of the Handbook in the Senior Management Arrangements, Systems and Controls Sourcebook ("SYSC"). Detailed financial resources and systems requirements are set out in the relevant section of the General Prudential Sourcebook or Prudential Sourcebook for Banks, Building Societies and Investment Firms.

1.3.3.5 *Suitability*

The person concerned must satisfy the FSA that he is a fit and proper person having regard to all the circumstances, including:

(a)   his connection with any person;
(b)   the nature of any regulated activity that he carries on or seeks to carry on; and
(c)   the need to ensure that his affairs are conducted soundly and prudently.

Threshold Condition 5 requires the firm to satisfy the FSA that it is "fit and proper" to have Part IV permission having regard to all the circumstances, including its connections with other persons, the range and nature of its proposed regulated activities and the overall need to be satisfied that its affairs are and will be conducted soundly and prudently.

The particular factors which the FSA will take into account include, but are not limited to, whether a firm:

(a)   conducts, or will conduct, its business with integrity and in compliance with proper standards;
(b)   has, or will have, a competent and prudent management; and
(c)   can demonstrate that it conducts, or will conduct, its affairs with the exercise of due skill, care and diligence.

13

1.3.4 Limitations and requirements

Section 42 FSMA 2000 states that the Authority may give permission for the applicant to carry on the regulated activity or activities to which this application relates. The FSA may incorporate in the description of a regulated activity which a firm is permitted to conduct such limitations (e.g., as to circumstances in which the activity may, or may not, be carried on) as it considers appropriate. A limitation is specific to a particular regulated activity (either to the specified activity, the specified investment or both). A limitation may be applied for by the applicant or, alternatively, imposed by the FSA. Examples of limitations include the following:

(a)   a limit on the types of client that a firm may deal with; or

(b)   a limit on the number of clients with whom a firm may carry on a particular regulated activity during, for example, an initial period of operation (perhaps because a firm's system is not yet adequate to be able to process a high volume of transactions); or

(c)   a limit on the types of specified investments that a firm can deal in; or

(d)   a limit on the type of insurance business which a firm may carry on in connection with certain categories of specified investments; or

(e)   in relation to the carrying on of designated investment business, carrying on such business in respect of certain customer classifications (e.g., only carrying on designated investment business in respect of intermediate customers and market counterparties but not private customers).

Section 43 states that a Part IV permission may include such "requirements" as the FSA considers appropriate. The requirements may be imposed on a firm to:

(a)   take a particular action; or

(b)   refrain from taking a particular action.

The FSA states that a requirement will either be unrelated to the performance of regulated activities (e.g., a requirement that relates to reporting) or will relate to all, or a number of, the regulated activities which an applicant wishes to carry on. This can be contrasted with a limitation, which is specific to one particular regulated activity.

Perhaps the most common requirement is one stating that the firm is not to hold or control client money. A requirement is also used by the FSA to define the scope of a number of regulated activities carried on by a firm so that a particular differentiated regulatory regime applies. For example, a different regulatory regime applies for locals, venture capital firms, corporate finance advisory firms and service companies. Consequently, an applicant may wish to apply for Part IV permission which includes a requirement defining the scope of each regulated activity so that it is able to benefit from this differentiated regime.

Examples of requirements which the FSA may impose in particular circumstances include the following:

(a) a requirement that a firm given Part IV permission obtains the approval of the FSA before payment of a dividend (in accordance with powers contained in Section 48 FSMA 2000); or

(b) a requirement to submit financial returns more often than normal, for example, during the firm's first months or years of business; or

(c) a requirement to submit audited financial accounts of a parent company; or

(d) a requirement, on the permission of an insurer, to carry on only reinsurance business; or

(e) a requirement to submit periodic independent compliance reviews, performed by an appropriate person, during the first months or years of business.

Chapter 2

Specified Investments

Michael Wainwright
Partner

David Bickley
Assistant Solicitor
Eversheds LLP

2.1 Overview

The Financial Services and Markets Act 2000 ("FSMA 2000") regulates the provision of financial services within and from the UK. For this purpose it defines the activities that are to be regulated and establishes a licensing regime for those activities. The extent of that regime is described in this Chapter and Chapter 3.

Section 19 FSMA 2000 provides that no person may carry on a regulated activity in the UK, or purport to do so, unless he is an authorised person or an exempt person. Breach of this provision is a criminal offence and resulting agreements cannot be enforced by the party in breach (Section 26 FSMA 2000). In addition, an agreement made by an authorised person will be unenforceable if it is made in consequence of a breach of this provision by a third party (Section 27 FSMA 2000). (Special provisions apply for this purpose in relation to deposit taking (Section 29 FSMA 2000).)

"Regulated activity" is defined in two ways. Some activities are regulated if they are carried on in relation to a specified investment, and some activities are regulated if they are carried on in relation to property of any kind. In order to describe regulated activities, it is necessary first to describe specified investments. That is the subject of this Chapter.

Schedule 2 FSMA 2000 sets out a list of specified investments. However, this Schedule only provides examples of investments that may be specified. It does not limit the power to specify investments by statutory instrument conferred by Section 22 FSMA 2000. Consequently Schedule 2 is completely eclipsed by the statutory instrument which has been made under Section 22 and it should therefore be ignored. Since the scope of the FSMA 2000 has expanded considerably since Schedule 2 was drafted, the Schedule does not refer to important categories of investments such as regulated mortgage contracts and personal pension schemes, which have come into FSMA regulation since 2001. Instead, in this Chapter we concentrate on the relevant statutory instrument, which is the Financial Services and Markets Act 2000 (Regulated Activities) Order 2001 (SI 2001/544) ("RAO") (as amended).

There is also a list of controlled investments in a different statutory instrument made for the purposes of the restriction on financial promotion in Section 21 FSMA 2000. This list is similar and much of what is said in this Chapter is equally applicable to that list. However, the two lists are not identical.

The list of specified investments can be summarised as follows:

- deposits;
- electronic money;
- insurance;
- shares, debentures, government bonds and other transferable securities;
- collective investments;
- rights under personal pension schemes (i.e., stakeholder pensions and personal pensions);
- options, futures and contracts for differences;
- Lloyd's participations;
- funeral plan contracts;
- residential mortgages, equity release plans and Islamic finance plans; and
- interests in any of the above.

There is no single unifying principle that determines whether a particular asset is to be treated as a specified investment. The contents of the list have been determined by policy considerations, which change with the times.

It is beyond the scope of this Guide to attempt to provide comprehensive definitions of each category of specified investment. This Chapter provides an initial guide which will assist in understanding the subsequent Chapters of this work and will serve as a starting point for further research if required.

The list of specified investments serves a dual purpose in practice. First it determines the extent of the licensing regime under the FSMA 2000. Second, the Financial Services Authority ("FSA") makes extensive use of the categorisation under this list in drafting its own rules and regulations. The FSA Handbook of Rules and Guidance contains extensive guidance on the categories of specified investments and regulated activities. This guidance is mostly contained in the Perimeter Guidance Manual (PERG) within the FSA Handbook of Rules and Guidance.

"Designated investment business" is a concept invented by the FSA. It represents a subset of the range of specified investments and regulated activities covered by the licensing regime under the FSMA 2000. This Chapter and Chapter 3 describe the full FSMA 2000 regime and then (at the end of Chapter 3) indicate which parts fall within the concept of designated investment business.

The following sections of this Chapter comment in more detail on each type of specified investment in turn. Further guidance is given by the FSA in section 2.6 of PERG.

2.2 Deposits

A deposit is a specified investment under Article 74 RAO. Article 5 RAO defines "deposit" as follows:

"(2) In paragraph (1), 'deposit' means a sum of money, other than one excluded by any of articles 6 to 9A, paid on terms –

(a) under which it will be repaid, with or without interest or premium, and either on demand or at a time or in circumstances agreed by or on behalf of the person making the payment and the person receiving it; and

(b)   which are not referable to the provision of property (other than currency) or services or the giving of security.

(3)   For the purposes of paragraph (2), money is paid on terms which are referable to the provision of property or services or the giving of security if, and only if –

(a)   it is paid by way of advance or part payment under a contract for the sale, hire or other provision of property or services, and is repayable only in the event that the property or services is or are not in fact sold, hired or otherwise provided;

(b)   it is paid by way of security for the performance of a contract or by way of security in respect of loss which may result from the non-performance of a contract; or

(c)   without prejudice to sub-paragraph (b), it is paid by way of security for the delivery up or return of any property, whether in a particular state of repair or otherwise."

This definition will catch simple loans and other forms of purely financial accommodation. In a situation where the parties wish to treat a particular payment as not constituting a deposit on the ground that it is an advance payment or a payment by way of security, it is advisable to ensure that there is a clear documented understanding between the parties to that effect. A party who wishes to rely on this exception will need to be able to demonstrate that it genuinely applies.

The exclusions under Articles 6 to 9A can be summarised as follows.

2.2.1 *Sums paid by certain persons (Article 6)*

A sum is not a deposit if it is paid by:

(a)   one of a range of institutions, including the Bank of England and other European central banks, UK and European banks and insurance companies, local authorities, the European Community and other international organisations;

(b) any other person in the course of a business consisting wholly or to a significant extent of lending money;

(c) a company to another company in the same group; or

(d) a person to a close relative or a business partner, or to a company which he controls or of which he is a director or manager.

2.2.2 Sums received by solicitors etc. (Article 7)

A sum is not a deposit if it is received by a practising solicitor acting in the course of his profession.

2.2.3 Sums received by authorised persons (Article 8)

A sum is not a deposit if it is received by an authorised or exempt person under the FSMA 2000 in the course of providing services to the payer consisting of any of the following regulated activities:

(a) dealing in investments as principal or as agent;

(b) arranging deals in investments;

(c) managing investments;

(d) establishing or operating a collective investment scheme or a stakeholder or personal pension scheme.

2.2.4 Sums received in consideration for the issue of debt securities (Article 9)

A sum is not a deposit if it is received by a person as consideration for the issue by him of investments falling within the categories of debentures or Government securities as described below. This exemption does not apply in relation to an issue of commercial paper (i.e., securities redeemable within one year) unless it is issued:

(a) to professional and/or institutional investors; and

(b) in units with a redemption value of not less than £100,000.

2.2.5 Exchange for electronic money (Article 9A)

A sum is not a deposit if it is received in exchange for the issue of electronic money.

2.3 Electronic money

Article 74A RAO provides that electronic money is a specified investment. This is defined in Article 3 RAO as:

"monetary value, as represented by a claim on the issuer, which is:

(a) stored on an electronic device;
(b) issued on receipt of funds; and
(c) accepted as a means of payment by persons other than the issuer."

2.4 Insurance

Article 75 RAO specifies as investments "Rights under a contract of insurance". The definition of a "contract of insurance" in Article 3 RAO is based on the common-law definition of insurance, but adds some contracts that are not insurance under the common law (e.g., certain contracts of guarantee and pension fund management contracts) and excluding funeral plans, which would be treated as insurance under the common law. In Chapter 6 of PERG the FSA has provided guidance on the identification of contracts of insurance.

Contracts of insurance are divided into general insurance and long-term insurance by reference to the lists of types of contract set out in Parts I and II of Schedule 1 to the RAO. These lists are taken from the EU insurance directives, which establish a harmonised framework for the regulation of insurance throughout the EU. The lists are comprehensive – if a contract does not fit into one of the categories, it is not a contract of insurance for the purposes of the FSMA 2000.

Under the directives, an insurance provider is subject to various prudential requirements, including a prohibition on carrying on any commercial business other than operations arising directly from its insurance business (in the FSA's Prudential Sourcebook for Insurers (INSPRU) at 1.5.13R). It follows from this that a person who provides insurance cannot provide other financial services; and, in general, a person who provides other financial services cannot also provide insurance.

Different types of insurance are regulated in different ways. Article 3 RAO contains a definition of a "qualifying contract of insurance". This is a long-term contract which is not reinsurance and which may have a significant savings or investment element. Most direct long-term insurance contracts are qualifying contracts. The most common example of those that are not is simple term life assurance.

All contracts of insurance are specified investments. When the FSMA 2000 was first brought into force, marketing, advice and intermediation activities were regulated in relation to qualifying contracts of insurance, but not other kinds of insurance. The RAO has since been amended so that these activities became regulated in relation to all kinds of insurance with effect from 14 January 2005 (or, in the case of long-term care insurance, from 31 October 2004).

2.5   Transferable securities

This section deals with a group of specified investments which are largely treated as being on a par with each other for the purpose of defining regulated activities under the FSMA 2000. For convenience, these investments are collectively referred to in this and the next Chapter as "transferable securities".

Note that Article 3 RAO defines the term "security" to include collective investments and rights under stakeholder and personal pensions, as well as these investments.

Article 76 (Shares etc.) defines the following instruments as specified investments:

"Shares or stock in the share capital of –

(a)   any body corporate (wherever incorporated), and
(b)   any unincorporated body constituted under the law of a country or territory outside the United Kingdom."

The definition excludes:

(a) shares in an open-ended investment company (*see* 2.6.3 below);
(b) shares in a building society, other than certain deferred shares issued by a UK building society; and
(c) shares in a UK or European Economic Area ("EEA") industrial and provident society, other than transferable shares.

Article 77 (Instruments creating or acknowledging indebtedness) specifies the following investments:

(a) debentures;
(b) debenture stock;
(c) loan stock;
(d) bonds;
(e) certificates of deposit;
(f) any other instrument creating or acknowledging indebtedness.

It expressly excludes assets that fall within the terms of Article 78 (Government and public securities). It also excludes the following:

(a) an instrument acknowledging or creating indebtedness for, or for money borrowed to defray, the consideration payable under a contract for the supply of goods or services;
(b) a cheque or other bill of exchange, a banker's draft or a letter of credit (but not a bill of exchange accepted by a banker);
(c) a banknote, a statement showing a balance on a current, deposit or savings account, a lease or other disposition of property, or a heritable security; and
(d) a contract of insurance.

Article 78 (Government and public securities) specifies the following investments: loan stock, bonds and other instruments creating or acknowledging indebtedness, issued by or on behalf of any of the following:

(a) Any government or local authority in the UK or elsewhere (including the Scottish Administration, the Executive Committee of the Northern Ireland Assembly and the National Assembly for Wales).
(b) A body the members of which comprise:

(i)   states including the UK or another EEA state; or
(ii)   bodies whose members comprise states including the UK or another EEA state.

The Article excludes the same specific items as are listed above in relation to Article 77, together with money received in connection with the business of the National Savings Bank or raised under the National Loans Act 1968.

Article 79 (Instruments giving entitlements to investments) specifies warrants and other instruments entitling the holder to subscribe for any investment of the kind specified by Articles 76, 77 or 78. It states that it is immaterial whether the investment to which the entitlement relates is in existence or identifiable.

The arrangements commonly referred to as "share options", under which a company agrees to issue shares at a point in the future, typically to employees, fall within this Article rather than Article 83, which is concerned with options to buy or sell securities.

Article 80 (Certificates representing certain securities) specifies certificates or other instruments which confer contractual or property rights:

(a)   in respect of an investment within Articles 76 to 79 (*see* above);
(b)   which are held by a person other than the person on whom the rights are conferred by the certificate or instrument; and
(c)   the transfer of which may be effected without the consent of the holder of the underlying investment.

It excludes any investment which:

(a)   falls within the terms of Article 83 (Options); or
(b)   confers rights in respect of two or more investments issued by different persons, or in respect of two or more different investments of the kind specified by Article 78 (Government and public securities) and issued by the same person.

For convenience, in the rest of this and the following Chapter, the investments specified by the following Articles in the RAO are referred to by the following terms:

(a) Article 76: shares;
(b) Article 77: debentures;
(c) Article 78: Government securities;
(d) Article 79: warrants;
(e) Article 80: certificates.

Note also that there is a convenient definition of "shares and debentures" in Article 71(6)(a) RAO.

2.6   Collective investments

In broad terms, a collective investment scheme is an arrangement under which a group of people contribute to a common investment and share the proceeds. The concept covers a broad range of arrangements, from retail unit trusts specifically designed as an investment vehicle to small informal clubs.

There are two important definitions: "collective investment scheme" and "open-ended investment company". An open-ended investment company is a subset of a collective investment scheme, but the definition is essentially independent and needs to be considered separately.

2.6.1   Collective investment scheme

The definition of "collective investment scheme" appears in Section 235 FSMA 2000 and is as follows:

> "(1)   In this Part 'collective investment scheme' means any arrangements with respect to property of any description, including money, the purpose or effect of which is to enable persons taking part in the arrangements (whether by becoming owners of the property or any part of it or otherwise) to participate in or receive profits or income arising from the acquisition, holding, management or disposal of the property or sums paid out of such profits or income.
>
> (2)   The arrangements must be such that the persons who are to participate ('participants') do not have day-to-day control over the management of the property, whether or not they have the right to be consulted or to give directions.

(3) The arrangements must also have either or both of the following characteristics –

(a) the contributions of the participants and the profits or income out of which payments are to be made to them are pooled;

(b) the property is managed as a whole by or on behalf of the operator of the scheme.

(4) If arrangements provide for such pooling as is mentioned in subsection (3)(a) in relation to separate parts of the property, the arrangements are not to be regarded as constituting a single collective investment scheme unless the participants are entitled to exchange rights in one part for rights in another."

This definition is supplemented by the Financial Services and Markets Act 2000 (Collective Investment Schemes) Order 2001 (SI 2001/1062). The Schedule to these regulations sets out a list of arrangements not amounting to a collective investment scheme, which can be summarised as follows:

- **Individual investment management arrangements**: arrangements confined to any of the following kinds of property:

  - transferable securities;
  - regulated collective investments;
  - contracts of long-term insurance;
  - cash awaiting investment;

  where there is no pooling of property and each participant is entitled to withdraw his property at any time.
- **Enterprise initiative schemes**: arrangements designed to take advantage of the special tax regime allowed for these schemes.
- **Pure deposit based schemes**: arrangements where each participant's contribution is a deposit accepted by an authorised person who holds permission to carry on the regulated activity of accepting deposits, or by a person who is exempt for this purpose.
- **Schemes not operated by way of business**.
- **Debt issues**: arrangements confined to debentures or government securities or related certificates issued by a single issuer, where certain detailed conditions are complied with.

- **Common accounts**: arrangements under which the rights or interests of participants are rights to or interests in money held in a common account; and the contribution of each participant is to be applied for the benefit of that participant.
- **Certain funds relating to leasehold property**: arrangements relating to a trust fund within the meaning of Section 42(1) of the Landlord and Tenant Act 1987 or in money held under a tenancy deposit scheme within the meaning of Section 212(2) Housing Act 2004.
- **Certain employee share schemes**: arrangements made for the purpose of facilitating transactions in shares or debentures issued by a group company, or the holding of such shares or debentures, by or for the benefit of bona fide employees or former employees of the group and their dependants, where certain detailed conditions are complied with.
- **Schemes entered into for commercial purposes related to existing business**: certain arrangements where each of the participants carries on a business which does not involve regulated activities and enters into the arrangements for commercial purposes related to that business.
- **Group schemes**: arrangements where each of the participants is a body corporate in the same group as the operator.
- **Franchise arrangements**.
- **Trading schemes**: certain "member-get-member" schemes, where participants are rewarded for introducing new members, the reward being funded out of the contributions of other participants, and the only element of pooling or joint management of property arises from the fact that, pending payment of this reward, the contributions of participants are managed as a whole by or on behalf of the operator of the scheme.
- **Certain timeshare schemes**.
- **Other schemes relating to use or enjoyment of property**: arrangements where:

  - the predominant purpose of the arrangements is to enable the participants to share in the use or enjoyment of property or to make its use or enjoyment available gratuitously to others; and
  - the property is not currency and does not consist of or include any specified investments (or assets which would be specified

investments but for an exclusion set out in the part of RAO that describes specified investments).

- **Schemes involving the issue of certificates representing investments**: arrangements relating to certificates covered by Article 80 RAO.
- **Clearing services**: provision of clearing services by an authorised person, a recognised clearing house or a recognised investment exchange.
- **Contracts of insurance**.
- **Funeral plan contracts**.
- **Individual pension accounts**.
- **Occupational and personal pension schemes**.
- **Bodies corporate**: it is expressly provided that no building society, industrial and provident society, friendly society or other body corporate (other than an open-ended investment company or a limited liability partnership established under the Limited Liability Partnerships Act 2000) amounts to a collective investment scheme.

2.6.2 *Identifying collective investment schemes*

Recognising a possible collective investment scheme and determining whether it actually falls within the definition is a refined art. The key indicators are:

(a) more than one participant;
(b) contributions made by participants;
(c) property pooled and/or managed as a whole;
(d) participants share in the proceeds.

The case of *Financial Services Authority* v *Fradley (t/a Top Bet Placement Services)* [2006] 2BCLC 616 illustrates the difficulties that can arise in practice. The FSA has issued specific guidance in Chapter 11 of PERG on the circumstances in which property investment clubs and land investment schemes may fall within the definition of a collective investment scheme. The general principles discussed in this guidance can also be relevant in other cases.

2.6.3 *Open-ended investment company*

An open-ended investment company is a body corporate that issues shares and looks for most practical purposes like a normal company, but is treated as a type of collective investment scheme under the FSMA 2000. The rules applying to promotion of and investment in these entities, and their tax treatment, differ radically from those applicable to normal companies. So it is important to be able to identify what is and is not an open-ended investment company.

The definition of "open-ended investment company" appears in Section 236 FSMA 2000 and is as follows:

> "(1) In this Part an 'open-ended investment company' means a collective investment scheme which satisfies both the property condition and the investment condition.
>
> (2) The property condition is that the property belongs beneficially to, and is managed by or on behalf of, a body corporate ('BC') having as its purpose the investment of its funds with the aim of –
>
> (a) spreading investment risk; and
> (b) giving its members the benefit of the results of the management of those funds by or on behalf of that body.
>
> (3) The investment condition is that, in relation to BC, a reasonable investor would, if he were to participate in the scheme –
>
> (a) expect that he would be able to realise, within a period appearing to him to be reasonable, his investment in the scheme (represented, at any given time, by the value of shares in, or securities of, BC held by him as a participant in the scheme); and
> (b) be satisfied that his investment would be realised on a basis calculated wholly or mainly by reference to the value of property in respect of which the scheme makes arrangements.
>
> (4) In determining whether the investment condition is satisfied, no account is to be taken of any actual or potential redemption of shares or securities under –

(a) the provisions of the Companies Act 1985 relating to redeemable shares and a company purchasing its own shares; or

(b) corresponding provisions in Northern Ireland or in any EEA state; or

(c) corresponding provisions in any other state which have been designated for this purpose by statutory instrument."

The main difficulty with this definition is in relation to the investment condition. The test of the expectations and opinions of the reasonable investor leaves a great deal of room for uncertainty. The FSA has issued guidance on how these uncertainties are to be resolved in Chapter 9 of PERG.

2.7 Rights under Pension Schemes

2.7.1 Stakeholder pensions

Article 3 RAO adopts the definition of "stakeholder pension scheme" given by Section 1 of the Welfare Reform and Pensions Act 1999. This makes provision for a scheme to be registered as a stakeholder scheme and sets out conditions which must be met for this purpose.

Under Article 82 RAO, rights under a stakeholder pension scheme are specified as a type of investment regulated under the FSMA 2000.

A stakeholder pension scheme can be established by contract or by trust.

2.7.2 Personal pensions

Article 3 defines a "personal pension scheme" as a scheme or arrangement which is not an occupational pension scheme (which is, broadly, as defined in Section 1 Pension Schemes Act 1993) or a stakeholder pension scheme and which is comprised in one or more instruments or agreements, having or capable of having effect so as to provide benefits to or in respect of people:

(a)   on retirement; or
(b)   on having reached a particular age; or
(c)   on termination of service in an employment.

The FSA has provided guidance on the definition of "personal pension scheme" in Chapter 12 of PERG.

2.8   Derivative instruments

Options, futures and contracts for differences represent a further group of specified investments which are largely treated as being on a par with each other for the purpose of defining regulated activities under the FSMA 2000. For convenience, these investments are collectively referred to in this and the next Chapter as "derivative instruments".

The basic definition of each type of derivative instrument is summarised below. Extended definitions apply in relation to activities carried on by certain professional firms operating within the scope of the Markets in Financial Instruments Directive ("MiFID"). These are explained at the end of this section.

Article 83 (Options) defines a type of specified investment consisting of options to acquire or dispose of:

(a)   a security or contractually based investment (other than another option);
(b)   currency of the UK or any other country or territory;
(c)   palladium, platinum, gold or silver; or
(d)   an option within paragraph (a), (b) or (c) above.

Article 84 (Futures) specifies futures contracts in the following terms:

"(1)   Subject to paragraph (2), rights under a contract for the sale of a commodity or property of any other description under which delivery is to be made at a future date and at a price agreed on when the contract is made.

(2)   There are excluded from paragraph (1) rights under any contract which is made for commercial and not investment purposes."

There are then a number of paragraphs that describe indicators as to whether a contract is made for commercial purposes or for investment purposes. There is also a paragraph confirming that the price of a contract will be taken to be agreed on when the contract is made even if it is left to be determined by reference to market prices at a later date specified in the contract.

Article 85 (Contracts for differences etc.) specifies rights under:

(a)   a contract for differences (which is not further defined); or
(b)   any other contract the purpose or pretended purpose of which is to secure a profit or avoid a loss by reference to fluctuations in:

   (i)   the value or price of property of any description; or
   (ii) an index or other factor designated for that purpose in the contract.

The following are specifically excluded from the above definition:

(a)   contracts where the parties intend actual delivery of the property to which the contract relates;
(b)   deposits made on terms that the return on the sum deposited will be calculated by reference to fluctuations in an index or other factor;
(c)   certain contracts made by the National Savings Bank or relating to money raised under the National Loans Act 1968;
(d)   rights under a qualifying contract of insurance.

However, there is no provision to prevent a debenture covered by Article 77 from also falling within this Article if it pays a return of the kind defined in Article 85.

2.8.1   MiFID extensions to the above categories

MiFID contains its own definitions of each category of derivative instrument. These cover the same ground as the pre-existing definitions summarised above, but are somewhat broader to cover more exotic instruments that were not commonly traded at the time when the predecessor to MiFID, the Investment Services Directive, was adopted. The RAO retains the pre-existing definitions for general purposes, but applies slightly broader definitions to the activities of certain professional traders operating within the scope of MiFID. Further guidance is provided by the FSA in Sections 2.6.20 to 2.6.24 and 13.4 of PERG.

2.9 Lloyd's underwriting interests

Article 86 RAO specifies the following as investments regulated under the FSMA 2000:

(a) the underwriting capacity of a Lloyd's syndicate;
(b) a person's membership (or prospective membership) of a Lloyd's syndicate.

In essence, these investments are the right of a member of a Lloyd's syndicate to participate in underwriting through that syndicate; and the right to determine what underwriting commitments a syndicate will accept. As such, these investments are relevant to members' agents and managing agents at Lloyd's.

2.10 Funeral plan contracts

Funeral plan contracts are defined in Articles 59 and 60 RAO. The basic definition is:

> "A 'funeral plan contract' is a contract (other than one excluded by Article 60) under which –
>
> (a) a person ('the customer') makes one or more payments to another person ('the provider'); and
> (b) the provider undertakes to provide, or secure that another person provides, a funeral in the United Kingdom for the customer (or some other person who is living at the date when the contract is entered into) on his death;
>
> unless, at the time of entering into the contract, the customer and the provider intend or expect the funeral to occur within one month."

Article 60 excludes from this definition the following arrangements where they are effected for the purpose of providing a funeral:

(a)   whole of life insurance provided by an authorised insurer;
(b)   establishment of a trust with independent trustees and an autho-rised fund manager, where certain additional specific require-ments are met.

Under Article 87 RAO, rights under a funeral plan are specified as a type of investment regulated under the FSMA 2000.

2.11   Residential mortgages, equity release and Islamic finance

2.11.1   *Residential mortgage contracts*

Under Article 88 RAO, rights under a regulated mortgage contract are specified as a type of investment regulated under the FSMA 2000. The expression "regulated mortgage contract" is defined in Article 61(3) RAO as follows:

"a contract is a 'regulated mortgage contract' if, at the time it is entered into, the following conditions are met –

(i)   the contract is one under which a person ('the lender') provides credit to an individual or to trustees ('the borrower');
(ii)   the contract provides for the obligation of the borrower to repay to be secured by a first legal mortgage on land (other than timeshare accommodation) in the United Kingdom;
(iii) at least 40% of that land is used, or is intended to be used, as or in connection with a dwelling by the borrower or (in the case of credit provided to trustees) by an individual who is a beneficiary of the trust, or by a related person."

There are various provisions clarifying the terminology used in the above definition. In essence, the definition refers to mortgages of resi-dential property where the mortgagee or a related person lives in the property. The delicate question of who is a "related person" is answered on the basis that the expression means:

(a)　a spouse or a civil partner;
(b)　a person (whether or not of the opposite sex) whose relationship with the relevant person has the characteristics of the relationship between husband and wife; or
(c)　a parent, brother, sister, child, grandparent or grandchild.

Regulation of mortgages under the FSMA 2000 took effect from 31 October 2004. A mortgage is only regulated if it was entered into on or after that date. The FSA has issued guidance, in the Mortgages and Home Finance: Conduct of Business Sourcebook ("MCOB") section of the FSA Handbook, on the circumstances in which changes made after that date to an existing mortgage will be treated as constituting a new contract which will then be a regulated mortgage. The FSA has also provided guidance on the definition of "regulated mortgage contract" in Chapter 4 of PERG.

2.11.2　*Home reversion plans (equity release)*

The definition of a regulated home reversion plan is intended to cover transactions under which a home owner realises part of the value of the home while retaining the right to continue to occupy it. Under Article 88A RAO, rights under a regulated home reversion plan are specified as a type of investment regulated under the FSMA 2000. The expression "regulated home reversion plan" is defined in Article 63B(3) RAO as follows:

"an arrangement comprised in one or more instruments or agreements, in relation to which the following conditions are met at the time it is entered into –

(i)　the arrangement is one under which a person (the 'plan provider') buys all or part of a qualifying interest in land (other than timeshare accommodation) in the United Kingdom from an individual or trustees (the 'reversion seller');

(ii)　the reversion seller (if he is an individual) or an individual who is a beneficiary of the trust (if the reversion seller is a trustee), or a related person, is entitled under the arrangement to occupy at least 40% of the land in question as or in connection with a dwelling, and intends to do so; and

(iii)   the arrangement specifies one or more qualifying termination events, on the occurrence of which that entitlement will end".

The FSA has provided guidance on the definition of "home reversion plan" in Chapter 14 of PERG.

2.11.3   Regulated home purchase plans (Islamic finance)

The definition of a regulated home purchase plan is intended to cover transactions to finance purchase of a home in a manner that complies with Islamic principles. Under Article 88B RAO, rights under a regulated home purchase plan are specified as a type of investment regulated under the FSMA 2000. The expression "regulated home purchase plan" is defined in Article 63F(3) RAO as follows:

"an arrangement comprised in one or more instruments or agreements, in relation to which the following conditions are met at the time it is entered into –

(i)   the arrangement is one under which a person (the 'home purchase provider') buys a qualifying interest or an undivided share of a qualifying interest in land (other than timeshare accommodation) in the United Kingdom;

(ii)   where an undivided share of a qualifying interest in land is bought, the interest is held on trust for the home purchase provider and the individual or trustees mentioned in paragraph (iii) as beneficial tenants in common;

(iii)   the arrangement provides for the obligation of an individual or trustees (the 'home purchaser') to buy the interest bought by the home purchase provider over the course of or at the end of a specified period; and

(iv)   the home purchaser (if he is an individual) or an individual who is a beneficiary of the trust (if the home purchaser is a trustee), or a related person, is entitled under the arrangement to occupy at least 40% of the land in question as or in connection with a dwelling during that period, and intends to do so".

The FSA has provided guidance on the definition of "home purchase plan" in Chapter 14 of PERG.

2.12 Rights to or interests in investments

Article 89 specifies a sweeping up category of investments consisting of rights to or interests in other investments (other than regulated mortgage contracts, home reversion plans and home purchase plans). The following specific categories are excluded:

(a) interests of a pension scheme member under the trusts of an occupational pension scheme;

(b) rights to and interests in the types of insurance contract and trust specifically excluded from the definition of funeral plans, as described above; and

(c) anything which already amounts to a specified investment under another provision of the RAO.

2.13 Overlap between different types of specified investments

There are a number of examples in Part III RAO of provisions included specifically to prevent a particular interest or asset from falling within more than one category of specified investment at the same time. For example, an investment which is a deposit or a qualifying contract of insurance cannot also be a contract for differences; and an investment which is a warrant cannot also be an option.

These provisions are important because they make it easier to use categories of investments in the provisions of RAO defining regulated activities and also in Conduct of Business Rules and other rules made by the FSA to regulate authorised persons. The fact that these provisions are included suggests that, where no such provision is made, it is possible for an investment to fall within two categories at once. Rights under a stakeholder pension scheme constituted by a contract of long-term insurance are a case in point. Presumably these rights are regulated as an investment in both of these categories, and neither excludes the other. Any other approach would lead to unexpected results where the relevant definitions are used elsewhere in the regulations and rules made under the FSMA 2000.

There are three important definitions which bring together several types of investment. These are:

(a) "security" – comprising shares, debentures, government securities, warrants, depositary receipts, collective investments, and rights under stakeholder and personal pensions;

(b) "contractually based investment" – comprising options, futures, contracts for differences, funeral plan contracts and qualifying contracts of insurance (i.e., long-term contracts other than those with no savings or investment element); and

(c) "relevant investment" – this is a similar concept to contractually based investment, but includes all kinds of insurance.

Chapter 3

Regulated Activities

Michael Wainwright
Partner

David Bickley
Assistant Solicitor
Eversheds LLP

3.1 Introduction

This Chapter explains which activities are regulated activities for the purposes of Section 22 of the Financial Services and Markets Act 2000 ("FSMA 2000"). It deals with each activity in turn, describing the activity, the investments to which it relates, and the special exclusions that apply in relation to that activity. It then describes 12 general exclusions, each of which applies to several different activities.

These matters are all dealt with in the Financial Services and Markets Act 2000 (Regulated Activities) Order 2001 (SI 2001/544) as amended ("RAO"), made pursuant to Section 22 FSMA 2000. The descriptions of each kind of specified investment, also set out in the RAO, are dealt with in Chapter 2. There is a list of regulated activities in Part I of Schedule 2 to FSMA 2000. However, that list is provided by way of example only and so is not considered further in this Chapter.

The order in which activities are described is as follows:

(a) the activities of accepting deposits, issuing electronic money and providing insurance, in relation to which special prudential requirements apply;

(b) activities that are specified in relation to designated investments generally;

(c) activities that are specified in relation to designated investments and other property;

(d)   activities that relate to five specialised areas – Lloyd's, funeral plans, residential mortgages, equity release plans and Islamic finance;

(e)   sweeping up provisions relating to agreeing to carry on regulated activities.

The sequence used in this Chapter is the same as in the RAO, except that advising has been promoted to be dealt with alongside other activities of similar scope. Exclusions that relate to a particular activity are described in conjunction with that activity. Exclusions that apply more generally are described in the following section of this Chapter. The final section of this Chapter explains which regulated activities constitute designated investment business.

As mentioned in Chapter 2, the Financial Services Authority ("FSA") Handbook of Rules and Guidance contains guidance on the categories of specified investments and regulated activities. This guidance is now mostly contained in the Perimeter Guidance Manual (PERG) within the Handbook. For example, PERG 4 contains guidance on regulated activities connected with mortgages; PERG 10 does the same for pension schemes; and PERG 14 covers home reversion and home purchase plans.

3.2   Accepting deposits (Article 5)

3.2.1   *The activity*

Article 5 RAO provides that accepting deposits is a specified kind of activity if:

(a)   money received by way of deposit is lent to others; or

(b)   any other activity of the person accepting the deposit is financed wholly, or to a material extent, out of the capital of or interest on money received by way of deposit.

3.2.2   *Investments to which the activity relates*

This activity only applies in relation to deposits. Authorised persons with permission to carry on this activity are subject to the special prudential regime that applies to banks pursuant to the EU banking directives.

3.2.3 Exclusions

The exclusions specified in relation to this activity relate to the definition of "deposit", rather than the description of the activity. Accordingly they are dealt with in Chapter 2.

3.3 Issuing electronic money (Article 9B)

3.3.1 The activity

Article 9B provides that issuing electronic money is a specified activity.

3.3.2 Investments to which the activity relates

This activity applies in relation to electronic money.

3.3.3 Exclusions

There is an exclusion for persons who are certified by the FSA as small issuers of electronic money. This applies where the maximum value that may be stored by a system user is not more than €150 and:

(a) the maximum value that the issuer may have outstanding under its system at any time will not normally exceed €5 million and will never exceed €6 million; or

(b) the maximum value outstanding will never exceed €10 million and either:

  (i) the system is only used for payments by members of the same group as the issuer; or

  (ii) the number of businesses that accept payments through the system is not more than 100 and those businesses are all located within the same site or area, or all have a close financial or business relationship with the issuer.

The FSA must grant a certificate on application if it is satisfied that the relevant conditions apply. It has a limited power to make rules requiring certified persons to provide information about their activities.

The Financial Services Compensation Scheme does not apply in relation to issuing electronic money.

3.3.4 FSA Guidance

The FSA has issued extensive guidance on the definition of electronic money and the activity of issuing electronic money in Chapter 3 of PERG.

3.4 Providing insurance (Article 10)

3.4.1 The activity

Article 10 provides that each of the following is a specified activity:

(a) effecting a contract of insurance as principal;
(b) carrying out a contract of insurance as principal.

3.4.2 Investments to which the activity relates

This activity applies in relation to all contracts of insurance. Authorised persons with permission to carry on this activity are subject to the special prudential regime that applies to insurance providers pursuant to the EU insurance directives.

3.4.3 Exclusions

3.4.3.1 Community co-insurers
There is a specific exclusion for a European Economic Area insurer providing insurance in the UK under co-insurance arrangements where it is not the lead insurer and is not acting through a branch in the UK.

3.4.3.2 Breakdown insurance
There is a specific exclusion for provision of breakdown insurance (which provides assistance in the event of accident to or breakdown of a vehicle) where the terms of the contract, the form of the assistance and the manner in which it is provided satisfy a number of detailed conditions.

3.4.4 Comment

The stipulation that this activity must be carried on "as principal" is important. The activities of insurance intermediaries, such as insurance brokers, are covered under the regulated activities of dealing as agent, arranging transactions and assisting in the administration and performance of contracts of insurance as discussed below.

3.5 Dealing as principal (Article 14)

3.5.1 The activity

Article 14 provides that buying, selling, subscribing for or underwriting certain investments as principal is a specified kind of activity.

3.5.2 Investments to which the activity relates

This activity applies in relation to securities and contractually based investments, other than funeral plan contracts and rights and interests in them.

3.5.3 Exclusions

3.5.3.1 Dealing in securities and qualifying contracts, but not on a professional basis

There is a broad general exclusion for dealing in securities and for making assignments of qualifying contracts of insurance, which applies in all cases, except where the relevant person carries on certain activities typical of dealing on a professional basis. Consequently, except in relation to derivative instruments, dealing as principal is only a regulated activity where the person dealing:

(a) holds himself out as willing, as principal, to buy, sell or subscribe for the relevant investments at prices determined by him generally and continuously rather than in respect of each particular transaction; or

(b) holds himself out as engaging in the business of buying the relevant investments with a view to selling them; or

(c) holds himself out as engaging in the business of underwriting the relevant investments; or

45

(d)   regularly solicits members of the public with the purpose of inducing them to deal in the relevant investments, and the particular transaction is entered into as a result of his having solicited members of the public in that manner.

In this context, "members of the public" means anyone other than:

(a)   authorised persons or persons who are exempt for the purposes of dealing in investments (note – this does not include appointed representatives, because dealing as principal is not one of the regulated activities that appointed representatives are permitted to perform);

(b)   where the person dealing is a company, other members of the same group;

(c)   persons participating in a joint enterprise with the person dealing;

(d)   any person contacted with a view to the acquisition by the person dealing of 20 per cent or more of the voting shares in a body corporate;

(e)   where the person dealing (together with other members of the same group) already owns more than 20 per cent of the voting shares in a body corporate, any person contacted with a view to acquiring further shares in that body corporate or disposing of such shares to the person contacted (or another member of the same group);

(f)   any person who (together with other members of the same group) already owns 20 per cent or more of the voting shares in a body corporate, where the person dealing is seeking to dispose of such shares to the person contacted or another member of the same group;

(g)   an overseas firm.

This exclusion does not apply where a person enters into a transaction as bare trustee on the instructions of the beneficial owner. In that case, an alternative exclusion applies, the only condition being that the trustee must not hold himself out as providing a service of buying and selling securities or contractually based investments (*see* Article 66(1)).

3.5.3.2   *Dealing in contractually based investments*

There is an exclusion for dealing in contractually based investments by persons who are not authorised, where they deal:

(a) with or through an authorised person;

(b) with or through an exempt person acting in the course of his exemption; or

(c) through a non-UK office of an overseas firm.

3.5.3.3 *Acceptance of instruments creating or acknowledging indebtedness*

There is a specific exclusion for accepting an instrument creating or acknowledging indebtedness in respect of any loan, credit, guarantee or other similar financial accommodation or assurance provided by the person accepting the instrument. For this purpose, "accepting" includes becoming a party to an instrument otherwise than as a debtor or a surety.

3.5.3.4 *Issue by a company of its own shares etc.*

There is an exclusion for the issue by a company (other than an open-ended investment company) of its own shares or share warrants, and the issue by any person of his own debentures or debenture warrants.

3.5.3.5 *Dealing by a company in its own shares*

There is an exclusion for a company purchasing its own shares under Section 162A Companies Act 1985 (from 1 October 2008, Section 724 Companies Act 2006) or dealing in its own shares as treasury shares in accordance with Section 162D of that Act (from 1 October 2008, Sections 727 or 729 Companies Act 2006).

3.5.3.6 *Risk management*

There is an exclusion for transactions in derivative instruments where the following conditions are satisfied:

(a) no party to the transaction is an individual;

(b) the sole or main purpose of the transaction (either by itself or in combination with other such transactions) is to limit the extent to which a relevant business will be affected by any identifiable risk arising otherwise than as a result of the carrying on of a regulated activity; and

(c) the relevant business consists mainly of activities other than regulated activities.

For this purpose, "relevant business" means a business carried on by the person seeking to rely on the exclusion or by:

(a)   a person participating in a joint enterprise with that person; or

(b)   where that person is a company, a member of the same group.

3.6   Dealing as agent (Article 21)

3.6.1   *The activity*

Article 21 provides that buying, selling, subscribing for or underwriting certain investments as agent is a specified activity.

3.6.2   *Investments to which the activity relates*

This activity applies in relation to securities and relevant investments, other than funeral plan contracts and rights and interests in them.

3.6.3   *Exclusions*

3.6.3.1   *Deals with or through authorised persons*
There is an exclusion for a person who is not authorised entering into a transaction as agent for another person (the "client") with or through an authorised person if:

(a)   the transaction is entered into on advice given to the client by an authorised person; or

(b)   it is clear, in all the circumstances, that the client, in his capacity as an investor, is not seeking and has not sought advice from the agent as to the merits of the client's entering into the transaction (or, if the client has sought such advice, the agent has declined to give it but has recommended that the client seek advice from an authorised person).

This exclusion does not apply if:

(a)   the transaction relates to a contract of insurance; or

(b)   the agent receives a reward or other advantage from a person other than the client as a result of the transaction, unless the agent accounts to the client for that benefit.

3.6.3.2   Risk management

There is an exclusion for transactions as agent in derivative instruments for risk management purposes. The terms of this exclusion are the same as for the corresponding exclusion in relation to dealing as principal, which is described at 3.5.3.6 above.

3.7   Arranging deals in investments (Article 25)

3.7.1   The activity

Article 25 provides that each of the following is a specified activity:

(a)   making arrangements for another person (whether as principal or agent) to buy, sell, subscribe for or underwrite certain investments;

(b)   making arrangements with a view to a person who participates in the arrangements buying, selling, subscribing for or underwriting any of those investments (whether as principal or agent).

In the case of *Re Inertia Partnership LLP* [2007] B.C.C. 656, the court took a broad view of the scope of the first limb of this specified activity. The FSA has commented extensively in PERG on this activity although, as a result of the way in which PERG is currently structured, these comments are made on a piecemeal basis in different parts of PERG rather than in a separate section dedicated to this subject.

3.7.2   Investments to which the activity relates

This activity applies in relation to securities, relevant investments and interests at Lloyd's.

3.7.3   Exclusions

3.7.3.1   Arrangements not causing a deal

There is a specific exclusion from paragraph (a) in 3.7.1 above for arrangements which do not or would not bring about the transaction to which the arrangements relate.

3.7.3.2 *Enabling parties to communicate*

There is a specific exclusion from paragraph (b) in 3.7.1 above for a person who merely provides the means by which one party to a transaction (or potential transaction) is able to communicate with other parties.

3.7.3.3 *Arranging transactions to which the arranger is a party*

There is a specific exclusion that applies where the relevant transaction or transactions are to be entered into by the person making the arrangements, whether as principal or as agent for some other person. The exclusion only applies in favour of a person who actually enters into the transaction(s). Other parties to the arrangements need to consider separately whether their involvement in the arrangements may constitute a specified activity under this Article.

This exclusion does not apply in relation to a contract of insurance unless the person making the arrangements is or will become the only policyholder under the contract.

3.7.3.4 *Arranging deals with or through authorised persons*

There is a specific exclusion for arrangements made by a person who is not an authorised person for or with a view to a transaction which is or is to be entered into by a person (the "client") with or through an authorised person if:

(a) the transaction is entered into on advice given to the client by an authorised person; or

(b) it is clear, in all the circumstances, that the client, in his capacity as an investor, is not seeking and has not sought advice from the arranger as to the merits of the client's entering into the transaction (or, if the client has sought such advice, the arranger has declined to give it and has recommended that the client seek advice from an authorised person).

This exclusion does not apply if:

(a) the transaction relates to a contract of insurance; or

(b) the arranger receives a reward or other advantage from a person other than the client as a result of the transaction, unless the arranger accounts to the client for that benefit.

3.7.3.5 Arranging transactions in connection with lending on the security of insurance policies

There is an exclusion for arrangements made by a money-lender under which either:

(a) an insurer or its agent will introduce or refer potential policy-holders to the money-lender; or
(b) an insurer gives an assurance to the money-lender as to the value of its policies as security for loans to potential policyhold-ers whom it introduces to the money-lender.

In this context, "money-lender" means:

(a) a money-lending company within the meaning of Section 209 of the Companies Act 2006;
(b) a UK building society; or
(c) a person whose ordinary business includes the making of loans or the giving of guarantees in connection with loans.

3.7.3.6 Arranging the acceptance of debentures in connection with loans

There is an exclusion for arrangements under which a person accepts an instrument creating or acknowledging indebtedness in respect of any financial accommodation provided by that person. The terms of this exclusion are the same as for the corresponding exclusion in relation to dealing as principal, which is described at 3.5.3.3 above.

3.7.3.7 Provision of finance

There is a specific exclusion from paragraph (b) in 3.7.1 above for arrangements having as their sole purpose the provision of finance to enable a person to buy, sell, subscribe for or underwrite investments.

3.7.3.8 Introducing

There is a specific exclusion from paragraph (b) in 3.7.1 above for arrangements under which people will be introduced to:

(a) an authorised person;
(b) an exempt person acting in the course of his exemption; or
(c) an overseas firm (*see* 3.29.7 below),

where, in each case, the introduction is made with a view to the provision of independent advice or the independent exercise of discretion in relation to investments generally or in relation to any class of investments to which the arrangements relate. This exclusion does not apply in relation to arranging insurance.

3.7.3.9   *Arrangements for the issue of shares etc.*
There is an exclusion for:

(a)   arrangements made by a company for the purpose of issuing its own shares or share warrants; and
(b)   arrangements made by any person for the purpose of issuing his own debentures or debenture warrants.

For the purposes of Article 25, a company is not, by reason of issuing its own shares or share warrants, and a person is not, by reason of issuing his own debentures or debenture warrants, to be treated as selling them.

3.7.3.10   *International securities self-regulating organisations*
There is an exclusion for arrangements made for the purposes of carrying out the functions of a body or association approved by the Treasury as an international securities self-regulating organisation. These are overseas bodies which facilitate and regulate international securities business between investment firms, but which do not satisfy the conditions for recognition as an overseas investment exchange or clearing house under Section 292(3) FSMA 2000.

The International Capital Market Association has been approved for this purpose in its capacity as operator of the TRAX system for trade matching and regulatory reporting of transactions.

3.8   Arranging mortgages (Article 25A)

3.8.1   *The activity*

Article 25A provides that each of the following is a specified activity:

(a)   making arrangements for another person to enter into a regulated mortgage contract as borrower or to vary the terms of his mortgage;

(b) making arrangements with a view to a person who participates in the arrangements entering into a regulated mortgage contract as borrower.

3.8.2 *Investments to which the activity relates*

This activity applies in relation to regulated mortgage contracts.

3.8.3 *Exclusions*

3.8.3.1 Exclusions similar to those for arranging deals in investments
There are exclusions from the regulated activity of arranging mortgages that mirror some of the exclusions described above in relation to arranging deals in investments. These are as follows and, except where specified otherwise, they apply in relation to paragraphs (a) and (b) in 3.8.1 above:

(a) arrangements not causing a deal (*see* 3.7.3.1 above): this exclusion only applies in relation to paragraph (a) in 3.8.1 above;
(b) enabling the parties to communicate (*see* 3.7.3.2 above): this exclusion only applies in relation to paragraph (b) in 3.8.1 above;
(c) arranging transactions to which the arranger is a party (*see* 3.7.3.3 above): this exclusion applies where the arranger is, or is to be, the lender or the borrower under the mortgage;
(d) arranging deals with or through authorised persons (*see* 3.7.3.4 above);
(e) introducing (*see* 3.7.3.8 above): this exclusion only applies in relation to paragraph (b) in 3.8.1 above.

3.8.3.2 Arrangements for administration by an authorised person
There is a specific exclusion from paragraph (a) in 3.8.1 for making arrangements to vary the terms of the mortgage. The exclusion applies where a person who is not authorised appoints an authorised person to administer a mortgage, or administers the contract himself for a period of up to a month after termination of the appointment.

3.8.3.3 Introducing to authorised persons etc.
There is a specific exclusion from paragraph (b) in 3.8.1 above for arrangements for introducing borrowers to an authorised person, an

appointed representative or an overseas firm (*see* 3.29.7 below) involved in arranging, advising on or providing regulated mortgages, where:

(a) the introducer does not receive any payment from the borrower in relation to the transaction, other than a payment to the introducer for his own account; and

(b) before introducing the borrower to the lender, the introducer discloses any commission or other remuneration that he or it may receive from the introduction and, where applicable, the fact that the introducer is a member of the same group as the lender.

3.9   Arranging regulated home reversion plans (Article 25B)

3.9.1   *The activity*

Article 25B provides that each of the following is a specified activity:

(a) making arrangements for another person to enter into a regulated home reversion plan as reversion seller or as plan provider or to vary the terms;

(b) making arrangements with a view to a person who participates in the arrangements entering into a regulated home reversion plan as reversion seller or as plan provider.

3.9.2   *Investments to which the activity relates*

This activity applies in relation to home reversion plans.

3.9.3   *Exclusions*

The exclusions in relation to this activity are similar to those described above in relation to arranging mortgages (*see* 3.8.3 above).

3.10 Arranging regulated home purchase plans (Article 25C)

3.10.1 *The activity*

Article 25C provides that each of the following is a specified activity:

(a) making arrangements for another person to enter into a regulated home purchase plan as house purchaser or to vary the terms;

(b) making arrangements with a view to a person who participates in the arrangements entering into a regulated home purchase plan as home purchaser.

3.10.2 *Investments to which the activity relates*

This activity applies in relation to regulated home purchase plans.

3.10.3 *Exclusions*

The exclusions in relation to this activity are similar to those described above in relation to arranging mortgages (*see* 3.8.3 above).

3.11 Operating a multilateral trading facility (Article 25D)

3.11.1 *The activity*

Article 25D provides that the operation of a multilateral trading facility on which Markets in Financial Instruments Directive ("MiFID") instruments are traded is a specified kind of activity.

A multilateral trading facility is, broadly, a trading platform that permits trading between participants but which is not a regulated market. Firms which operated multilateral trading facilities (formerly known as alternative trading systems) before the implementation of MiFID were deemed to be conducting regulated activities under Articles 14, 21 and 25 RAO. These activities have now been amended to exclude activities falling under Article 25D.

3.11.2   Investments to which the activity relates

This activity applies in relation to "MiFID instruments" (set out in Schedule 2 of the RAO). These comprise all transferable securities, collective investments and derivative instruments (and rights to or interests in any of them) that fall within the scope of MiFID.

3.11.3   Exclusions

This activity is only subject to the overseas persons exclusion (Article 72).

3.12   Advising on investments (Article 53)

3.12.1   The activity

Article 53 provides that advising a person is a specified activity if the advice:

(a)   is given to the person in his capacity as an investor or potential investor, or in his capacity as agent for an investor or a potential investor; and

(b)   is advice on the merits of his doing any of the following (whether as principal or agent):

   (i)   buying, selling, subscribing for or underwriting a particular investment; or

   (ii)   exercising any right conferred by an investment to buy, sell, subscribe for or underwrite an investment.

3.12.2   Investments to which each activity relates

Article 53 applies in relation to securities and relevant investments.

3.12.3   Exclusions

3.12.3.1   Advice given in newspapers etc.
There is an exclusion for advice given in writing or other legible form:

(a)   in a newspaper, journal, magazine or other periodical publication; or

(b) by way of a service comprising regularly updated news or information,

but only if the principal purpose of the publication or service, taken as a whole and including any advertisements or other promotional material contained in it, is not:

(a) to give investment advice or mortgage advice as described at 3.12.1 above; or
(b) to lead or enable persons to deal in investments or to borrow under or renegotiate a mortgage.

There is a further exclusion for advice given in any service consisting of the broadcast or transmission of television or radio programmes, but once again only if the principal purpose of the service satisfies the test set out above.

It is possible to apply to the Financial Services Authority ("FSA") for a certificate (which will be conclusive if granted) that a particular publication or service falls within this exclusion. The cost of such a certificate is currently £2,000 for the application and an annual fee of £1,000.

3.12.4 *FSA Guidance*

The FSA has issued guidance on financial promotion and related activities in Chapter 8 of PERG. Parts of this guidance provide useful interpretation of the scope of the regulated activities that apply to advising and the related exclusions. The FSA has also issued guidance on the scope of the exclusion for advice given in newspapers etc. and the availability of certificates under this exclusion. This is contained in Chapter 7 of PERG.

3.13 Advising on mortgages (Article 53A)

3.13.1 *The activity*

Article 53A provides that advising a person is a specified activity if the advice:

(a) is given to the person in his capacity as a borrower or potential borrower; and

(b) is advice on the merits of his entering into a particular mortgage or varying his obligations under a mortgage.

3.13.2 Investments to which each activity relates

Article 53A applies in relation to regulated mortgage contracts.

3.13.3 Exclusions

There is an exclusion for mortgage advice where a person who is not authorised ("A") appoints an authorised person ("B") to administer mortgages on his behalf. The exclusion applies in relation to:

(a) anything done by B in the course of administering mortgages on A's behalf; and

(b) anything done by A in the course of administering mortgages during the period of up to one month after B's appointment is terminated.

3.14 Advising on regulated home reversion plans (Article 53B)

The provisions describing this activity and the specific exclusions that apply in relation to it are similar to those for advising on regulated mortgage contracts (*see* 3.13 above).

3.15 Advising on regulated home purchase plans (Article 53C)

The provisions describing this activity and the specific exclusions that apply in relation to it are similar to those for advising on regulated mortgage contracts (*see* 3.13 above).

3.16 Providing basic advice on stakeholder products (Article 52B)

3.16.1 *The activity*

Article 52B provides that providing basic advice to a retail consumer on a stakeholder product is a specified kind of activity. A person ("P") provides "basic advice" when:

(a) he asks a retail consumer questions to enable him to assess whether a stakeholder product is appropriate for that consumer; and

(b) relying on the information provided by the retail consumer, P assesses that a stakeholder product is appropriate for the retail consumer and:

    (i) describes that product to that consumer;

    (ii) gives a recommendation of that product to that consumer; and

(c) the retail consumer has indicated to P that he has understood the description and the recommendation in sub-paragraph (b).

A "retail consumer" is any person who:

(a) is advised by P on the merits of opening or buying a stakeholder product in the course of a business carried on by P; and

(b) does not receive the advice in the course of a business carried on by him.

3.16.2 *Investments to which each activity relates*

Article 52B applies in relation to stakeholder products, which are defined as:

(a) an account which qualifies as a stakeholder child trust fund within the meaning given by the Child Trust Funds Regulations 2004;

(b) rights under a stakeholder pension scheme;

(c) any other investment of a kind specified in regulations made by the Treasury.

3.17   Managing investments (Article 37)

3.17.1   *The activity*

Article 37 provides that managing assets belonging to another person, in circumstances involving the exercise of discretion, is a specified activity if:

(a)   the assets consist of or include securities or contractually based investments; or
(b)   the arrangements for their management are such that the assets may consist of or include those investments, and either the assets have at any time since 29 April 1988 done so, or the arrangements have at any time (whether before or after that date) been held out as arrangements under which those investments would be included.

3.17.2   *Investments to which the activity relates*

This activity applies primarily in relation to securities and contractually based investments, but can also cover other assets.

3.17.3   *Exclusions*

3.17.3.1   *Attorneys*
There is an exclusion for a person appointed to manage assets under a power of attorney where all routine or day-to-day decisions, as far as relating to investments, are taken on behalf of that person by:

(a)   an authorised person with permission to carry on the regulated activity of managing investments;
(b)   an exempt person whose exemption covers that activity; or
(c)   an overseas firm (*see* 3.29.7 below).

3.18   Administration of insurance (Article 39A)

3.18.1   *The activity*

Article 39A provides that assisting in the administration and performance of a contract of insurance is a specified activity.

3.18.2 *Investments to which the activity relates*

This activity applies in relation to contracts of insurance.

3.18.3 *Exclusions*

There is a specific exclusion for provision of claims management services. This covers the following activities:

(a) expert appraisal;
(b) loss adjusting on behalf of an authorised insurer; and
(c) managing claims on behalf of an authorised insurer.

3.19   Custody services (Article 40)

3.19.1 *The activity*

Article 40 provides that the activity consisting of both:

(a) safeguarding assets belonging to another person; and
(b) administering those assets,

is a specified activity if:

(a) the assets consist of or include securities and/or contractually based investments; or
(b) the arrangements are such that the assets may consist of or include those investments, and either the assets have at any time since 1 June 1997 done so, or the arrangements have at any time (whether before or after that date) been held out as ones under which those investments would be included.

Arranging for another person to carry on the above activity is also a specified activity in its own right.

For these purposes:

(a) it is immaterial that title to the assets safeguarded and administered is held in uncertificated form; and
(b) it is immaterial that the assets safeguarded and administered may be transferred to another person, subject to a commitment

by the person safeguarding and administering them, or arranging for their safeguarding and administration, that they will be replaced by equivalent assets at some future date or when so requested by the person to whom they belong (i.e. under stock-lending or similar arrangements).

3.19.2 Investments to which the activity relates

This activity applies primarily in relation to securities and contractually based investments, but can also cover other assets.

3.19.3 Exclusions

3.19.3.1 Acceptance of responsibility by third party

There is an exclusion that applies where custody services are provided by a person who does not have permission to carry on this activity, but arrangements are made for a qualifying custodian to undertake to the owner of the assets to be personally responsible for that activity to the same extent as if the qualifying custodian were itself carrying on that activity.

For this purpose a "qualifying custodian" means:

(a) an authorised person with permission to provide the custody services; or

(b) an exempt person whose exemption covers that activity,

and who, in either case, is acting in the course of carrying on that activity in the UK.

3.19.3.2 Introduction to qualifying custodians

There is an exclusion for arrangements pursuant to which a person (the "arranger") introduces customers to a qualifying custodian with a view to the qualifying custodian providing custody services to the customer in the UK, where the qualifying custodian (or other person who is to safeguard and administer the assets in question) is not connected with the arranger.

For this purpose:

(a) "qualifying custodian" has the meaning given in 3.19.3.1 above; and

(b) a person is connected with the arranger if either he is a member of the same group as the arranger, or the arranger is remunerated by him.

3.19.3.3 *Activities not constituting administration*

The following activities do not constitute the administration of assets for these purposes:

(a) providing information as to the number of units or the value of any assets safeguarded;

(b) converting currency;

(c) receiving documents relating to an investment solely for the purpose of onward transmission to, from or at the direction of the person to whom the investment belongs.

3.20 Sending dematerialised instructions (Article 45)

3.20.1 *The activity*

Article 45 provides that making use of CREST (or any similar system to which the Uncertificated Securities Regulations 2001 apply) to send dematerialised instructions on behalf of another person, is a specified activity. This activity also covers a system-participant causing dematerialised instructions to be sent through such a system on behalf of another person.

3.20.2 *Investments to which the activity relates*

This activity applies in relation to securities and contractually based investments.

3.20.3 *Exclusions*

3.20.3.1 *Instructions on behalf of participating issuers, settlement banks and offerors*

There are exclusions for sending a dematerialised instruction on behalf of:

(a)   a participating issuer in CREST (within the meaning of the 2001 Regulations);
(b)   a settlement bank (as defined in the 2001 Regulations) in its capacity as such; or
(c)   an offeror making a takeover offer.

For this purpose, "takeover offer" includes, broadly speaking:

(a)   an offer which is a takeover offer within the meaning of Chapter 3 of Part 28 of the Companies Act 2006 (or would be such an offer if that Part of that Act applied in relation to the particular target company);
(b)   an offer to acquire all or substantially all the shares, or all the shares of a particular class, in a body corporate incorporated outside the UK; or
(c)   an offer made to all the holders of shares, or shares of a particular class, in a body corporate to acquire a specified proportion of those shares.

3.20.3.2   *Instructions in the course of providing a network*
There is an exclusion for sending a dematerialised instruction as a necessary part of providing a network, the purpose of which is to carry dematerialised instructions which are at all times properly authenticated (within the meaning of the 2001 Regulations).

3.20.3.3   *Investments held by a trustee or personal representative*
There is an exclusion for a person sending or causing to be sent a dematerialised instruction, if the instruction relates to an investment which that person holds as trustee or personal representative (*see* Article 66(5)).

3.21   Providing collective investments (Article 51)

3.21.1   *The activity*

Article 51 provides that the following are specified activities:

(a)   establishing, operating or winding up a collective investment scheme;

(b) acting as trustee of an authorised unit trust scheme;
(c) acting as the depositary or sole director of an open-ended investment company.

3.21.2 *Investments to which the activity relates*

This activity applies in relation to property of any description.

3.22 Providing a pension scheme (Article 52)

3.22.1 *The activity*

Article 52 provides that establishing, operating or winding up a
stakeholder pension scheme or a personal pension scheme is a specified activity.

3.22.2 *Investments to which the activity relates*

This activity applies in relation to property of any description.

3.23 Lloyd's (Articles 56–58)

3.23.1 *The activity*

Articles 56 to 58 provide that each of the following is a specified
activity:

(a) advising a person to become, or continue or cease to be, a
member of a particular Lloyd's syndicate;
(b) managing the underwriting capacity of a Lloyd's syndicate as a
managing agent at Lloyd's;
(c) the arranging, by the society of Lloyd's, of deals in contracts of
insurance written at Lloyd's.

3.23.2 *Investments to which the activity relates*

This activity applies in relation to interests at Lloyd's and to contracts
of insurance.

3.24 Funeral plans (Article 59)

3.24.1 *The activity*

Article 59 provides that entering as provider into a funeral plan contract is a specified activity.

3.24.2 *Investments to which the activity relates*

This activity applies in relation to funeral plan contracts.

3.25 Regulated mortgage contracts (Article 61)

3.25.1 *The activity*

Article 61 provides that each of the following is a specified activity:

(a)   entering into a regulated mortgage contract as lender;
(b)   administering a regulated mortgage contract.

For this purpose, administering a regulated mortgage contract means either or both of the following:

(a)   notifying the borrower of matters requiring to be notified to him under the contract, including changes in interest rates or payments; and
(b)   taking steps for collecting or recovering payments under the contract,

but does not include merely being entitled to enforce the contract.

3.25.2 *Investments to which the activity relates*

This activity applies in relation to regulated mortgage contracts.

3.25.3 *Exclusions*

3.25.3.1 *Arranging administration by an authorised person*
There is an exclusion which applies where a person who is not authorised:

(a)   arranges for a regulated mortgage contract to be administered by an authorised person with permission to carry on that activity; or

(b)   administers the contract himself during a period of not more than one month beginning with the day on which any such arrangement comes to an end.

3.25.3.2   Administration pursuant to agreement with an authorised person

There is an exclusion which applies where a person who is not authorised administers a regulated mortgage contract pursuant to an agreement with an authorised person who has permission to carry on that activity.

3.26   Regulated home reversion plans (Article 63B)

3.26.1   *The activity*

Article 63B provides that each of the following is a specified activity:

(a)   entering into a regulated home reversion plan as plan provider;
(b)   administering a regulated home reversion plan.

For this purpose, administering a regulated home reversion plan means either or both of the following:

(a)   notifying the reversion seller of matters requiring to be notified to him under the plan;
(b)   taking any necessary steps for the purposes of making payments to the reversion seller; and
(c)   taking steps for collecting or recovering payments under the plan,

but does not include merely being entitled to enforce the contract.

3.26.2   *Investments to which the activity relates*

This activity applies in relation to regulated home reversion plans.

3.26.3   *Exclusions*

There are exclusions in relation to this activity similar to those provided in relation to regulated mortgage contracts (*see* 3.25 above).

3.27 Regulated home purchase plans (Article 63F)

3.27.1 *The activity*

Article 63F provides that each of the following is a specified activity:

(a) entering into a regulated home purchase plan as home purchase provider;
(b) administering a regulated home purchase plan.

For this purpose, administering a regulated home purchase plan means either or both of the following:

(a) notifying the home purchaser of matters requiring to be notified to him under the contract, including payments due under the plan; and
(b) taking steps for collecting or recovering payments due under the plan from the home purchaser,

but does not include merely being entitled to enforce the contract.

3.27.2 *Investments to which the activity relates*

This activity applies in relation to regulated home purchase plans.

3.27.3 *Exclusions*

There are exclusions in relation to this activity similar to those provided in relation to regulated mortgage contracts (*see* 3.25 above).

3.28 Agreeing to carry on regulated activities (Article 64)

3.28.1 *The activity*

Article 64 provides that agreeing to carry on any of the activities specified above, other than accepting deposits, issuing electronic money, providing insurance, providing collective investments and providing stakeholder pensions, is a specified activity.

3.28.2   *Investments to which the activity relates*

This activity applies in relation to all specified investments.

3.29   General exclusions

Each of the following general exclusions applies in relation to a range of specified activities.

3.29.1   *Trustees, nominees and personal representatives (Article 66)*

There is a set of exclusions that apply in relation to a person acting as a trustee or a personal representative (the "trustee"). Except for dealing as principal and sending dematerialised instructions, they do not apply if the trustee is remunerated for what he does in addition to any remuneration he receives as trustee or personal representative. For these purposes, the trustee is not to be regarded as receiving additional remuneration merely because his remuneration is calculated by reference to time spent.

These exclusions apply in relation to all kinds of specified investments; and in relation to the following regulated activities.

Dealing as principal: the exclusion applies where a person enters into a transaction as bare trustee, acting on instructions from the beneficiary, but it does not apply if the trustee holds himself out as providing a service of buying and selling securities or contractually based investments.

Arranging deals in investments and arranging mortgages: the exclusion covers arrangements made by a trustee for or with a view to a transaction entered into:

(a)   by the trustee and a fellow trustee or personal representative (acting in their capacity as such); or
(b)   by a beneficiary under the trust, will or intestacy.

Managing investments: there is a general exclusion for any activity carried on by a person as trustee or personal representative, unless:

(a) he holds himself out as providing the service of managing investments; or

(b) he is acting as trustee of an occupational pension scheme, and, under the Financial Services and Markets Act 2000 (Carrying on Regulated Activities by Way of Business) Order 2001 (SI 2001/1177), he is treated as carrying on that activity by way of business.

Administration of insurance: there is a general exclusion for any activity carried on by a person as trustee or personal representative, unless he holds himself out as providing insurance administration services.

Custody services: there is a general exclusion for any activity carried on by a person as trustee or personal representative, unless he holds himself out as providing the service of safeguarding and administering investments.

Sending dematerialised instructions: there is a general exclusion for a person giving instructions in relation to an investment which he holds as trustee or as personal representative.

Advising on investments and advising on mortgages: there is a general exclusion for giving advice to:

(a) a fellow trustee or personal representative for the purposes of the trust or the estate; or

(b) a beneficiary under the trust, will or intestacy concerning his interest in the trust fund or estate.

Lending under and administering mortgages: there is a general exclusion for a person as trustee or personal representative where the borrower is a beneficiary under the trust, will or intestacy.

3.29.2 *Activities carried on in the course of a profession or non-investment business (Article 67)*

There is a general exclusion for any activity which:

(a) is carried on in the course of carrying on any profession or business which does not otherwise involve carrying on regulated activities in the UK; and

(b) may reasonably be regarded as a necessary part of other services provided in the course of that profession or business,

unless the activity in question is remunerated separately from the other services.

This exclusion applies in relation to all specified investments, but only in relation to the following regulated activities:

(a) dealing as agent;
(b) arranging deals in investments and arranging mortgages;
(c) advising on investments and advising on mortgages;
(d) administration of insurance; and
(e) custody services.

3.29.3 *Activities carried on in connection with the sale of goods or supply of services (Article 68)*

There is a general exclusion for certain activities carried on for the purposes of or in connection with the sale of goods or supply of services by a supplier to a customer, where the "supplier" is a person whose main business is to sell goods or supply services and not to carry on any regulated activities (other than activities that relate solely to deposits, electronic money, mortgages and/or interests at Lloyd's). Where the supplier is a company, the exclusion can apply for the benefit of other members of the same group. (However, the benefit of the exclusion may be lost if another member of the group carries on regulated activities as part of its business.)

The exemption only applies where the customer is a person other than an individual. Where the customer is a company, the exclusion can apply in relation to activities carried on with another member of the same group as the customer.

The exclusion can also apply in relation to a sale of goods or supply of services to the customer by a person other than the supplier and members of its group, where this is closely connected with the sale or supply by the supplier. For convenience, the sale or supply by the supplier and any connected sale or supply by a third party are together referred to below as the "relevant supply".

The exclusion does not apply in relation to contracts of insurance or units in a collective investment scheme, except as far as it applies to custody services. Otherwise it applies in relation to all kinds of specified investments to which the relevant regulated activities apply. It applies to regulated activities as follows.

Dealing as principal: the exclusion applies to any transaction entered into between the supplier and the customer for the purposes of or in connection with the relevant supply.

Dealing as agent: the exclusion applies to any transaction entered into by the supplier as agent for a customer for the purposes of or in connection with the relevant supply, provided that:

(a) where the investment to which the transaction relates is a security, the supplier does not hold himself out (other than to the customer) as engaging in the business of buying securities of the relevant kind with a view to selling them, and does not regularly solicit members of the public for the purposes of inducing them to buy, sell, subscribe for or underwrite securities;

(b) where the investment to which the transaction relates is a contractually based investment, the supplier enters into the transaction:

    (i) with or through an authorised person, or an exempt person acting as such; or

    (ii) through an office outside the UK maintained by a party to the transaction, and with or through an investment firm whose head office is outside the UK.

In paragraph (a) above, the reference to soliciting members of the public is to be interpreted in the same way as the corresponding expression in Article 15 (*see* 3.5.3.1 above).

Arranging transactions: the exclusion covers arrangements made by the supplier for, or with a view to, a transaction which is or is to be entered into by the customer for the purposes of or in connection with the relevant supply.

Managing investments: the exclusion covers any activity carried on by the supplier where the assets in question belong to the customer and are managed for the purposes of or in connection with the relevant supply.

Custody services: the exclusion covers any activity carried on by the supplier where the assets in question are safeguarded and administered for the purposes of or in connection with the relevant supply.

Advising on investments: the exclusion covers the giving of advice by the supplier to the customer for the purposes of or in connection with the main supply or a related supply, or to a person with whom the customer proposes to enter into a transaction for the purposes of or in connection with the relevant supply.

3.29.4   Groups and joint enterprises (Article 69)

Article 69 sets out a series of exclusions that apply between members of a group of companies. The exclusions also apply in the same way between participators in a joint enterprise. For convenience, where the following paragraphs refer to members of a group, they should be read as also including participators in a joint enterprise.

These exclusions apply in relation to all kinds of specified investments, but not in relation to insurance intermediation activities. They apply to regulated activities as follows.

Dealing as principal: there is an exclusion for any transaction entered into between two members of the same group, where both are acting as principal.

Dealing as agent: there is an exclusion for a person entering into a transaction as agent for another member of the same group where that person is acting as principal, provided that:

(a)   where the investment to which the transaction relates is a security, the agent does not hold himself out (other than to members of the same group) as engaging in the business of buying securities of the relevant kind with a view to selling them, and does not regularly solicit members of the public for the purpose of inducing them to buy, sell, subscribe for or underwrite securities;

(b)   where the investment to which the transaction relates is a contractually based investment, the agent enters into the transaction:

(i)   with or through an authorised person or an exempt person acting as such; or

(ii)   through an office outside the UK maintained by a party to the transaction, and with or through an investment firm whose head office is outside the UK.

In paragraph (a) above, the reference to soliciting members of the public is to be interpreted in the same way as the corresponding expression in Article 15 (*see* 3.5.3.1 above).

Arranging deals in investments: there is an exclusion for arrangements made by a person for, or with a view to, a transaction which is to be entered into by another member of the same group as principal.

Managing investments and **Custody services**: there is an exclusion for any activity carried on by a person in relation to assets belonging to another member of the same group.

Sending dematerialised instructions: there is an exclusion which covers sending a dematerialised instruction, or causing one to be sent, on behalf of another member of the same group, if the investment to which the instruction relates is one in respect of which a member of the same group is registered as holder in the appropriate register of securities, or will be so registered as a result of the instruction.

Advising on investments: there is an exclusion for giving advice to another member of the same group.

3.29.4.1   Comment

As mentioned above, this exclusion does not apply in relation to insurance intermediation activities. The FSA has issued a statement, primarily directed to group risk managers but relevant in other contexts, to the effect that certain insurance intermediation services provided between members of a group of companies will not be regulated because they do not satisfy the "by way of business test" applicable to insurance mediation activities. This statement tends to compensate for the fact that the groups exclusion does not apply in relation to insurance mediation activities. However, it is not currently reflected in the FSA's formal guidance in PERG on the "by way of business" test for insurance mediation activities.

3.29.5 *Activities carried on in connection with the sale of a body corporate (Article 70)*

Article 70 defines a type of transaction and provides a series of exclusions for transactions of that kind and related preparatory activities.

The transaction is an acquisition or disposal of shares in a body corporate (other than an open-ended investment company), which satisfies either of the following conditions, or a transaction entered into for the purposes of such an acquisition or disposal. The conditions are:

(a) the shares, together with any already held by the person acquiring them, consist of or include at least 50 per cent of the voting shares in the body corporate; and the acquisition or disposal is between parties each of whom is a body corporate, a partnership, a single individual or a group of connected individuals; or

(b) the object of the transaction may reasonably be regarded as being the acquisition of day-to-day control of the affairs of the body corporate, despite the fact that the conditions at (a) above are not satisfied.

For the purposes of paragraph (a) above, "a group of connected individuals" means:

(a) in relation to a party disposing of shares in a body corporate, a single group of persons each of whom is:

    (i) a director or manager of the body corporate;

    (ii) a close relative of any such director or manager;

    (iii) a person acting as trustee for any person falling within paragraph (i) or (ii); and

(b) in relation to a party acquiring shares in a body corporate, a single group of persons each of whom is:

    (i) a person who is or is to be a director or manager of the body corporate;

    (ii) a close relative of any such person; or

    (iii) a person acting as trustee for any person falling within paragraph (i) or (ii).

There are exclusions for transactions falling within the above definition from the regulated activities of dealing as principal, dealing as agent, arranging transactions and advising on investments. These cover not just the transaction itself but also arrangements and dealings with a view to a transaction of this kind and advice in connection with a proposed transaction. These exclusions do not apply in relation to any aspects of the transaction that involve insurance.

The exclusion at paragraph (a) above is by no means as broadly applicable as might appear at first sight, because of the requirement that the acquirer and the disposer must each fall within a particular description, with no ability to "mix and match".

The exclusion under paragraph (b) above is much broader and will cover many corporate transactions. It is not confined to transactions of a private character and even seems capable of applying to transactions involving public companies.

3.29.6 *Activities carried on in connection with employee share schemes (Article 71)*

There is a series of exclusions that apply in relation to a transaction the purpose of which is to enable or facilitate:

(a) transactions in shares in, or debentures issued by, a body corporate (the "issuer") between, or for the benefit of, relevant employees and their dependants; or
(b) the holding of such shares or debentures by, or for the benefit of, relevant employees and their dependants.

The exclusions apply to activities carried on by:

(a) the issuer;
(b) a member of the same group as the issuer;
(c) a person who holds shares or debentures of the issuer as trustee pursuant to arrangements made for the above purpose.

For this purpose, the relevant employees and their dependants are:

(a) bona fide employees or former employees of the issuer or of another member of the same group; and

(b) wives, husbands, widows, widowers, or children or step-children under the age of 18 of those employees or former employees.

The exclusions apply in relation to dealing as principal or as agent, arranging transactions and custody services. The exclusions do not apply in relation to managing investments or advising on investments. Where an employee share scheme is constituted as a trust, the trustee may also be able to rely on the specific exclusions in relation to trustees, in particular in relation to managing and advising on investments.

For the purposes of these exclusions, "shares" and "debentures" are defined to include warrants and certificates relating to shares and debentures as specified in Articles 76 and 77 RAO. However, the exclusions do not apply in relation to options or other contractually based investments; or in relation to shares in an open-ended investment company.

This broad definition of an employee share scheme is also used in other contexts. In particular, there is a corresponding exclusion from the definition of a collective investment scheme.

The definition has its limitations. It does not cover a scheme which extends to persons other than employees – for example, a scheme that includes self-employed consultants and/or non-executive directors. In connection with acquisitions, the exclusion arguably does not apply in relation to activities carried on before a group relationship has been established between the issuer of the securities (typically in the acquirer group) and the employer company (typically in the acquired group). Similarly in relation to disposals, it is not clear whether a scheme which includes in its beneficiaries employees of a company which is no longer part of the issuer group will fall within the exclusion.

3.29.7   Overseas firms (Article 72)

There is a series of exclusions that can be relied on by overseas financial services firms. The exclusions can apply where the overseas firm does not have a permanent place of business in the UK and deals with or through an authorised or exempt person; or provides services to another person as the result of a legitimate approach made by or to the person in the UK to whom the services are provided.

For this purpose, a "legitimate approach" means:

(a) an approach made to the overseas firm which has not been solicited by it in any way, or has been solicited by it in a way which does not contravene Section 21 FSMA 2000 (restrictions on financial promotion); or

(b) an approach made by or on behalf of the overseas firm in a way which does not contravene Section 21 FSMA 2000.

For this purpose, an overseas firm (referred to in RAO as an overseas person) is a person who carries on any of the following regulated activities within or outside the UK:

*   dealing as principal or agent;
*   arranging deals in investments and/or arranging mortgages;
*   advising on investments and/or advising on mortgages;
*   managing investments;
*   administration of insurance;
*   custody services;
*   sending dematerialised instructions;
*   providing collective investments and/or stakeholder pensions;
*   lending under and/or administering mortgages,

but who does not do so from a permanent place of business in the UK.

There is an exclusion for an overseas firm dealing as principal where it:

(a) enters into a transaction as principal with or through an authorised person, or an exempt person acting as such; or

(b) enters into a transaction as the result of a legitimate approach.

There is an exclusion for an overseas firm dealing as agent where it:

(a) deals with or through an authorised person, or an exempt person acting as such; or

(b)   enters into a transaction with X as agent for Y, unless:

   (i)   either X or Y is in the UK; and
   (ii) the transaction is the result of an approach (other than a legitimate approach) made by or on behalf of, or to, whichever of X or Y is in the UK.

In relation to arranging transactions:

(a)   there is an exclusion from Article 25(1) RAO (arranging a particular transaction) for arrangements made by an overseas firm with an authorised person, or an exempt person acting as such; and

(b)   there is an exclusion from Article 25(2) RAO (arrangements with a view to transactions generally) for arrangements made by an overseas firm with a view to transactions which are, as respects transactions in the UK, confined to transactions entered into by authorised persons or by exempt persons acting as such.

There is an exclusion for the giving of advice by an overseas firm as a result of a legitimate approach.

There is an exclusion from Article 64 RAO (agreeing to carry on regulated activities) for any agreement made by an overseas firm to carry on certain regulated activities (namely arranging transactions, managing investments, custody services, administration of insurance and sending dematerialised instructions) if the agreement is the result of a legitimate approach.

In the case of arranging mortgages, there are exclusions covering:

(a)   arranging a mortgage under which the borrower (or each of them, if more than one) is an individual who is not normally resident in the UK (a "non-resident individual");

(b)   arranging to vary a mortgage under which the borrower (or each of them) was a non-resident individual at the time when the mortgage was originally entered into;

(c)   arranging mortgage lending to non-resident individuals;

(d)   administering mortgages under which each borrower was a non-resident individual at the time when the mortgage was originally entered into.

3.29.8 Information society services (Article 72A)

There is a general exclusion for activities consisting of the provision of an information society service from an EEA state other than the UK. The exclusion applies to all regulated activities except provision of insurance by an EEA authorised insurer. An information society service is a service covered by the E-Commerce Directive (2000/31/EC). Very broadly it is:

(a) normally provided for remuneration;
(b) provided at a distance;
(c) so provided by means of electronic equipment for the processing (including digital compression) and storage of data; and
(d) so provided at the individual request of a recipient of the service.

3.29.9 Supply of goods or services and related insurance (Article 72B)

There is a general exclusion for travel agents and providers of goods (other than motor vehicles) who offer complementary insurance and do not carry on any other regulated activities. The insurance must satisfy the following conditions:

(a) it must not be long-term insurance (although the policy may include subsidiary long-term benefits);
(b) the total duration should be five years or less;
(c) the annual premium (or annual equivalent) should be €500 or less;
(d) it should cover travel risks or risk of breakdown, loss or damage to the goods supplied by the provider;
(e) it must not cover liability risks (except on an ancillary basis in relation to travel risks);
(f) it should be simple enough that the salesman only needs to be trained on the terms of cover in order to sell it.

The exclusion covers advising on, arranging, selling as agent and administering contracts of insurance that satisfy the above conditions. In December 2007, the Treasury announced that it intended to modify this exemption so that it will cease to apply in relation to travel insurance sold alongside a holiday with effect from 1 January 2009 onwards.

3.29.10   *Introducing insurance (Article 72C)*

There is a general exclusion for provision of information about insurance to a policyholder or potential policyholder by a person who carries on a profession or business which does not involve other regulated activities, where the provision of information is incidental to that profession or business. The exclusion covers arranging insurance, administration of insurance, managing investments and custody services.

3.29.11   *Large risks situated outside the EEA (Article 72D)*

There is a general exclusion covering the activities of advising on, arranging, dealing as agent in and administration of insurance where they relate to certain commercial insurances in respect of a risk or commitment which is not situated in an EEA state. The type of insurance, and in some cases the policyholder, must satisfy criteria set out in Article 72D RAO.

3.29.12   *Business angel-led enterprise capital funds (Articles 72E and 72F)*

There is a general exclusion covering the activities of advising, arranging, dealing as agent in, managing, safeguarding, and administering and establishing, operating or winding up a collective investment scheme for "business angels".

A business angel is an EEA incorporated limited liability entity, which operates a business angel-led enterprise capital fund. This fund must only invest in securities of unlisted companies. Both the entity operating the fund and the fund itself must only have members/participants of a kind specified in Article 72F RAO.

3.30   Certain exclusions not available to MiFID and IMD firms

The RAO contains two provisions intended to ensure that the exclusions described in this Chapter do not compromise the proper implementation of the Markets in Financial Instruments Directive (2004/39/EC) ("MiFID") and the Insurance Mediation Directive (2002/92/EC) ("IMD").

3.30.1 MiFID

MiFID requires the UK to regulate investment firms and credit institutions providing and carrying on investment services and activities on a professional basis. It does not permit some of the exclusions provided for in the RAO. Accordingly Article 4(4) RAO provides that such firms and institutions may not rely on certain specific exclusions relating to dealing, arranging deals in and managing investments, and the general exclusions set out in Articles 67 to 70 and 72E RAO, all of which are described above. The consequence is that the activities of those firms and institutions will be regulated, even where they would otherwise fall within the terms of an exclusion.

3.30.2 IMD

The IMD requires the UK to regulate insurance intermediation activities which are carried on for remuneration. Accordingly Article 4(4A) RAO contains a provision that (subject to a specific exception for warranty and travel business) the following exclusions do not apply in favour of an insurance intermediary carrying on business for remuneration:

(a) the exclusion for arranging finance on the security of an insurance policy (Article 30);
(b) the trustee exclusion (Article 66);
(c) the exclusion for activities in the course of a profession or non-investment business (Article 67).

The FSA gives guidance on this provision and its implications for professional firms in section 5.14.3 of PERG.

3.31   Designated investment business

The remainder of this Guide is concerned specifically with "designated investment business". This concept is not recognised in the RAO. It is defined in the FSA Handbook as follows:

"Designated investment" is defined as a security or a contractually based investment (other than a funeral plan contract and a right to or interest in a funeral plan contract). It comprises:

- life policy (subset of Article 75 (Contracts of insurance));
- share (Article 76);
- debenture (Article 77);
- government and public security (Article 78);
- warrant (Article 79);
- certificate representing certain securities (Article 80);
- unit (Article 81);
- stakeholder pension scheme or personal pension scheme (Article 82);
- option (Article 83);
- future (Article 84);
- contract for differences (Article 85);
- rights to or interests in the above investments (Article 89).

"Designated investment business" comprises the following activities:

- dealing in designated investments as principal (Article 14), but disregarding the exclusion in Article 15 (Absence of holding out etc);
- dealing in designated investments as agent (Article 21);
- arranging deals in designated investments (Article 25);
- operating a multilateral trading facility (Article 25D);
- managing investments (Article 37), but only if the assets consist of or include (or may consist of or include) designated investments;
- assisting in the administration of a contract of insurance, but only when the insurance contract is a designated investment;
- custody services (Article 40), but only if the assets consist of or include (or may consist of or include) designated investments;
- sending dematerialised instructions (Article 45);
- establishing, operating or winding up a collective investment scheme (Article 51);
- establishing, operating or winding up a stakeholder pension scheme or a personal pension scheme (Article 52);
- providing basic advice on stakeholder products (Article 52B);
- advising on designated investments (Article 53);
- agreeing to carry on a regulated activity (Article 64), where the activity is one of the kinds of designated investment business listed above.

Chapter 4

Further Orders

Daniel Tunkel
Partner
Financial Services Group
SJ Berwin LLP

4.1 Introduction

The purpose of this Chapter is to consider the impact of three more of the statutory instruments made pursuant to the provisions of the Financial Services and Markets Act 2000 ("FSMA 2000"). These are:

(a)   the Financial Services and Markets Act 2000 (Professions) (Non-Exempt Activities) Order 2001 (SI 2001/1227);
(b)   the Financial Services and Markets Act 2000 (Carrying on Regulated Activities By Way of Business) Order 2001 (SI 2001/1177); and
(c)   the Financial Services and Markets Act 2000 (Appointed Representatives) Regulations 2001 (SI 2001/1217).

Each of these instruments has undergone a measure of amendment over the six or so years since they were first made, and the commentary below addresses these amendments in context.

As with the majority of the Orders and Regulations which are made under the provisions of the FSMA 2000, these instruments came into force when the FSMA 2000 itself came into force, on 1 December 2001 (with certain exceptions, as explained below).

These instruments are not conceptually connected, other than through their purpose of implementing aspects of the FSMA 2000 regime which are not contained in the primary legislation. But it is convenient to review them in this Chapter since, compared with the instruments reviewed in earlier Chapters of this Guide, they are reasonably short and self-contained.

4.2 The Financial Services and Markets Act 2000 (Professions) (Non-Exempt Activities) Order 2001 (the "Professions Order")

4.2.1 The recognised professional bodies regime under the Financial Services Act 1986

Previous editions of this Guide summarised, by way of background, the regime that applied under the Financial Services Act 1986 ("FS Act 1986") to the activities of various professions in the investment business sector. Since the FS Act 1986 was repealed with effect from 30 November 2001, it is probably not necessary to dwell on this at length.

In summary, the manner in which those in the legal, accounting and actuarial professions carried on investment business activities fell under the FS Act 1986 to be treated in one (or more) of three ways:

(a)   First and foremost, it was always open to law firms, accounting practices and actuaries to seek to be regulated by one of the self-regulatory entities established under the aegis of that legislation, though in practice not many ever did.

(b)   Various professional bodies (termed "recognised professional bodies" or "RPBs") developed their own investment business regulation regimes under the aegis of the FS Act 1986. RPBs had to be accepted by the Securities and Investments Board and comply with certain standards laid down in the FS Act 1986.[1]

(c)   In addition to the regime for RPB regulation for investment business carried on by lawyers, accountants and the like, there were also specific exclusions in Schedule 1 to the FS Act 1986 for certain limited activities which were, essentially, functions performed in a fashion wholly ancillary to professional services.

4.2.2 The FSMA 2000 simplification

The position of professionals under FSMA 2000 Part XX is in principle simplified, to the extent that there is no longer any significant

---

[1] *See* FS Act 1986 Schedule 3.

function for the various professional bodies to discharge. Broadly speaking, the professional person is now either deemed to be carrying on a regulated activity or its activities are excluded from the scope of regulation altogether.[2] Where a professional firm carries on a regulated activity which is not carved out of the FSMA 2000 regime for its benefit, the firm now needs to be directly regulated by the Financial Services Authority ("FSA").

4.2.3 *Part XX FSMA 2000*

To set the Professions Order in its context, it is necessary to look at the framework of Part XX. It has to be said that the structure of Sections 325–327 is unnecessarily complicated and creates a clear circularity of logic in relation to what sort of activities are intended to fall outside the scope of FSA authorisation when carried on by the professions.

(a)   There is provision under Section 326 for a Treasury Order to be made determining which entities shall be considered "Designated Professional Bodies" ("DPBs")[3] as a part of the new process of regulation of professional persons. The legislation goes on to provide a "basic condition" and a series of "additional conditions" which a would-be DPB must satisfy in order to justify the making of an order constituting it a DPB. However, one of the additional conditions is that bodies established in other European Economic Area ("EEA") Member States with regulatory powers over their professions in those States may fall within the scope of such an Order: thus, the regime of Part XX will apply to the UK offices of professional firms constituted and regulated professionally in other EEA Member States.

(b)   DPBs are expected to make regulations which govern the carrying on by members of the relevant professions of so-called

---

[2] As will be seen from 4.2.8 below, however, there is still a potentially significant problem in relation to acts of financial promotion under FSMA 2000 Section 21.

[3] The Financial Services and Markets Act 2000 (Designated Professional Bodies) Order 2001 (SI 2001/1226). Article 2 specifies 10 DPBs: the original eight from the 2001 Order included the UK's three Law Societies, three Institutes of Chartered Accountants, the Institute of Actuaries and the Association of Certified Chartered Accountants. To these were added the Council for Licensed Conveyancers (Financial Services and Markets Act 2000 (Designated Professional Bodies) (Amendment) Order 2004 (SI 2004/3352)) with effect from 14 January 2005; and the Royal Institution of Chartered Surveyors (Financial Services and Markets Act 2000 (Designated Professional Bodies) (Amendment) Order 2006 (SI 2006/59)) as from 10 February 2006.

"exempt regulated activities". This term is defined[4] as activities which, though within the scope of the concept of regulated activities under the FSMA 2000, may be carried on by a person who is a member of any profession supervised and regulated by a DPB without that person needing FSA regulation as well. By way of clarification, "member" refers to a member of the relevant profession who is answerable to the rules and regulations of the DPB; he need not be a member of the DPB itself.

(c)　The FSA's principal duty[5] is to "keep itself informed" of the manner in which members of relevant professions carry on exempt regulated activities and more specifically the manner of their supervision by the DPBs in question.

(d)　However, the "basic condition" referred to at (a) above is that a body seeking DPB status must have rules in relation to regulated activities which, if it became a DPB, would be exempt regulated activities.[6] This clearly achieves a circularity with the stated definition of "exempt regulated activities", and since the legislation provides no further detail as to how this sub-set of regulated activities should be defined or identified,[7] it is necessary to have regard to the mechanism under the FSMA 2000 for determining what regulated activities are non-exempt.

(e)　Section 327(6) FSMA 2000 then goes on to state that any exemption for members of the professions from the general prohibition[8] does not apply in relation to the carrying on of those regulated activities specified by the Treasury in an Order made for the purpose. Simply put, for a professional to carry on any activity which that Order specifies necessarily requires the professional to be FSA-regulated (absent reliance on some other exclusion or qualification in, for example, the Regulated Activities Order). The Professions Order has been made for this purpose. Its scope is considered in more detail in 4.2.4 below.

(f)　There are a few further points in Section 327 which should be mentioned. This Section provides a framework under which a

---

[4] FSMA 2000 Section 325(2).
[5] Ibid. Section 325(1).
[6] Ibid. Section 326(4).
[7] Although under FSMA 2000 Section 332(3) DPBs "must" make regulations which define the regulated activities which members of the professions may carry on.
[8] That is, the prohibition against carrying on a regulated activity without requisite authorisation: *see* ibid. Section 19.

member of one of the professions supervised by a DPB (or one who is "controlled or managed" by such a member)[9] may carry on regulated activities without being in breach of the general prohibition:

(i)   he must not receive payments for provision of such services from a third party (unless he accounts for them to his client);[10]

(ii) the carrying on of a regulated activity must be incidental to the provision of professional services[11] (i.e. services which do not constitute a regulated activity and which are subject to regulation in accordance with the rules of a DPB);

(iii) the only regulated activities which that person carries on are activities which are subject to rules made by the relevant DPB pursuant to FSMA 2000 Section 332(3) (other than where the activities are ones in respect of which the person is an exempt person).[12]

There are powers under FSMA 2000 Sections 328–329 for the FSA to intervene and/or make specific regulations which have the effect in specific cases or more generally of suspending the regime under Section 327. To date, these have not been exercised.

4.2.4   The specified activities

Articles 4 to 8 of the Professions Order sets out details of various regulated activities which, should they be carried on by a professional person, require that person to be authorised directly by the FSA. These are referable to regulated activities as set out in the Regulated Activities Order, which has been considered in Chapter 3 of this Guide, and therefore further elaboration here as to the provisions of the Regulated Activities Order will be kept to a minimum.

Broadly, the non-exempt activities to which the Professions Order relates are either completely non-exempt (*see* Article 4 of the

---

[9] Ibid. Section 327(2)(b).
[10] Ibid. Section 327(3). The FSA is understood to take the view that in this context "accounts for" means nothing less than "hands over", although this has never been tested in the courts.
[11] Ibid. Section 327(4).
[12] Ibid. Section 327(5).

Professions Order) or non-exempt if certain further conditions are satisfied (*see* Articles 4A–8). Various amendments introduced to the Professions Order since it first came into force largely reflect the impact of the extension of the FSA's jurisdiction in relation to electronic money, insurance intermediation and mortgage services.

4.2.5 Completely non-exempt activities

The list in Article 4 reads as follows:

(a) accepting deposits (pursuant to Article 5 of the Regulated Activities Order);

(b) issue of electronic money (ibid. Article 9B);[13]

(c) effecting and carrying out contracts of insurance (ibid. Article 10);

(d) dealing in investments as principal (ibid. Article 14);

(e) establishing, operating or winding up a collective investment scheme, acting as trustee of an authorised unit trust scheme, acting as a depositary or sole director of an open-ended investment company (ibid. Article 51);

(f) establishing, operating or winding up a pension scheme (ibid. Article 52);[14]

(g) providing basic advice on stakeholder products (ibid. Article 52B);[15]

(h) managing the underwriting capacity of a Lloyd's syndicate as managing agent at Lloyd's (ibid. Article 57); and

(i) providing funeral plan contracts (ibid. Article 59).[16]

However, the blanket non-exemption in relation to entering into a regulated mortgage contract as lender or administering a regulated

---

[13] Para. (aa) of Article 4 was added by SI 2002/682 Article 7(1), with effect from 27 April 2002, as part of the process of implementing the EC Electronic Money Directive.

[14] Originally para. (e) of Article 4 referred to the establishment etc. of *stakeholder* pension schemes. The "stakeholder" word was deleted by the Financial Services and Markets Act 2000 (Regulated Activities) (Amendment) Order 2006 (SI 2006/1969), Article 11, with effect, subject to certain transitional provisions, from 6 April 2007. The same Order provided for the term "pension scheme" to be generally defined with respect to Section 1 Pension Schemes Act 1993.

[15] Paragraph (ea) of Article 4 was added by the Financial Services and Markets Act 2000 (Regulated Activities) (Amendment) (No. 2) Order 2004 (SI 2004/2737), Articles 5(3) and (4), with effect from 6 April 2005. The meaning of "stakeholder product" in the context of Article 52B of the Regulated Activities Order has been considered in Chapter 3 at 3.16 (above).

[16] This provision came into force on 1 January 2002.

mortgage (ibid. Article 61) has now been repealed, the matter being operatively addressed in Article 6B of the Professions Order (*see* 4.2.6 below).

The effect of this list of complete non-exemptions is that, for example, should a law firm wish to take deposits or an accountant to underwrite insurance or deal as principal in investments etc., this now clearly requires FSA authorisation; there is nothing further that liaison with the relevant professional body can accomplish.[17]

4.2.6 *Non-exemptions subject to conditions*

Over and above the complete non-exemptions in 4.2.5 above, there are some more non-exempt activities which are subject to certain further qualifications. In order of their appearance in the Professions Order, these are as follows:

(a)   Article 4A of the Professions Order[18] gives effect to the EC Insurance Mediation Directive, and simply provides that the professional's general right to arrange investment deals or to make arrangements for persons to buy or sell investments is curtailed to the extent this involves transactions in rights under a contract of insurance and the professional is not himself on the FSA's Record of Insurance Intermediaries.[19]

(b)   Article 5 of the Professions Order addresses the activity of managing "relevant investments" (Article 37 of the Regulated Activities Order).[20] The term "relevant investment" is used in the Professions Order as a shorthand for securities and contractually based investments. The expressions "security" and "contractually based investment" are defined in accordance

---

[17] Having said that, the professional body is of course free to make its own professional rules concerning what sort of areas its members can work within: thus it is highly likely that the Law Society would wish to prevent a firm of solicitors from acting as a bank, even though under the FSMA 2000 regime there is nothing explicit to prohibit this state of affairs if the firm applied to the FSA for requisite authorisation.

[18] Added by SI 2003/1476 Article 16(1) and (3). Article 4A of the Professions Order comes into force on 31 October 2004 in relation to long-term care insurance and on 14 January 2005 in relation to other types of insurance.

[19] This Register is required to be maintained by the FSA pursuant to Article 93 of the Regulated Activities Order, added by SI 2003/1476.

[20] Professions Order, Article 5(1).

with Article 3(1) of the Regulated Activities Order. There are some further qualifications:

(i)   managing is only non-exempt in relation to the buying or subscribing for of securities or contractually based investments. While it is difficult to envisage a management arrangement as involving only selling and no buying at all, it is conceivable that a solicitor or accountant might have instructions to realise a portfolio in an estate in order to distribute cash to the beneficiaries, and this would not appear to amount to non-exempt management (i.e. the professional will be able to sell for cash without requiring FSA authorisation);

(ii) if the professional arranges for all routine or day-to-day activities in relation to managing to be carried out by a duly authorised or exempt person[21] or the activity is carried out in accordance with the advice of such a person,[22] whatever remains for him to manage is taken outside the scope of the Order.

- In relation to the first limb, it clearly matters to consider what amounts to "routine" and "day-to-day" decisions. It is suggested that the comparison is being made here with strategic or one-off decisions. So, a decision to appoint a particular valuer with expertise in a certain type of security, or to appoint a custodian, is almost certainly not a day-to-day matter, whereas any decision to make an investment should be considered a day-to-day decision, since it implies a duty to keep that investment under review on a regular basis.
- This might equally be true where a decision to move into or out of a particular market is taken, since this also needs to be kept under regular review.
- Whether investing in a collective investment scheme is considered to fall within the day-to-day or the one-off category is open to debate. The safer view is that this is also day-to-day, since the person who makes this

---

[21] Professions Order, Article 5(2)(a).
[22] Ibid. Article 5(2)(b).

decision is just as duty-bound to keep this under peri-odical review as if it were a holding of a share or a bond.

- However, overriding all of these considerations is the fact that if the professional acts in tandem with an appropriately authorised investment adviser, then it would seem he can make day-to-day as well as strategic investment management decisions.

(c) Article 5A of the Professions Order[23] has the effect of requiring a professional to be on the FSA's Record of Insurance intermediaries in order to assist in the administration or performance of an insurance contract. As already noted, this had effect from 31 October 2004 in relation to long-tern healthcare insurance and from 14 January 2005 in relation to all other insurance contracts.

(d) Advising on investments is a specified activity under Article 6 of the Professions Order (and may therefore not be carried on by a member of a profession without FSA authorisation) if:

(i) the advice consists of a recommendation to a member of a personal pension scheme[24] or his agent to dispose of any rights or interests in the scheme[25] (other than where all that the professional is doing is endorsing a recommendation that the professional or his client has received from an appropriately authorised person);[26] or

(ii) the advice is given to an individual,[27] and it consists of a recommendation to buy or subscribe for a particular security or contractually based investment[28] and the relevant transaction associated with that advice would be made:

- with a person who deals with the investment in the course of business; or
- on an investment exchange or other market; or
- in response to an invitation to subscribe for the investment which is to be admitted onto such an exchange.[29]

---

[23] Inserted by SI 2003/1476 Article 16.
[24] As defined in Section 1 Pension Schemes Act 1993.
[25] Professions Order Article 6(3).
[26] Ibid. Article 6(4).
[27] Ibid. Article 6(2)(a).
[28] Ibid. Article 6(2)(b).
[29] Ibid. Article 6(2)(c).

Providing advice in such circumstances does not fall within the scope of the Professions Order if the recipient of that advice carries on business by himself or carries on business through an undertaking which he already controls by virtue of the transaction to which the advice relates (or would do so if the transaction proceeds).[30] Similarly the advice would not fall within the scope of the Professions Order if the recipient receives the advice in his capacity as a trustee of an occupational pension scheme ("OPS")[31] or if it endorses a recommendation from an authorised person with respect to the advised person's personal pension scheme.

Once again, any advice in relation to dealings in policies of insurance currently falls outside the Professions Order, as does advice purely in relation to disposal of securities or derivatives. Advising on sale or purchase of rights under a contract of insurance has, however, been added to the Professions Order, and the amendment operates in broadly the same way as the other amendments already encountered which give effect to the regime for the registration etc. of insurance intermediaries.[32]

(e) Article 6A was added to the Professions Order[33] to take account of the coming into force of the regime under which the FSA in October 2004 acquired responsibility for regulation of various activities related to retail mortgages.

   (i) Advising on regulated mortgage contracts[34] (per Article 53A of the Regulated Activities Order) is specified (i.e. the professional will require direct FSA authorisation to provide this service) where:

   • it consists of a recommendation, given to an individual, to enter as a borrower into a regulated mortgage contract with a particular mortgagee;[35] and

---

[30] Ibid. Article 6(2)(a)(i).
[31] Ibid. Article 6(2)(a)(ii).
[32] Ibid. Article 6(5), inserted by SI 2003/1476 Article 16. Consequential amendments and repeals have been made to the remaining provisions of Article 6 of the Professions Order.
[33] The provisions of Articles 6A and 6B of the Professions Order came into force on 31 October 2004, when the FSA acquired its powers to regulate the mortgage industry. *See* SI 2004/1475 Article 1(3).
[34] Professions Order Article 6A.
[35] Ibid. Article 6A(2)(a).

- that mortgagee, in so acting, carries on the regulated activity of entering into regulated mortgage contracts (Regulated Activities Order Article 61);[36]

unless[37] the recommendation from the professional merely endorses a corresponding recommendation from a person who is already authorised by the FSA to provide advice in relation to mortgages (or a person who is exempt from the requirement to be regulated to do this). It might appear from this that the conveyancing solicitor advising his client on the purchase of a property financed by a mortgage will need to ensure that his client is advised by the mortgagee or an independent mortgage advisory agent in order to escape the need to be regulated. However, advising on the purely *legal* impact of a mortgage (and, for example, the consequences in law of failure to maintain repayments to the mortgagee) surely continues to fall within the realm of advice completely excluded from regulation on account of its being wholly incidental to legal services; and realistically, it is this sort of advice (rather than financial advice) which the client typically seeks from his legal adviser.

(ii) As a consequence, the original blanket prohibition on actually effecting mortgage contracts in former Article 4(h) has been revoked, and a version of this in qualified form appears as Article 6B.[38]

(f) Articles 6C–6F were added to the Professions Order[39] in order to extend the qualified non-exemption provisions to the regulated activities associated with regulated home reversion plans and regulated home purchase plans. In essence:

(i) Article 6C (advising on regulated home reversion plans: Regulated Activities Order Article 53B) and Article 6E (advising on regulated home purchase plans: ibid. Article

---

[36] Ibid. Article 6A(2)(b).
[37] Ibid. Article 6A(3).
[38] Ibid. Article 6B.
[39] These provisions were added by the Financial Services and Markets Act 2000 (Regulated Activities) (Amendment) (no. 2) Order 2006 (SI 2006/2383) with effect (subject to transitional provisions) from 6 April 2007. For commentary on the relevant regulated activities and the definitions of "regulated home reversion plan" and "regulated home purchase plan", *see* 4.2.6 above.

      53C) work for these investment types in the same way as Article 6A does in relation to advising on regulated mortgage contracts; and

(ii)   Articles 6D (entering into and administering a regulated home reversion plan: Regulated Activities Order Article 63B) and 6F (entering into and administering a regulated home purchase plan: ibid. Article 63B) work for these investment types in the same way as Article 6B does in relation to entering into and administering regulated mortgage contracts).

(g)   Advising a person to become a member of a particular Lloyd's syndicate is a specified activity unless that advice merely endorses the advice of a duly authorised or exempt person.[40]

(h)   There is a sweeper provision which catches activities that amount to agreeing to carry on any of the activities addressed by Articles 4–8 of the Professions Order, except for those in Article 4(a), (aa), (b), (d) and (e)[41] (*see* 4.2.5 above). Merely agreeing to deal in investments, manage investments or advise on investments (to the extent covered under Articles 4–8) will therefore be specified activities and accordingly will be non-exempted for the purposes of FSMA 2000 Part XX.[42]

4.2.7   What, in summary, can a professional do?

The arrangement of FSMA 2000 Part XX and the Professions Order establishes what is in effect a structure with three layers of negatives, the semantics of which are ungainly and rather unnecessary. The summary is as follows:

(a)   Consider first of all the scope of the Professions Order and the activities set out there which, come what may, a professional will only be able to carry on if he accepts direct regulation from the FSA. It is quite clear that, absent direct FSA regulation, professionals cannot run banks, e-money businesses or insurance underwriting services, for example, nor deal directly in investments in any

---

[40] Ibid. Article 7.
[41] Ibid. Article 8.
[42] Paradoxically, though, not para. (ea) of Article 4, so agreeing to provide basic advice on stakeholder products is not treated as a non-excluded activity.

fashion. Nor can they operate collective investment schemes or pension schemes of any variety or act in various capacities with respect to regulated collective investment schemes.[43]

(b) Capacity to manage investments or advise on investments is restricted, though clearly there is no obstacle to much of this activity in circumstances where the professional acts in accordance with the advice which an appropriately authorised person or exempt person provides. Thus, there is no conceptual difficulty in a professional passing on to a private client advice which is clearly derived from an investment report from a UK investment firm.

(c) Two heads of activity are barely contemplated by the Professions Order:[44]

    (i) the first is arrangement of deals in investments. This should allow firms of lawyers, accountants etc., to be involved in setting up arrangements whereby their clients can deal, and would appear to permit such firms to engage in corporate finance activities up to the point where what is involved is actual investment dealing as principal. However, care has to be taken to ensure that the activity is not in the first instance caught by the carefully drawn limitations on the sort of investment advice that can be given (*see* 4.2.6(d) above). It would seem that a group of individuals can instruct their accountant in the making of arrangements for them to acquire control of a company, but since no one of them will be that controller, there has to be some doubt as to whether the strict wording of Article 6(2)(a)(i) of the Professions Order will allow the accountant to advise them individually or collectively if he is not FSA regulated. It has been noted of course that arrangement of transactions in insurance contracts falls within the scope of the Professions Order with the coming into force of Article 4A;

---

[43] Though in practice this last point need not have been included, since authorised corporate directors, trustees and depositaries of regulated collective investment schemes are all required by other provisions in the FSMA 2000 or made thereunder to be corporate entities.

[44] Actually, to be fair, nor is the sending of dematerialised instructions within the scope of the Professions Order; but it is altogether unlikely that a law firm or accountancy practice will be a member of CREST system as presently constituted, so it is not relevant to consider this further in this context.

(ii) safe-keeping and administration arrangements are not discussed in the Order at all. In principle therefore, this is not a non-exempt activity and is something which should fall within the scope of DPB regulation and thus be permitted to professionals without their requiring to be authorised by the FSA.

(d) Where there is a provision in the Regulated Activities Order which carves an exclusion out of any given regulated activity, the professional world is in principle entitled to take advantage of this. The nature of the exclusions from the Regulated Activities Order has been discussed in Chapter 3 already, and no more need be said about them at this point.

(e) There remains, of course, a conceptual lacuna in the system. It might be thought that if a regulated activity is not mentioned in the non-exempt list in the Professions Order it is therefore one that a member of the professions can carry on without concern for breaching the general prohibition. This is clearly not the case. Section 327(5) requires that he not carry on any regulated activity unless he is exempt or it is subject of rules made by his DPB. Should his DPB *not* make relevant rules, or should their scope be tailored so as to limit the nature of his conduct in a particular area, the professional could find that specific aspects of regulated activities, while not non-exempted, are not provided for in the relevant rules and are therefore off limits for him just as effectively as if they had been specified in the Professions Order.

(f) What complicates matters even further is that although professional regulators in other EEA Member States are expected to fashion rules for their professionals in the UK (this is the clear implication of Section 326(5)(d)), the FSA clearly contemplates that rules will be made which address the activities as they are spelt out in the Regulated Activities Order. Other EEA Member States do not characterise their investment activities in the same fashion as is the case in the UK.[45] Despite the length of time since the coming into force of the FSMA 2000, it still remains to be seen how the framework of Part XX will work

---

[45] Note, for example, the mismatch between arrangement of deals in investments pursuant to Article 25 of the Regulated Activities Order and the concept of reception and transmission of orders pursuant to the EC Markets in Financial Instruments Directive.

with respect to overseas professionals from other Member States.

4.2.8 *The catch: financial promotion*

The Part XX regime is concerned with regulated activities. There is another fundamental reason why a person might wish (or *need*) to be FSA regulated, which is in order to be freely able to communicate financial promotions under the FSMA 2000 Section 21 regime. Alternatively, those members of the professions who are not FSA-authorised (and do not wish to pray in aid authorised firms for all their promotional activities) will need to assure themselves that such promotions as they do carry out are subject to an exemption from the financial promotion restrictions. This is not the appropriate context to review the financial promotion regime in detail. There are opportunities for any unregulated person to promote investment opportunities to certain categories of exempt recipient, which have been considered in outline in Chapter 1 of this Guide. What regrettably does not exist is a foolproof blanket exemption in relation to promotion by professionals in relation to activities which themselves fall within the scope of the Part XX exempt regime.

The first edition of this Chapter was written shortly after the FSMA 2000 and the financial promotion regime came into force, and reviewed two exemptions in the Financial Promotion Order which were of particular relevance to professionals. The limitations of these provisions apparent at that time, from a first consideration of the Financial Promotion Order, were discussed. It is still worth considering these provisions, although guidance from the FSA in Appendix 1 to its Authorisation Manual has to some extent softened the blow of the provisions in question. This guidance was under discussion for much of 2002 and was finalised some time after the first edition of this Guide went to print.

(a) Article 55 of the Financial Promotion Order exempts a real-time communication of any nature made by a member of the professions to a recipient who has previously engaged the professional to provide professional services, provided of course that it touches upon the carrying on of a regulated activity by the professional which by virtue of FSMA 2000 Section 327 does not cause him to breach the general prohibition.

(b) Article 55A of the Financial Promotion Order[46] extends the effect
of Article 55 to non-real time communications, which in this case
may be made by the professional to any person (not merely his
pre-existing client), but provided that there is a written notification on each such communication in the form specified in Article
55A(2). Since the warning wording required mentions that the
provider of the communication must be doing so "as an incidental part of the professional services we have been engaged to
provide", it would seem that even though the communication
can be made to persons other than clients, there must be a relevant client retainer in place.

In 2001/02 these provisions were considered to be of potentially
significant difficulty to the professional firms (in particular the larger
commercial law practices). Examples of the sort of difficulties
perceived were provided to the FSA as part of its process of consideration of guidance on the financial promotion regime:

(a) At a negotiation meeting or a conference call, the professional's
client may be accompanied by others, such as the client's counterparties and intermediaries of different sorts, and all are party
to any real-time communication made at such an occasion: but
Article 55 only extends to own clients.
(b) In principle, the same applies in court, arbitration or mediation
proceedings, where several parties may be involved in relation
to what is in effect the acquisition and disposal of investments.
(c) Any document concerning an investment may be a communication, since FSMA 2000 Section 21 refers to invitations or inducements to engage in investment activity. As a result, while a legal
agreement was not considered under the FS Act 1986 to amount
to an "investment advertisement", it is clearly a communication if
sent to other persons and may induce them to invest (even if it is
far-fetched to consider it to be an invitation to this effect). Would
this mean that compliance with Article 55A requires every travel-
ling draft of an agreement for the purchase and sale of shares to
bear the requisite legend? What about draft completion board
minutes? Indeed, what about internal communications between

---

[46] Added by the Financial Services and Markets Act 2000 (Financial Promotion) (Amendment)
Order 2001 (SI 2001/2633).

different members of a large firm where the subject matter is the circumstances of a public offer to be made by a client?

The consequence of non-compliance with this regime by a professional firm is, among other things, that investment transactions can be unravelled and compensation may be due to investors. The position was wholly unsatisfactory, as was made very clear by representatives of the professions in a number of approaches to the Treasury and the FSA. It was particularly undesirable that merely for the sake of clarification of the position with the financial promotion regime, primary authorisation might have been necessary. Such authorisation would entail compliance by professional firms with capital adequacy regimes, regulatory compliance and all manner of other controls applicable to investment professionals but wholly alien to the structure of professional operation.

4.2.9 *Summary of the effect on financial promotion by professionals of the FSA Guidance*

Notwithstanding the concerns described above, the guidance located in the Perimeter Guidance Manual ("PERG") has in some respects provided clarification for the professions of the scope of the two tailor-made exemptions. While some of this merely clarifies that the professions' fears of 2001/02 are borne out by the narrowness of the language in the FP Order, other aspects of the Guidance do provide some comfort.[47] It is not appropriate in the context of this Chapter to go into great detail, but the following few points may offer some explanation:

(a) PERG 8.15 offers commentary on Articles 55 and 55A, and they are as narrowly drawn, and to be as narrowly interpreted, as the professions had reason to fear in 2001/02. That said, even though there are going to be circumstances under which these two exemptions will simply not work for the professional concerned, there are other exemptions which can be relied upon instead.

---

[47] It is probably also fair comment that since the FSMA 2000 came into force, practitioners have generally become more relaxed with the way that the financial promotion exemptions regime works in practice.

(b)   Probably more important than these two specific exemptions is the FSA's general understanding of what is required for something to constitute an "inducement". PERG 8.4 (and in particular PERG 8.4.7G) addresses (with numerous examples) what is meant by the word "inducement" as used in FSMA 2000 Section 21. The FSA looks for the "inducement" to be a significant step in the critical path towards the consummation of the investment. In this respect:

(i)   PERG 8.4.19G states in terms that legal agreements will only rarely be inducements. If the terms of a deal have been agreed and the agreement in writing serves merely to document those terms, the inducement phase has passed;

(ii)   PERG 8.4.24G indicates that a document that explains the terms of an agreement need not be an inducement unless it specifically contains further language that steers the reader towards a decision to invest.

These two provisions alone should afford the legal profession comfort in relation to circulation of draft agreements for review etc.

The truth is that the lacuna in the Part XX regime referred to above does remain – if for no other reason than that the FSA's guidance is only that, and it could be attacked by a court asked to rule on the matter. A better-argued regime for professionals would improve matters further, and it is a little disappointing that the Treasury's review of the financial promotion regime during the course of 2004–05 did not really address this concern.

4.3   Financial Services and Markets Act 2000 (Carrying on Regulated Activities by Way of Business) Order 2000 (the "Business Order")

4.3.1   Background

Under the FS Act 1986, there was a prohibition on the carrying on of "investment business" in the UK. On the principle that the greater includes the lesser, it was always understood that a person not operating by way of business *at all* could not be carrying on an investment business. However, the FS Act 1986 provided no clear guidance as to what "business" meant in such circumstances, and one was reduced to considering questions of whether the activity was "business-like" in its conception: was the person concerned acting in a professional manner, taking money for his troubles, regularly seeing people with respect to the same or similar activities, filing tax returns etc?

The FSMA 2000 regime is intended to resolve some of these difficulties. FSMA 2000 Section 22 provides that an activity is "regulated for the purposes of this Act if it is an activity of a specified kind which is carried on by way of business". Section 419(1) affords the Treasury scope to make an Order which determines where a person not ordinarily considered to be operating by way of business is in fact deemed to be doing so and vice versa. Accordingly, the Business Order determines the circumstances in which persons are to be regarded or not, as the case may be, as carrying on regulated activities by way of business.

4.3.2 Scope of the Business Order

The Business Order relates to regulated activities only. This is an important point to note, since the relevance of "business" occurs in another context, namely that of financial promotion, and the Business Order does not apply here at all.[48]

The scope of the Business Order may be summarised as follows:

(a) Articles 2 and 3 of the Business Order make provision as to the circumstances in which a person who accepts a deposit or carries on certain kinds of dealing and other investment activities may be regarded as not doing so by way of business.

(b) Articles 3A, 3B and 3C have been variously added to make provision as to the circumstances in which a person who arranges or advises on, respectively, regulated mortgage contracts, regulated home equity reversion plans and regulated

---

[48] The financial promotion restriction applies to communications issued in the course of business. FSMA 2000 Section 21(4) allows the Treasury to say more clearly what this means in context, but the Treasury has declined to do so to date, and has given indications in the consultative process that led to the finalisation of the financial promotion regime that it considers the point to be self-explanatory.

home equity purchase plans may be regarded as not doing so by way of business.

(c)   Article 4 makes provision for the exceptional circumstances in which a person who manages the assets of an OPS is not regarded as doing so by way of business.

4.3.3   Deposit taking not by way of business

A person who accepts deposits is not regarded as doing so by way of business if two conditions are fulfilled:

(a)   he must not hold himself out as accepting deposits on a day-to-day basis;[49] and

(b)   the deposits must only be accepted on particular occasions.[50] Whether an occasion is particular or not is determined by the frequency of those occasions or any other feature which might distinguish them.[51]

What this achieves is not entirely clear. It is clearly insufficient that the person concerned is not holding himself as a regular deposit-taker. There has to be some sort of form and system to the irregularity with which deposits are accepted. The definitions of "deposit" and "accepting deposits" are found for these purposes in Article 5(1) and (2) of the Regulated Activities Order.[52]

What the Business Order achieves in relation to the taking of deposits is more likely to be circumstances under which an investment firm may be considered to accept deposits that fall outside regulation (meaning that the firm does not also have to register as a credit institution). It is altogether less likely that the provisions in Article 2 of the Business Order sanction opportunities for informal deposit-taking by an entity that is outside of regulation altogether. Nor, of course, is it intended through Article 2 to create circumstances under which an entity that remains unregulated in respect of "informal deposit taking" somehow avoids regulation altogether.

---

[49] Business Order Article 2(1)(a).
[50] Ibid. Article 2(1)(b).
[51] Ibid. Article 2(2).
[52] And, in fact, these formulations are taken directly from the Banking Act 1987 Sections 5 and 6.

4.3.4 *Carrying on investment business not by way of business*

This sounds like a contradiction in terms. In fact, what Article 3 of the Business Order achieves is an official formulation of the principle mentioned at 4.3.1 above as having been an informal but logical conclusion drawn from the meaning of "investment business" in the FS Act 1986. Thus, a person is only to be regarded as carrying on a range of listed regulated activities by way of business if he is engaged in doing so as a business. The list of activities holds no surprises, and includes:

(a) dealing in investments as principal (Article 14 of the Regulated Activities Order). Considering that Article 15 of the Regulated Activities Order already carves out from the activity of dealing as principal circumstances under which the person concerned does not "hold himself out" (*see* 4.3.3 above), it is not entirely clear how much further the Business Order needs to take this point. It is true that the "holding out" provisions do not apply to derivatives, of course, so the exclusion in the Business Order would now appear to make it clear that a company which enters into an off-market swap or option of some sort as a principal in relation to commercial arrangements does not do so by way of business and therefore falls outside the scope of FSMA 2000 regulation. (There was probably never any doubt of this in the first place, but it is comforting to know that this is covered expressly in regulations, and not merely by implication);

(b) dealing in investments as agent (ibid. Article 21). Essentially the same point applies to the analysis of this provision as to dealing as principal in (a) above in relation, say, to the arrangement of derivatives for companies within a group by a centralised treasury function;

(c) arranging deals in investments (ibid. Article 25), other than where the investments concerned are Lloyd's syndicate participations or rights and interests in other investments;

(d) operating a multilateral trading facility (ibid. Article 25D);[53]

(e) managing investments (ibid. Article 37). Note that this is not pertinent to the management of the assets of an OPS, which is

---

[53] Added by the Financial Services and Markets Act 2000 (Regulated Activities) (Amendment) (No. 3) Order 2006 (SI 2006/3384) Article 37, with effect from 1 November 2007. The concept of a multilateral trading facility is derived from the EC Markets in Financial Instruments Directive, and it has to be said that it is bizarrely improbable that one of these can be run or operated other than as, or as an integral part of, a business.

considered further in Article 4 of the Business Order. This should be understood to relate to discretionary and non-discretionary management activities, and would appear to carve out from FSMA 2000 regulation informal management activities undertaken by unremunerated trustees of a settlement or family trust, for example;

(f) safeguarding and administering investments (ibid. Article 40). This offers latitude to firms which can offer safekeeping services in relation to investments as an added free feature of an overall service which might itself be a business. For example, a solicitor or accountant can offer services in relation safekeeping of securities in a family trust where he is appointed (on a pro bono basis) as trustee;

(g) sending dematerialised instructions (ibid. Article 45). Here again, it is not easy to see how this sort of activity is likely to be carried on other than by way of business, since the sort of undertakings which interface with the CREST system are most likely to do so by substantial way of business. It is not inconceivable that individual independent investors might become members of the CREST system and thereby be involved in sending their own trading instructions into CREST for settlement;

(h) establishing, operating or winding up a collective investment scheme, acting as trustee of an authorised trust scheme and acting as the depositary or sole director of an open-ended investment company (ibid. Article 51). It is frankly rather difficult to imagine that, with the various requirements to be undertaken in order to operate etc. a regulated collective investment scheme. But this carve-out does have one useful effect. Many limited partnership arrangements provide for their winding-up to be overseen by a "liquidating trustee". Provided that this entity does not operate by way of business in such capacity, it ought to be possible to structure arrangements so that the general partner of the limited partnership could be appointed to this function and would not require authorisation under the FSMA 2000 to do so;

(i) establishing, operating or winding up a pension scheme (ibid. Article 52).[54] Again, it is not really all that likely that, in view of

---

[54] The "stakeholder" word was deleted by the Financial Services and Markets Act 2000 (Regulated Activities) (Amendment) Order 2006 (SI 2006/1969), Article 9, with effect, subject to certain transitional provisions, from 6 April 2007. *See* further note 14 above.

the regulation underpinning pensions, this sort of activity could be carried on by a person other than in a business context;

(j)   provision of investment advice (ibid. Article 53);

(k)   agreeing (ibid. Article 64) to do any of the activities mentioned in (a) to (j).

There is one curious semantic problem with Article 3 of the Business Order, however. The precise wording of Article 3(1) reads as follows:

"A person is not to be regarded as carrying on by way of business an activity to which this article applies, unless he carries on the business of engaging in one or more such activities."

This wording seems to suggest that if the person concerned carries on one of the regulated activities enumerated above as a part of his business, then he cannot argue that he has capacity to carry on any other or others of them not by way of business. It is unclear whether this was intended in practice. But the effect seems to be, for example, that an entity which deals or manages as part of its business cannot purport to offer a safeguarding and administration service as a non-business.

4.3.5   No amendments in relation to e-money activities

Another slightly curious thing is that no amendments have been made to the Business Order in relation to the regulated activity of issue of e-money. This is curious. The capital requirements of an e-money issuer prescribed under the FSA's Electronic Money Sourcebook ("ELM") are prohibitive, and are essentially designed to ensure that entities who wish to issue e-money are effectively restricted to the major European and worldwide banks. However, it is increasingly the case that smaller organisations engage, in a quite non-businesslike fashion, in the issue of electronic equivalents to cash. This is becoming popular in respect of universities, for example, whose students and fellows can use electronic cash to make on-campus purchases (e.g. at lunch counters or in university shops). While it is possible that some such organisations are excluded from the regulation of electronic money by virtue of the terms of the Electronic Money Directive, there are bound to be borderline cases in the future, and it seems sensible that an amendment to the Business

Order to take borderline cases completely out of regulation should be introduced at some point.

Article 9C of the Regulated Activities Order offers a way out of regulation for certain small e-money issuers, but it is restricted in its sweep. For example, it can only apply to small issuers who are companies or partnerships with a head office in the UK, and it depends upon the issue of a certificate of exemption by the FSA (rather than automatically in accordance with the sort of activities the entity carries on).

4.3.6 Insurance mediation

Amendments to Article 3 of the Business Order provide that a person is not considered to carry on any insurance mediation activity by way of business unless "he takes up or pursues that activity for remuneration".[55]

4.3.7 Mortgages and home equity plans

The last edition of this Chapter noted that no provision had been made for taking the arrangement of or advice upon mortgages out of the definition of regulated activities where conducted other than by way of business. This omission has been addressed,[56] and further provisions have been added to extend this to similar services in relation to regulated home reversion plans[57] and regulated home purchase plans.[58] The same formulation is used in all three provisions: a person is not to be regarded as carrying on by way of business:

(a) arranging regulated mortgage contracts (Regulated Activities Order Article 25A), regulated home reversion plans (ibid. Article 25B) or regulated home purchase plans (ibid. Article 25C); or

---

[55] Business Order Article 3(4), added by SI 2003/1476 Article 18. As with the various amendments so far reviewed which implement the insurance mediation regime, this provision came into force on 31 October 2004 in relation to long-term care insurance and on 14 January 2005 in relation to all other classes of insurance.
[56] Business Order, Article 3A.
[57] Ibid. Article 3B.
[58] Ibid. Article 3C.

(b)   advising on regulated mortgage contracts (Regulated Activities Order Article 53A), regulated home reversion plans (ibid. Article 53B) or regulated home purchase plans (ibid. Article 53C); or

(c)   agreeing to do any of the above (ibid. Article 63),

unless he carries on the business of engaging in such activity.

4.3.8   *Managing investments in relation to occupational pension schemes*

The FSMA 2000 handles the regulation of occupational pension scheme ("OPS") trustees through the Business Order. Thus, a person who manages investments for OPSs[59] will be deemed to do so by way of business[60] unless one of two conditions applies:

(a)   Either he is a trustee *and* beneficiary of the same "relevant scheme". There are two types of relevant scheme for these purposes, and it will be clear from these definitions the sort of pension scheme arrangements which are now sought to be taken outside regulation:

(i)   one of these[61] is a scheme constituted as an irrevocable trust with no more than 12 relevant members (i.e. employees or former employees who are making contributions and/or receiving pension benefits), all of whom (barring incapacity or some other disqualification) are trustees. All or a majority of those persons must be involved in the day-to-day[62] decision-making process (whether or not in conjunction with an authorised person etc.). This is obviously directed at small senior executive schemes within large organisations, as well as much smaller schemes in family and small companies, and is intended to provide a framework where the trustee/beneficiaries are able to

---

[59] The definition of "occupational pension scheme" was changed with effect from 6 April 2005 through an amendment introduced by the Financial Services and Markets Act 2000 (Carrying on Regulated Activities by Way of Business) (Amendment) Order 2005 (SI 2005/92).

[60] Business Order, Article 4(1).

[61] Ibid. Article 4(4).

[62] The words "routine or" were deleted from this provision by the Financial Services and Markets Act 2000 (Carrying on Regulated Activities by Way of Business) (Amendment) Order 2005 (SI 2005/92) Article 2 with effect from 6 April 2005.

       manage their own affairs with a minimum of regulatory interference;

  (ii) the other type of relevant scheme[63] is one having 50 or fewer members, all of whom have the opportunity to select a life assurance or annuity contract to which their contributions will be subscribed, and no other investment management decisions are taken. This definition has a trap for the unwary: no other decisions means that uninvested cash cannot be used for the acquisition of any investments (e.g. government securities). Bank deposits may not fall within this, since the deposit of uninvested cash is not typically considered to be an act of investment management, but the trustees cannot do anything more sophisticated than this.

(b) Or, the other circumstances where the manager of OPS assets is not considered to operate by way of business is if he takes no day-to-day[64] decisions relating to the management of any "relevant assets",[65] having taken care to arrange that all day-to-day decisions are taken on his behalf by:

  (i) a person authorised[66] to manage investments pursuant to Article 37 of the Regulated Activities Order or exempt[67] from the requirement to be authorised; or

  (ii) an overseas person.[68]

Note, however, that this carve-out need not now be forced to apply to a decision[69] to buy, sell or subscribe for units in any collective investment scheme, interests in a contract of insurance or shares, debentures or warrants issued by a body corporate which operates on the premise of risk-spreading and which are intended to afford their investors the benefit of the management of their investment portfolios. This will therefore include open-ended investment companies of the sort specified in FSMA 2000 Section 236, as well as closed-ended

---

[63] Business Order, Article 4(5).
[64] Once again, the words "routine or" are deleted: see note 62 above..
[65] That is, securities and contractually based investments, as defined in Article 3(1) of the Regulated Activities Order.
[66] Article 4(1)(b)(i).
[67] Article 4(1)(b)(ii).
[68] Article 4(1)(b)(iii).
[69] Per ibid. Article 4(6).

investors such as investment trusts, VCTs and REITs. That decision to invest must be taken in accordance with the advice of a duly authorised, exempt or overseas person. However, the exempt status may, for the avoidance of doubt, also derive from the Part XX FSMA 2000 regime for the exemption of professional firms. This carve-out was recast, in a rather more permissive fashion, with effect from 6 April 2005.[70]

What does the carve-out for collective investment schemes achieve? Undoubtedly the earlier iteration of the provisions of Article 4(6) and (7) of the Business Order represented another aspect in which the policy behind the FSMA 2000 has been fashioned so as to promote private equity opportunities. If the trustees of an OPS wish to make a day-to-day or routine decision to invest in (and for this, understand to remain invested in) a private equity limited partnership or a body corporate such as a venture capital trust, the earlier iteration was designed to avoid their having to appoint an authorised investment manager to oversee this investment, provided that they act on the recommendation of an appropriately authorised investment advisory firm. The revision to this context with effect from April 2005 extended this exercise to all manner of collective investment schemes and all corporate entities which operate as open-ended investment companies.

4.4   The Financial Services and Markets Act 2000 (Appointed Representatives) Regulations 2001 (the "AR Regulations")

4.4.1   *Background*

This section considers the regulations which apply in relation to appointed representatives under the FSMA 2000. The framework for the appointed representative regime is found in FSMA 2000 Section 39. An appointed representative ("AR") is a person (natural or legal) which is contracted to an authorised person to do the bidding of the latter, and for whom the latter accepts responsibility in regulatory terms. Conventionally, one finds ARs most frequently in relation to

---

[70] Per Financial Services and Markets Act 2000 (Carrying on Regulated Activities by Way of Business) (Amendment) Order 2005 (SI 2005/92).

the distribution of retail financial products such as life assurance, pensions and unit trusts. But the concept can in principle be used in relation to a number of different investment or related services. By virtue of AR status, the AR is exempt from the requirement to be personally regulated by the FSA, and the firm to which he or it is tied takes full personal responsibility for the AR's acts and omissions as though they were that firm's own.

FSMA 2000 Section 39 provides no indication that there are to be regulations which determine the sorts of activities that an AR can carry on yet remain an exempt person. Section 39(1) talks in terms of the agreement between the parties having to relate to the carrying on of business "of a prescribed description" and compliance with "such requirements as may be prescribed", and from reading this, one might expect this to refer to the terms of the agreement alone. However, FSMA 2000 Section 417(1) explains that where the FSMA 2000 uses the word "prescribed" and does not attach a context to this (as is the case in Section 39), this is intended to indicate prescription in Treasury regulations; hence, there is after all a basis for the making of the AR Regulations.

4.4.2 Scope of the AR Regulations

The AR Regulations have two functions:

(a) They prescribe the types of business which the ARs of authorised persons may carry on without themselves requiring authorisation under the FSMA 2000. It will be important for the AR to endeavour to remain within the scope of the AR Regulations, since under the FSMA 2000 regime it is not possible for the same person or entity to be an AR for certain purposes and authorised for certain others.
(b) The AR Regulations prescribe the requirements with which a contract between an authorised person and his AR must comply, in order for the latter to be exempt from regulations.

4.4.3 Regulation 2 (as amended several times): what can an AR do?

An AR, without himself requiring authorisation under the FSMA 2000, may in the context of an agreement with his principal:

(a)   deal as agent in relation to contracts of general insurance;[71]

(b)   arrange deals in investments, if the transactions relate to securities, contractually based investments and insurance contracts;[72]

(c)   arrange regulated mortgage contracts;[73]

(d)   arrange regulated home reversion plans;[74]

(e)   arrange regulated home purchase plans;[75]

(f)   assist in the administration and performance of a contract of general insurance;[76]

(g)   safeguard and administer investments;[77]

(h)   provide basic advice on stakeholder products;[78]

(i)   advise on investments;[79]

(j)   advise on regulated mortgage contracts;[80]

(k)   advise on regulated home reversion plans;[81]

(l)   advise on regulated home purchase plans;[82] and

(m)   agree to do any activity falling under (a), (b), (c), (f) ,(g), (i) or (j) above.[83]

Article 2(1A) adds two further categories to the list above, in circumstances where the AR is tied to a principal that is an investment firm or a credit institution from another EEA Member State, namely:

(a)   placing financial instruments; and

(b)   providing advice to clients on the placing of financial instruments.

---

[71] AR Order Regulation 2(1)(aa), inserted by SI 2003/1476 Article 14, and coming into force on 31 October 2004 in relation to long-term care insurance and on 14 January 2005 in relation to all other classes of insurance.

[72] Ibid. Regulation 2(1)(a).

[73] Ibid. Regulation 2(1)(ab), inserted by SI 2003/1475 Article 23, and coming into force on 31 October 2004.

[74] Ibid. Regulation 2(1)(aba), inserted by SI 2006/2383 Article 31 with effect from 6 April 2007.

[75] Ibid. Regulation 2(1)(abb), inserted by SI 2006/2383 Article 31 with effect from 6 April 2007.

[76] Ibid. Regulation 2(1)(ac), inserted by SI 2003/1476 Article 14, and coming into force on 31 October 2004 in relation to long-term care insurance and on 14 January 2005 in relation to all other classes of insurance.

[77] Ibid. Regulation 2(1)(b).

[78] Ibid. Regulation 2(1)(ca), inserted by SI 2004/2737 Article 5 as from 6 April 2005.

[79] Ibid. Regulation 2(1)(c).

[80] Ibid. Regulation 2(1)(ca), inserted by SI 2003/1475 Article 23, and coming into force on 31 October 2004.

[81] Ibid. Regulation 2(1)(cb), inserted by SI 2006/2383 Article 31 with effect from 6 April 2007.

[82] Ibid. Regulation 2(1)(cc), inserted by SI 2006/2383 Article 31 with effect from 6 April 2007.

[83] Ibid. Regulation 2(1)(d), as amended.

The terms "client" and "financial instrument" are derived from Article 4 of the EC Markets in Financial Instruments Directive.[84]

4.4.4 Regulation 3: content of AR contracts

The contract between the principal and the AR, unless it prohibits the AR from representing counterparties (i.e. persons apart from the principal),[85] must:

(a) contain a provision to enable the principal to make such a prohibition;[86] and

(b) impose the restrictions as to the other counterparties which the representative may represent or the types of investment in relation to which the representative may represent other counterparties.[87]

A representative will be treated as representing counterparties[88] if he makes arrangements for persons to enter into investment transactions with other counterparties, arranges for other counterparties to safeguard and administer assets[89] or gives advice on the merits of entering into investment transactions with other counterparties.[90]

An investment transaction for the purposes of Regulation 3 means a transaction to buy, sell, subscribe for or underwrite an investment which is a security or a contractually based investment.

Regulation 3 has been extended in a fashion similar to Regulation 2(1) to address circumstances where the AR would be deemed to be representing counterparties in relation to mortgage, home reversion plan, home purchase plan or insurance-related activities. In relation to insurance mediation and related activities, a further condition of the terms of the AR's agreement is that the AR is not permitted or

---

[84] 2004/39/EC.
[85] AR Regulations Regulation 3(1).
[86] Ibid. Regulation 3(1)(a).
[87] Ibid. Regulation 3(1)(b).
[88] Ibid. Regulation 3(2)(a).
[89] Ibid. Regulation 3(2)(b).
[90] Ibid. Regulation 3(2)(c).

required to carry on the requisite business unless the AR is himself included in the FSA's record of insurance firms maintained by virtue of Article 93 to the Regulated Activities Order.

Regulation 3 is stated (*see* Para. (1A)) to apply expressly also where the principal is an EEA investment firm or credit institution.

Chapter 5

Scope and General Application of Conduct of Business Rules

Arun Srivastava

Partner

Sandra Zivcic

Associate
Baker & McKenzie LLP

5.1 Introduction

Chapter 1 of the FSA's new Conduct of Business Sourcebook ("COBS") sets out the scope and general application of the FSA's conduct of business rules. Chapter 2 of COBS prescribes general conduct obligations that apply to firms carrying on designated investment business.

The rules in COBS came into force on 1 November 2007, replacing the FSA's previous Conduct of Business Sourcebook ("Old COB"). The triggers to the changes to COB were two-fold. The first was the FSA's commitment to reform the COB Sourcebook given in the FSA's Business Plan for 2006/2007 and its Better Regulation Action Plan. The general approach of the FSA in its reforming of COB was, wherever possible, to move to a more principles-based form of regulating conduct of business requirements. The intention of the FSA has been to focus on regulatory outcomes with a recognition that prescriptive rules have failed to address the root causes of regulatory failures.

However, the ability of the FSA to move away from detailed conduct of business rules has been limited by the second trigger for change, which has been the UK's obligation to implement the conduct of business requirements contained in the Markets in Financial Instruments Directive ("MiFID") and its implementing legislation (Regulation 2004/39/EC and Directive 2006/73/EC) ("MiFID Implementing

Legislation") by 1 November 2007. MiFID and its Implementing Legislation contain detailed rules designed to bring about a high degree of harmonisation between the rules applicable to MiFID business in the Member States of the European Economic Area ("EEA"). In particular, Section 2 of Chapter II of MiFID sets out various conduct of business obligations that apply to firms within the scope of MiFID. Certain of the more significant changes introduced by MiFID, such as the MiFID best-execution requirement, suitability obligations and appropriateness obligations on non-advised sales, are contained within this Part of MiFID and accordingly the changes that have been introduced into COBS to reflect these matters represent material developments.

The types of business that fall within the scope of MiFID are narrower than the types of business that were covered by the Old COB rules. In particular, designated investment business covers a broader range of activities than the activities that fall within the scope of MiFID. One of the issues that the FSA has therefore been required to consider is the extent to which MiFID conduct of business requirements should be applied to non-MiFID business. Pensions and life policies, for example, do not fall within the scope of MiFID but were subject to conduct of business requirements contained in Old COB.

The FSA has decided to apply certain MiFID requirements contained in COBS to firms carrying on non-MiFID business for reasons of consistency and to ensure a coherent approach to products which share similar characteristics. Products are substitutable, so that services carried on in relation to units in UCITS (which are within MiFID) and those carried on in relation to unit-linked life products (which are outside MiFID) should be subject to the same regulatory requirements. Accordingly, for example, MiFID rules relating to suitability will provide the basis for the rules relating to life policies. A further example of where MiFID requirements have been applied more broadly are the rules under COBS relating to client agreements. The FSA decided to apply MiFID requirements relating to client agreements to both firms within the scope of MiFID and those outside its scope.

UK branches of third-country firms will be subject to MiFID conduct of business requirements in respect of business falling within MiFID scope. Third-country firms are not MiFID firms on the basis that they do not have their head office in an EEA state. However, the FSA is required to ensure that branches of such firms do not receive more favourable treatment than branches of firms from other EEA states.

Although certain MiFID requirements have been applied to non-MiFID business, in other areas COBS distinguishes between MiFID and non-MiFID business, applying different requirements to the different categories of business. This has introduced a layer of complexity that previously did not exist. For example, the definition of a "professional client" for client categorisation purposes under Chapter 3 of COBS will differ depending on whether the relevant activities fall within or outside the scope of MiFID.

The FSA's consultation process in reforming COB was initiated with Consultation Paper 06/19 Reforming Conduct of Business Regulation published in October 2006 ("CP 06/19") and Consultation Paper 06/20 Financial Promotions and Other Communications also published in October 2006 ("CP 06/20"). Both CP 06/19 and CP 06/20 proposed revised conduct of business rules. For the purposes of the discussion below, the FSA's final position on its approach proposed in CP 06/20 is found in Policy Statement 07/06: Conduct of Business regime: Feedback on CP 06/19 and CP 06/20 published in May 2007 ("PS 07/06") and Policy Statement 07/14 which sets out the FSA's final feedback on the consultation process initiated by CP 06/19 published by the FSA in July 2007.

As with the other sourcebooks in the FSA Handbook, COBS contains rules (identified by an "R" suffix), evidential provisions (identified by an "E" suffix) and guidance (identified by a "G" suffix).

The rules, together with the Principles for Businesses, are "general rules" for the purposes of Section 138 of the Financial Services and Markets Act 2000 ("FSMA 2000"). A breach of these rules will expose a firm (i.e. an authorised person) to FSA enforcement proceedings. Given the move towards principles-based regulation, enforcement proceedings might also be brought solely in respect of a breach of the Principles for Businesses, whereas previously the FSA would be unlikely to bring a case solely on this basis.

A breach of the rules, other than the Principles for Businesses, may also give rise to a right of action to a "private person" under Section

150 FSMA 2000 (a "private person" being defined in the FSA Handbook Glossary and the Financial Services and Markets Act 2000 (Rights of Action) Regulations 2001 (SI 2001/2256)). The circumstances in which such a right of action will arise are qualified in that a private person, who is an individual, will not have a right of action if, broadly, they have suffered a loss in the course of carrying on a regulated activity. Likewise, where the "private person" is not an individual, then no right of action will arise if the loss is suffered in the course of carrying on business of any kind.

The evidential provisions, which are issued pursuant to Section 149 FSMA 2000, do not create binding obligations. However, contravention of, or compliance with, an evidential provision may be relied upon as tending to establish compliance with the rule to which it relates.

The guidance provisions are often used to indicate possible means of compliance with a rule or to recommend particular courses of action or arrangements. However, guidance provisions are not binding on those to whom FSMA 2000 and the rules apply, nor do they have an "evidential" effect. Further assistance with the interpretation of the status of rules, the evidential provisions and the guidance is set out in the FSA's *Reader's Guide to the FSA Handbook*.

Chapter 1 of COBS is an introductory Chapter that sets out the "general application rule" for COBS which in broad terms identifies the firms that are subject to COBS, the activities that are covered and the general territorial scope of the application of COBS. COBS 1 Annex 1 ("the Annex") is part of COBS. The Annex is divided into three parts. Part 1 of the Annex sets out modifications to the general application rule according to the activities carried on by a firm. Part 2 of the Annex modifies the general application rule according to the location from which a firm carries on business, while Part 3 provides guidance with regard to the scope of the general application rule, the modifications to it, and its interaction with the territorial scope of relevant EU Directives.

Chapter 2 of COBS focuses on the COBS provisions that apply to all firms engaging in "designated investment business". It is the first Chapter of COBS that contains substantive provisions relating to conduct of business. However, some provisions distinguish between non-MiFID and MiFID business. In addition, it should be borne in mind that the definition of "designated investment business" does not include deposit taking or carrying on insurance business (i.e., carrying out or effecting a contract of insurance as principal). At the same time, the definition includes dealings by an FSA-authorised firm as principal which would otherwise be excluded from the scope of the Financial Services and Markets Act 2000 (Regulated Activities) Order 2001 ("RAO") by Article 15 of the RAO.

Many firms whose activities constitute regulated activities within the scope of FSMA 2000 and the RAO will therefore not be covered by the "overreaching" provisions of COBS 2 to the extent that their business does not constitute designated investment business.

The COBS provisions which generally apply across the board to all firms conducting designated investment business are those which relate to acting honestly, fairly and professionally, disclosing information about the firm before providing services, inducements and reliance on others. Even these overreaching provisions are subject to numerous exceptions and limitations on their application which are discussed below.

Conduct of business requirements relating to business that falls outside the scope of COBS, including general insurance and mortgage business, are contained in other parts of the FSA Handbook, such as MCOB and ICOB.

5.2 COBS Chapter 1 – application and general provisions

According to the FSA, the application provisions of COBS serve a dual purpose. First, the provisions determine the areas that the FSA intends to be regulated under COBS. Secondly, they are intended to be used by readers as indicators of the rules which may be relevant to them. This dual purpose has influenced the manner in which COBS 1 has been drafted.

As mentioned above, COBS 1 sets out the general application rule and describes the modifications to that rule. More specifically, COBS 1 addresses the following issues:

(a) the application of COBS;
(b) defining who is subject to COBS;
(c) defining the type of activities that are covered by COBS;
(d) defining the territorial scope of COBS; and
(e) identifying circumstances in which COBS will have a reduced application to particular types of business or activity.

5.2.1 The general application rule

The general application rule in COBS 1.1.1R provides that COBS applies to a firm with respect to accepting deposits, designated investment business and long-term insurance business in relation to life policies (and activities connected with them), where those activities are carried on from an establishment maintained by the firm, or its appointed representative, in the UK.

In principle, COBS applies to a broad range of firms. However, not all of the provisions in COBS apply to all firms carrying on the activities specified in COBS 1.1.1R. The general application rule is modified and narrowed in its application to specific types of firms and in relation to specific types of activities. Individual Chapters within COBS contain rules relating to and scoping the application of the Chapters concerned and regard must therefore be had both to the general application rule and any individual rules contained within other Chapters of COBS.

Chapter 18 of COBS ("Specialist Regimes") tailors the obligations in COBS to particular types of firms by applying only particular rules in COBS to those firms.

For example, COBS has only limited application for UCITS qualifiers[1] and service companies.[2] According to COBS 18.10.1R, only COBS 5.2 (which deals with electronic commerce activity

---

[1] That is, a firm which is an operator, trustee or depository of a recognised scheme under Section 264 FSMA 2000 (which applies to EEA collective investment schemes established outside the UK).

[2] Which is a type of firm whose authorisation is limited to arranging transactions in investments or agreeing to make such arrangements (other restrictions also apply, for which *see* the definition of service company in the FSA Handbook Glossary). It typically covers firms such as information vendors.

providers), COBS 4 (which relates to communication with clients) and COBS 12.4 (which deals with required disclosures for the distribution of investment research) together with the provisions of COBS which are incorporated into COBS 5.2 or COBS 4 and COBS 12.4 by reference, apply to such firms. The conduct of business rules for UCITS qualifiers are nonetheless supplemented by guidance for UCITS qualifiers and provisions in the Collective Investment Schemes Sourcebook ("COLL") at COLL 9.4 (which deals with facilities that need to be maintained by operators of recognised schemes).

5.2.2 *Type of activity covered by COBS*

As mentioned above, most of COBS applies to regulated activities conducted by firms where the activities in question fall within the definition of "designated investment business" (*see* Chapter 2, 2.1 above). By contrast, COBS only has limited application in relation to other regulated activities such as deposit-taking business, pure protection contracts (which are a type of long-term insurance contract) and general insurance contracts.[3] The scope of the regulated activities to which COBS applies is in turn determined by the description of the activity as set out in the RAO. A firm will not ordinarily be subject to COBS in relation to any aspect of its business activities which falls within an exclusion established by the RAO. However, there are exceptions to this general rule. For example, as mentioned above, the definition of designated investment business includes activities falling within the exclusion covered by Article 15 of the RAO (which deals with the absence of holding out, etc.) for firms dealing in investments as principal.

Most of COBS also has only limited application to Lloyd's related activities, which are specified in Chapter XIII of Part II of the RAO. However, there is a dedicated section of COBS (COBS 18.6) which deals specifically with Lloyd's and Lloyd's related activities.

---

[3] However, it should be noted that general insurance business is subject to separate conduct of business requirements pursuant to the FSA's Insurance: New Conduct of Business Sourcebook ("ICOBS"), which gives effect to relevant provisions of the Insurance Mediation Directive. These provisions have also been amended and came into force on 1 November 2007.

The application of COBS is modified with respect to activities carried on with certain categories of clients. In particular, the Annex modifies the application of COBS to eligible counterparty business in accordance with Article 24(1) of MiFID. In broad terms, a firm carries on "eligible counterparty business" when it deals on own account, executes orders on behalf of clients, or receives and transmits orders with or for an eligible counterparty. Any ancillary service that is directly related to these activities will also constitute eligible counterparty business, as will the activity of arranging where it is carried on with or for an eligible counterparty in relation to business which is not MiFID or equivalent third-country firm business.

Paragraph 1.1R of Part 1 of the Annex lists the particular COBS provisions that do not apply to eligible counterparty business. The provisions that are disapplied to eligible counterparty business are:

(a) COBS 2 (other than COBS 2.4). COBS 2 contains overreaching obligations such as the obligation to act honestly, fairly and professionally;

(b) COBS 4 (other than COBS 4.4.1R and COBS 4.4.2G). COBS 4 contains rules on communications with clients, including financial promotions;

(c) COBS 6.1, which concerns the provision to clients of information relating to the firm and its services;

(d) COBS 8, which sets out obligations relating to client agreements;

(e) COBS 10, which concerns appropriateness obligations for non-advised sales;

(f) COBS 11.2, COBS 11.3, COBS 11.6, which refer to best execution, client order handling and use of dealing commission;

(g) COBS 12.3.1R to 12.3.3R, which relates to obligations concerning the labelling of non-independent research,

(h) COBS 14.3, which concerns obligations to provide product information to clients; and

(i) COBS 16, which sets out client reporting obligations.

The regime for eligible counterparty business effectively replaces the regime under the Old COB rules for interprofessional business. MAR3, which set out the rules for interprofessional conduct is no longer in force.

As mentioned above, each Chapter in COBS also has its own application provisions which may provide that the Chapter or particular provisions apply only to customers (which encompasses both retail and professional clients, but not eligible counterparties) or to only retail clients.

The relevance of distinguishing between customers and eligible counterparties of a firm for the purposes of determining the application of COBS reflects recital 41 of MiFID. Although recital 40 states that "eligible counterparties should be considered as acting as clients", recital 41 indicates that it is appropriate to clarify that conduct of business rules may be waived in the case of transactions entered into or brought about between eligible counterparties. Recital 41 indicates that this is to ensure that conduct of business rules are enforced in respect of those investors most in need of these protections, and to reflect well-established market practice throughout the Community.

Less onerous obligations relating to consumer protection therefore apply in respect of certain regulated activities which firms conduct with eligible counterparties than would apply to activities with customers covered by COBS. Eligible counterparties, on the basis of being deemed the most sophisticated participants in the financial markets and that such business is conducted in accordance with established market practice in so far as MiFID business is concerned, require a lower level of consumer protection than customers.

COBS is therefore designed to apply to the provision of investment services primarily to retail and professional clients. While, as a general rule, most of COBS applies to business with retail clients, without any right for a firm to disapply the rules set out in COBS, the ability of clients to request categorisation into a higher client category, with fewer regulatory protections, introduces, at least in principle, an element of flexibility in relation to the application of the rules to all types of clients. For example, by conferring on certain types of retail clients the option to become elective professional clients, the application of particular COBS rules will be modified in their application to that client.

In this connection, it should be noted that clients cannot be categorised as per se or elective eligible counterparties for certain types of business. For example, where the service being provided comprises investment management or the provision of investment advice, the firm must categorise the client either as a retail client or as a professional client. Thus, in many instances, MiFID effectively operates a two-tier client categorisation regime with both tiers coming within the scope of COBS provisions.

Other modifications to the general application rule are provided for in Part 1 of the Annex regarding specific activities. The main driver for these modifications is the scope of COBS regulation under MiFID. In accordance with Articles 14(3) and 42(2) of MiFID, the COBS provisions in paragraph 1.1R of the Annex and the rule regarding client limit orders in COBS 11.4 are also generally disapplied to:

(a)   transactions between a multilateral trading facility ("MTF") operator and its users (*see* paragraph 2.1R); and
(b)   transactions concluded under the rules governing an MTF between members or participants of the MTF (*see* paragraph 3.1R), although if the member or participant is acting on behalf of a client in executing orders on an MTF, these rules are not disapplied as between the MTF member or participant and its client.

In addition, members and participants of a regulated market are not obliged to apply to each other the COBS provisions in paragraph 1.1R of the Annex and the rule on client limit orders in COBS 11.4. Again, if the member or participant is acting on behalf of a client in executing orders on a regulated market, these rules are not disapplied as between the member or participant and its client.

Paragraph 5.1R of the Annex also provides for further modifications with regard to the conduct of consumer credit business by credit institutions which are not subject to MiFID. Article 19(9) of MiFID provides that the conduct of business obligations should not apply to a firm where an investment service is offered as part of a financial product which is already subject to other provisions of Community legislation or common European standards related to credit institutions and consumer credit with respect to the risk assessment of clients and/or information requirements. Paragraph 5.1R purports to give effect to Article 19(9) of MiFID by removing the obligation of a firm to comply with the COBS rules to the extent that they implement Article 19 of MiFID. However, the FSA's guidance indicates that the exclusion for consumer credit products should be construed narrowly and that it does not apply where the investment service is the essential or leading part of the financial product. Paragraph 5.2G also indicates that the exclusion is not intended to apply where the service provided is a combination of an investment service and an ancillary service (for example granting credit for the execution of an order where the credit is instrumental to the buying or the selling of a financial instrument) or the sale of a financial instrument for the purpose of enabling a client to invest money to repay obligations under a loan, mortgage or home reversion.

The final modification of the general application rule in Part 1 of the Annex applies in relation to the use of third-party processors in relation to life mediation activities. Paragraph 6.1R provides that, unless the third-party processor is advising on investments, if a firm (or its appointed representative or, where applicable, its tied agent) outsources insurance mediation activities to a third-party processor, the firm will be responsible for the acts and omissions of the processor. In addition, any COBS rule requiring the processor's identity to be disclosed to clients applies as though it were a requirement to disclose the firm's identity.

5.2.3 Territorial scope rules

After setting out the general application rule and the modifications to it, which have the effect of reducing the application of COBS to certain types of firms and clients, Part 2 of the Annex goes on to consider the territorial scope of COBS.

Part 2 of the Annex sets out the EEA territorial scope rule which is intended to ensure that the rules in COBS are compatible with European law with respect to the same subject matter. The EEA territorial scope rule provides that the territorial scope of COBS is modified to the extent necessary to be compatible with European law and that the rule overrides every other rule in COBS. The EEA territorial scope rule is essentially concerned with allocation of supervisory responsibilities between home and host state authorities where activities are carried on cross-border within the EEA, either on the basis of a services or branch passport. Part 3 of the Annex sets out guidance in relation to the application of the various Single Market Directives and their effect on territorial scope of the application of UK conduct of business rules to those activities. The starting point for the consideration of the territorial application of COBS is that COBS applies to activities carried on from an establishment maintained by a firm or its appointed representative in the UK. This basic rule is modified in a number of respects.

To the extent that an FSA-authorised firm carries on business with a client in the UK from an establishment overseas, COBS will apply to the firm in respect of the relevant activities carried on from the overseas establishment. This extension in the scope of COBS' territorial application is, however, limited. Accordingly, COBS does not apply to activities carried on from an overseas establishment if the activities would fall within the overseas persons exclusion in Article 72 of the RAO, or would not be regarded as carried on in the UK (whether by virtue of Section 418 FSMA 2000 or otherwise), were the overseas establishment to be regarded as a separate person. In broad terms, activities will fall within the scope of the overseas person exclusion where the activities are carried on as a result of an approach that has not been solicited by the firm or the firm has solicited the client or the counterparty but in a manner that does not contravene the restrictions on financial promotions contained in Section 21 FSMA 2000. Part 3 of the Annex provides some limited further guidance on this.

As noted in the FSA guidance in paragraph 2.2G of the Annex, one of the effects of the EEA territorial scope rule is to override the application of COBS to the overseas establishments of EEA firms in a number cases. In general terms, the EEA territorial scope rule should only be relevant where there is a non-UK element to the business of the firm. Where activities are carried on by a UK firm, from within the UK for a UK client, the EEA territorial scope rule should not be relevant. However, where there is a non-UK element to the conduct of a firm's business and it would appear that any one or more of the Single Market Directives (e.g., the Banking Consolidation Directive, MiFID, the Insurance Directives, the Insurance Mediation Directive or the UCITS Directive) could be relevant, in order to determine whether a particular COBS rule is applicable to the firm, paragraph 2.2G advises firms to consider:

(a)   whether the firm is subject to a directive;
(b)   whether the directive applies to the business that the firm is performing; and
(c)   whether the particular COBS rule is within the scope of the directive.

If the answer to all three questions is "yes", then the EEA territorial scope rule may affect the general application rule.

One of the difficulties with this approach can be in establishing whether a COBS rule is within the scope of one of the Single Market Directives. This is particularly the case with those provisions which may not have been enacted in order to give effect to an obligation that applies under a Directive but which appear to fall within the scope of a Single Market Directive owing to the broad nature of the drafting in many EU Directives. The complexity of this situation is lessened with regard to some Directives, such as MiFID, because each COBS rule that is within the scope of MiFID is followed by a "Note" with a cross-reference to the relevant article in MiFID. Accordingly, the process for determining whether the EEA territorial scope rule modifies the application of a particular COBS rule where there is a non-UK element will require a careful analysis of EU legislation.

In PS 07/06 the FSA has acknowledged the problems presented by the broadly drafted EEA territorial scope rule when it is applied to particular circumstances. In deciding on its approach, the FSA has weighed the competing interests of those who seek more detail about the application of a rule and those "who see the rules as sensible and usable". However, the FSA has avoided providing more detail on the basis that it would be difficult to give greater clarity without prejudicing the accessibility of COBS.

In relation to MiFID, the FSA explains in the guidance set out in paragraph 3.3G of the Annex that for a UK MiFID investment firm, rules in COBS that are within the scope of MiFID generally apply to the firm's MiFID business carried on from an establishment in the UK and that they also generally apply to the firm's MiFID business carried on from an establishment in another EEA state but only where that business is not carried on within the territory of that other EEA state. MiFID has generally taken a country of origin approach to the regulation of conduct of business, meaning that the conduct of business rules applicable to particular activities will be the rules in force in the state from which the services are being provided. Accordingly, in relation to business conducted from a UK establishment cross-border into another EEA state on a services basis, UK conduct of business rules contained in COBS will apply. Where a UK firm conducts business from a branch located in another EEA state, in accordance with the country of origin approach, the conduct of business rules applicable in the EEA state in which the branch is located will generally apply. However, the position in relation to services provided from a branch is complicated, as in determining which conduct of business rules apply regard must be had to whether or not the relevant business is carried on within the territory of the state in which the branch is located. If the business is carried on within the territory of the state in which the branch is located, the conduct of business rules of that state (i.e., the branch's host state) will apply. If the business is not carried on within the territory of the state in which the branch is located then the UK's conduct of business rules in COBS will apply. It should, however, be noted that UK rules on investment research, non-independent research and personal transactions contained in COBS 12.2, 12.3 and 11.7 respectively will apply on a home state basis, that is, to the activities of a UK MiFID investment firm whether carried on from the UK or from a branch located in another EEA Member State.

Concern has been expressed about the uncertainty relating to the particular conduct of business rules to be applied to branch activities. Whether home state or host state conduct of business rules will apply will depend on whether the activities are carried on within the territory of the host state. For example, if a UK firm's branch in Paris was dealing with a client located in Spain, would French or UK conduct of business rules apply? The uncertainty arises from the fact that the client is located in Spain, which raises the issue of whether the branch's activities are being carried on within the territory of its host state. These matters have been considered by the Committee of European Securities Regulators ("CESR"). In its May 2007 paper on Recommendations on the Passport under MiFID, the CESR acknowledged this uncertainty and the desire of industry participants to have a single set of conduct of business rules applicable to services provided through a branch. The CESR asked the European Commission to provide clarification of this point, which arises from Article 32(7) of MiFID. In June 2007, the Commission published its response to this request and subsequently the CESR published a Protocol on the supervision of branches under MiFID (October 2007), which provides for a dual model of supervision based on individual agreement between the Competent Authorities for each Member State under MiFID. Branches may therefore either be supervised under a "Common Oversight Request" or a "Standing Request for Assistance" between the national regulators in question. Absenting such agreement between the home and host state, therefore, the question of which is the applicable law remains a grey area.

The Annex also provides guidance on the effect on the territorial scope rule of the Insurance Mediation Directive, the Consolidated Life Directive, the Distance Marketing Directive, the Electronic Commerce Directive, the Investor Compensation Directive and the UCITS Directive in Sections 4 to 9 of Part 3 of the Annex.

In the case of the Electronic Commerce Directive, the FSA points out in its guidance in Part 3 of the Annex that a key element of the Directive is the ability of a person from one EEA state to carry on an electronic commerce activity freely into another EEA state. The Electronic Commerce Directive applies to electronic commerce activities, which, broadly, involve the provision of financial services electronically from a distance in return for remuneration from recipients who have requested the service. Every rule in COBS is therefore within the Directive's scope. The territorial scope of COBS is modified so that its rules will apply to a firm that carries on electronic commerce activities from an establishment in the UK with or for a person in the UK or another EEA state: COBS 5.2.1. However, for firms carrying on an electronic commerce activity from another EEA state to UK recipients, the rules and guidance contained in COBS do not apply.

5.2.4 Application of COBS to specific activities

As stated above, there are particular areas of activity that are subject to a modified application of the COBS Rules. Chapter 18 of COBS deals in particular with the application of COBS to certain Specialist Regimes. These include trustee firms, energy market activity and oil market activity, corporate finance business, stock lending activity, operators of collective investment schemes, Lloyd's, depositaries, OPS firms (non-scope business), ICVCs, UCITS qualifiers, and service companies and authorised professional firms. The Old COB rules provided for concessionary treatment of certain types of activities. To the extent that these activities fall within the scope of MiFID, certain concessions have been removed where these were inconsistent with the provisions contained in MiFID.

A summary of the regimes relating to stock lending activity, corporate finance business and oil and energy market activities is given at 5.2.5–5.2.7 below.

5.2.5   Stock lending activity

COBS 18.4.1R provides that, in respect of any stock lending activity undertaken by a firm which is MiFID or equivalent third-country business, the provisions of COBS set out in the table at COBS 18.4.1R do not apply. These are shown in Table 5.1.

Table 5.1   *Chapters in COBS that do not cover stock lending activity*

COBS	Description
6.2	Describing the breadth of a firm's advice on investments
6.3	Disclosing information about services, fees and commission – packaged products
6.4	Disclosure of charges, remuneration and commission
9.4	Suitability reports
9.6	Special rules for providing basic advice on a stakeholder product
11.6	Use of dealing commission
16.3.9	Guidance on contingent liability transactions
16.5	Quotations for surrender values
16.6	Life insurance contracts – communications to clients
16 Annex 1R(1) 14	Information to be provided in accordance with COBS 16.2.1R and 16.3

In addition, COBS 18.4.2G lists in tabular format the COBS provisions that are unlikely to apply to stock lending activity carried on by firms doing MiFID or equivalent third-country business.

5.2.6 Corporate finance business

COBS 18.3.1R also provides that certain COBS provisions do not apply to corporate finance business[4] undertaken by a firm, which is MiFID or equivalent third-country business. The COBS provisions in question are set out in Table 5.2.

Again, COBS 18.3.2G lists the COBS provisions that are unlikely to be relevant to corporate finance business undertaken by a firm carrying on MiFID or equivalent third-country business.

In addition, COBS 18.3.3R provides that certain COBS provisions do apply to corporate finance business[5] undertaken by a firm which is

Table 5.2   *Chapters in COBS that do not apply to corporate finance business undertaken by a firm which is MiFID or equivalent third-country business*

COBS	Description
6.2	Describing the breadth of a firm's advice on investments
6.3	Disclosing information about services, fees and commission – packaged products
6.4	Disclosure of charges, remuneration and commission
9.4	Suitability reports
9.6	Special rules for providing basic advice on a stakeholder product
11.6	Use of dealing commission
16.3.9	Guidance on contingent liability transaction
16.5	Quotations for surrender values
16.6	Life insurance contracts – communications to clients
16 Annex 1R(1) 14	Information to be provided in accordance with COBS 16.2.1R and 16.3

---

[4] The extensive definition of which is set out in the FSA Handbook Glossary.
[5] The extensive definition of which is set out in the FSA Handbook Glossary.

Table 5.3 *Chapters in COBS that do apply to corporate finance business undertaken by a firm which is not MiFID or equivalent third-country business*

COBS	Description
1	Application
2.1.1	Acting honestly, fairly and professionally
2.3	Inducements
2.4	Acting as client and reliance on others
3	Client categorisation
4	Communication to clients including financial promotions, except COBS 4.5–COBS 4.11
5.1	The information and other requirements of the Distance Marketing Directive, but only in relation to distance contracts concluded with consumers
5.2	E-commerce
11.7	Personal account dealing
12	Investment research
15	Cancellation, but only in relation to distance contracts concluded with consumers

not MiFID or equivalent third-country business. The COBS provisions in question are also set out in Table 5.3.

5.2.7 *Oil market and energy market activities*

COBS also has limited application in respect of:

(a) oil market activities; and
(b) other energy market activities.

The limited COBS provisions that apply to oil market activity and energy market activity and the provisions of COBS that do not apply in relation to any energy market activity or oil market activity carried on by a firm which is MiFID or equivalent third-country business are shown in Table 5.4.

COBS has an even more limited application in relation to oil market and energy market activities undertaken by any firm where, if the

Table 5.4 *Chapters in COBS that cover oil market and energy market activity*

COBS	Description
6.2	Describing the breadth of a firm's advice on investments
6.3	Disclosing information about services, fees and commission – packaged products
6.4	Disclosure of charges, remuneration and commission
9.4	Suitability reports
9.6	Special rules for providing basic advice on a stakeholder product
11.6	Use of dealing commission
16.3.9	Guidance on contingent liability transaction
16.5	Quotations for surrender values
16.6	Life insurance contracts – communications to clients
16 Annex 1R(1) 14	Information to be provided in accordance with COBS 16.2.1R and 16.3

firm were not authorised, the activity would not be a regulated activity because of:

(a) Article 16 of the RAO (dealing in contractually-based investments); or
(b) Article 22 of the RAO (deals with or through authorised persons, etc.).

This further limitation of COBS provides that only the COBS Chapters shown in Table 5.5 apply.

Table 5.5 *COBS Chapters that apply following limitation of application*

COBS	Subject
1	Application
2.4	Agent as client and reliance on others
4.12	Unregulated collective investment schemes
5.2	E-commerce

5.3 COBS Chapter 2 – conduct of business obligations

5.3.1 *Provisions which apply to all firms conducting designated investment business*

COBS 2 sets out the rules which apply to all firms conducting "designated investment business" (as to which, *see* above). COBS 2 sets out four principal areas of COBS that apply to firms. The areas in question relate to:

(a) acting honestly, fairly and professionally;
(b) information disclosure before providing services;
(c) inducements; and
(d) agent as client and reliance on others.

The purpose of the rules is to set high-level conduct of business requirements concentrating on a limited number of overarching matters. They are also intended to impose relevant high-level conduct of business obligations, as set out in Article 19 of MiFID, on firms that provide investment services that are subject to MiFID. Although COBS 2 is expressed to apply to all firms, this is nonetheless subject to the provisions of COBS 1 which, as discussed above, can have the effect of narrowing the application of COBS in particular circumstances. In addition, some rules are specifically expressed to apply to "MiFID or equivalent third-country business", rather than to all firms who carry on designated investment business. This is to ensure that, where the FSA has intended this to be the case, only firms that are subject to MiFID are obliged to comply with the relevant obligation. In addition, it also ensures that a branch of a non-EEA firm that has been established in the UK that carries on MiFID-type activities is treated the same as a branch of a firm with its head office in the EEA, even though MiFID does not, according to its terms, apply to branches of non-EEA firms.

"MiFID or equivalent third-country business" is defined in the Glossary of the FSA Handbook as "MiFID business or the equivalent business of a third-country investment firm". In general terms, a firm carries on "MiFID business" if it is a firm which has its head office in an EEA Member State and its business includes providing investment services and activities that are regulated under MiFID and, where relevant, ancillary services.

The investment firms to whom MiFID is intended to apply, by definition, excludes branches established in the EEA of firms from non-EEA jurisdictions. During consultation, the FSA expressed its view that the position under MiFID with regard to EEA branches of non-EEA firms is the same as has prevailed under Article 5 of the Investment Services Directive. That is, while MiFID does not apply directly to third-country branches, Member States must not treat such branches more favourably than branches of investment firms from other EEA Member States. This view is shared by the European Commission. Accordingly, as a minimum, the FSA considers itself obliged to apply to the UK branch of a third-country firm the same requirements that it applies to the UK branch of an EEA firm under MiFID.

In terms of the approach taken in COBS 2, this means that MiFID obligations will apply also to branches of third-country firms where the business carried on by the firm from an establishment in the UK would be MiFID business if that firm were a MiFID investment firm.

5.3.2 Acting honestly, fairly and professionally

COBS 2.1 imposes three core obligations on firms conducting both MiFID and non-MiFID business that together are intended to ensure that firms conduct their designated investment business in a manner that is honest, fair and professional. These obligations should be read in conjunction with Principle 6 (A firm must pay due regard to the interests of its customers and treat them fairly) and Principle 7 (A firm must pay due regard to the information needs of its clients, and communicate information to them in a way which is clear, fair and not misleading).

The three core obligations are:

(a) the obligation to act honestly, fairly and professionally;
(b) a prohibition that prevents firms from seeking to exclude or restrict the firm's duties or liabilities to a client under the regulatory system; and

(c)   an obligation to provide certain basic information to clients about the firm and its business.

5.3.3   *Honestly, fairly and professionally*

The first of these obligations is in COBS 2.1.1R(1). It requires firms to act "honestly, fairly and professionally" in accordance with the best interests of their clients. This is referred to as the "client's best interest rule". COBS 2.1.1R(2) distinguishes the circumstances in which this rule applies depending on the nature of the client for whom designated investment business is carried on. Where the firm is carrying on MiFID or equivalent third-country business, the obligation will apply to business carried on for all client categories and is an overriding obligation in the conduct of the firm's business. This is consistent with the obligation prescribed by Article 19(1) of MiFID. Where the firm is carrying on designated investment business activities that fall outside the scope of MiFID, then the obligation only applies in relation to retail clients. It should also be borne in mind that where the activities come within the scope of eligible counterparty business, COBS 2 is disapplied.

The FSA has acknowledged that there is a similarity between Article 19(1) of MiFID and Principle 6 (Customers' interests), but has also expressed the view, in PS 07/6, that the overlap is not complete. The FSA has therefore considered it necessary to "copy out" the Article in order to ensure proper implementation of MiFID.

5.3.4   *Exclusion of liability*

In addition to the client's best interest rule, COBS 2.1.2R sets out the rules on the exclusion of liability by a firm in relation to any kind of communication made by a firm with a client relating to "designated investment business". The Section ties in with Principle 6 (customers' interests) of the FSA Principles for Businesses, which requires firms to pay due regard to the interests of their customers and to treat them fairly. COBS 2.1.2R provides that a firm must not seek to exclude or restrict, or to rely on any exclusion or restriction of, any duty or liability that it may have to a client under the regulatory system. The regulatory system is defined in the FSA Handbook Glossary as the arrangements for regulating a firm, or other persons, in or under

FSMA 2000, including the threshold conditions, the Principles and other rules, the Statements of Principle (which apply to individuals) and codes and guidance.

In relation to retail clients, the restriction would appear to be more far reaching. The FSA's guidance in COBS 2.1.3G provides that a firm should not in any communication to a retail client relating to designated investment business seek to exclude or restrict, or to rely on any exclusion or restriction of, any duty or liability that it may have to a client *other than under the regulatory system,* unless it is reasonable for it to do so. The rule as it applies to retail clients is therefore broader in scope in that it does not relate solely to duties or liabilities arising under the regulatory system. In particular, this means that firms dealing with retail clients must have regard not only to the duties and liabilities that arise under the FSA Rules, but elsewhere such as under the Unfair Terms in Consumer Contracts Regulations 1999 which also impose limitations on the ability of a firm to exclude or restrict any duty or liability that it has towards the customer.

Prior to the implementation of MiFID, COB 2.5 contained rules prohibiting a firm from seeking to exclude or restrict any duty or liability it has to customers under the regulatory system or under general law. The FSA has scaled back the previously detailed provisions on the basis that the objective that the rules sought to achieve is the subject of other general consumer protection legislation. Nevertheless, the FSA considered it desirable to include a high-level rule to act as a "further deterrent" to this practice. In addition, it should be noted that, under the former COB rules, the extension of the obligation with regard to retail clients was imposed by way of a rule. The obligation is now the subject of FSA guidance, but would nevertheless appear to carry the same force given that firms will be lawfully obliged to comply with consumer protection provisions that exist outside the regulatory system.

5.3.5 Disclosures about the firm

The final obligation appears in COBS 2.2.1R. Under COBS 2.2.1R(1), firms are obliged to provide "appropriate information" in a comprehensible form to a client about the firm and its services, designated investments and proposed investment strategies (including appropriate guidance on and warnings of the risks associated with investments in those designated investments or in respect of particular investment strategies), execution venues and costs and associated charges.

This rule is derived from Article 19(3) of MiFID and is expressed to apply in relation to MiFID or equivalent third-country business rather than to firms generally. That said, the application of the rule is extended to firms carrying on non-MiFID business by COBS 2.2.1R(4). COBS 2.2.1R(4) applies the disclosure obligations in COBS 2.2.1R(1) to firms carrying on designated investment business for a retail client in relation to a derivative, a warrant or stock lending activity.

The information must be provided so that the client is reasonably able to understand the nature and risks of the service to be provided and of the specific type of designated investment that is being offered and, consequently, to make investment decisions on an informed basis. Clearly, the type of information that the firm provides to its clients to achieve this purpose will vary depending on the nature of the client. For example, a retail client will usually need more information about the risks attaching to a particular designated investment than an eligible counterparty. Again, even within the category of retail client, some may require more information than others, given that clients in this category will per se include individuals who might in practical terms be regarded as sophisticated professional investors. However, there is no obligation to tailor the disclosure to the particular needs of each client, and COBS 2.2.1R(2) permits information to be provided in a standardised format. There is therefore scope for firms to adapt standardised disclosures based on the type of designated business that they carry on and the clients with which they deal.

The guidance in COBS 2.2.2G is particularly important as the obligation to provide clients with information about itself and its services, costs and associated charges and designated investments is extended by COBS 6.1. COBS 6.1 is relevant to firms conducting MiFID business and those who carry on non-MiFID business for retail clients. In addition, COBS 14.1 prescribes additional disclosure requirements for non-MiFID business. Both of these Chapters of COBS are discussed in greater detail elsewhere.

5.3.6   Inducements

This Section of Chapter 2 applies to any firm that conducts desig-nated investment business with or for a client which is MiFID or non-MiFID business. In the case of MiFID or equivalent third-country business, the obligations in this Section also apply to an ancillary service provided by the firm. The new rule on inducements set out below replaces the Old COB rules in COB 2.3 and is intended to give effect to Article 26 of the MiFID Implementing Directive. The FSA has taken a "copy out" approach of the MiFID inducement provisions and retained, as guidance, the substance of the former COB rules dealing with the sale of packaged products for both MiFID and non-MiFID business. In terms of the scope of the new inducement rules, the FSA has not applied some of the detailed MiFID requirements to retail non-MiFID business and firms.

The guidance in COBS 2.3.3G cross-refers to Principles 1, 2 and 6 of the FSA Principles for Businesses, which require a firm to conduct busi-ness with integrity, to conduct its business with due skill, care and dili-gence, to pay due regard to the interests of its customers and to treat them fairly. Additional obligations apply to investment managers with regard to the use of dealing commission in COBS 11.6 and investment managers are required to comply with both Sections of COBS.

The general prohibition on inducements is set out at COBS 2.3.1R. This provides that, other than in certain prescribed circumstances (which are set out below), a firm must not pay or accept any fee or commission, or provide or receive any non-monetary benefit ("Payment"), in relation to designated investment business or, in the case of its MiFID or equivalent third-country business, another ancil-lary service, carried on for a client.

5.3.7   Exceptions to the rule on inducements

There are three circumstances where a payment may be made or received by a firm without breaching the rule against inducements. These are consistent with Article 26 of the Implementing Directive. The first is in COBS 2.3.1R(1) and it provides that a payment may be paid by or provided to or by the client, or a person on behalf of the client (this is Article 26(a) of the Implementing Directive).

The second, in COBS 2.3.1R(2), is intended to give effect to Article 26(b) of the Implementing Directive, and modifies relevant provisions for non-MiFID business. The effect of these provisions is that a payment may be paid or provided to or by a third party or a person acting on behalf of a third party provided that all of the following three conditions are met:

(a) Condition 1: the payment of the fee or commission, or the provision of the non-monetary benefit, does not impair compliance with the firm's duty to act in the best interests of the client.

(b) Condition 2: the existence, nature and amount of the fee, commission or benefit, or, where the amount cannot be ascertained, the method of calculating that amount, is clearly disclosed to the client, in a manner that is comprehensive, accurate and understandable, before the provision of the service. However, this requirement does not apply in every case. In particular, it does not apply to a firm when it gives basic advice.

In addition, with regard to firms carrying on business which is not MiFID or equivalent third-country business, the requirement to provide such disclosure will only apply where the firm is giving a recommendation in relation to a packaged product (e.g., life policy or pension product). Where a firm is obliged to give this disclosure, the firm is not required to provide disclosure of information relating to non-monetary benefits that are permitted by paragraph (a) above, provided that the benefit is reasonable in accordance with the Table set out in COBS 2.3.15G (*see* the discussion below).

According to COBS 2.3.2R, the disclosure obligation under COBS 2.3.1R will be satisfied if the firm:

(i) discloses the essential arrangements relating to the fee, commission or non-monetary benefit in summary form;

(ii) undertakes to the client that further details will be disclosed on request; and

(iii) honours the undertaking in (ii).

In terms of the content that should be included in the "summary form", the FSA has indicated in PS 07/6 that it is for firms to decide what information needs to be contained in the summary form disclosure. The FSA expects that the contents of the disclosures will vary with business activities and client types and that further guidance may be needed at some point in the future to help firms adjust to the changes, in particular in the retail market. The FSA also indicated in PS 07/6 that a firm's disclosure must provide adequate information for the client to make an informed decision on whether to proceed with the investment or ancillary service provided by the firm and whether to ask for the full information. It is noted that generic disclosure that the firm may or will receive or pay or provide benefits will not be sufficient to enable a client to make an informed decision.

(c) Condition 3: in relation to MiFID or equivalent third-country business, the payment of the fee or commission, or the provision of the non-monetary benefit must be designed to enhance the quality of the service to the client. Guidance in COBS 2.3.6G indicates, consistently with recital 39 of the MiFID Implementing Directive, that an investment firm that is in receipt of a commission in connection with a personal recommendation or a general recommendation, in circumstances where the advice or recommendation is not biased as a result of the receipt of commission, should be considered as designed to enhance the quality of the recommendation to the client.

Note that a non-monetary benefit would include the direction or referral by a firm of an actual or potential item of designated investment business to another person, whether on its own initiative or on the instructions of an associate: COBS 2.3.5G.

In PS 07/6, the FSA expresses the view that the expression "designed to enhance" makes it clear that a judgement about a fee or payment, or arrangements for fees or payments, can be made at the time the arrangement is proposed rather than only after a payment has been made. In addition, in the FSA's view, it is not necessary that the payment must benefit the particular client that is receiving the investment service. Rather, it may also benefit other clients or groups of clients, so that a requirement to "enhance the quality" of the relevant service to the client is met at the level of the service.

The FSA further indicates that, although this assessment could be performed at the level of a service provided under a particular business line, firms should not take this approach because the assessment should not be performed at a level that would convert the test into a meaningless exercise.

The third circumstance where a payment may be made or received by a firm without breaching the rule against inducements is in COBS 2.3.1R(3). COBS 2.3.1R(3) is a "copy out" of Article 26(c) and provides that the payment or receipt by a firm of proper fees which enable or are necessary for the provision of designated investment business or ancillary services, such as custody costs, settlement and exchange fees, regulatory levies or legal fees will not be regarded as a breach of the rule on inducements. These fees are considered, by their nature, not to give rise to conflicts with the firm's duties to act honestly, fairly and professionally in accordance with the best interests of the client.

It should also be noted that the rule in COBS 2.3.1R is unlikely to be relevant to small gifts and minor hospitality received by an individual in their personal capacity below a level specified in the firm's conflicts of interest policy: COBS 2.3.8G.

5.3.8 *Packaged products and reasonable non-monetary benefits*

Sections COBS 2.3.9G to 2.3.13G contain specific guidance in relation to packaged products. COBS 2.3.10E contains evidential provisions in relation to the sale of packaged products (being, *inter alia*, units in regulated collective investment schemes and interests in investment trust savings schemes). It states that a firm should not enter into certain types of arrangements (set out below) with an independent intermediary in relation to the sale of a packaged product if any commission is required to be disclosed. Two of these arrangements are:

(a) volume overrides, if commission paid in respect of several transactions is more than a simple multiple of the commission payable in respect of one transaction of the same kind; and

(b) an agreement to indemnify the payment of commission on terms that would or might confer an additional financial benefit on the recipient in the event of the commission becoming repayable.

This evidential provision is relevant to determining whether there has been a breach of COBS 2.3.1R, which is the rule setting out the prohibition on inducements referred to above. It is also relevant to determining whether the firm has breached the rules on disclosure of charges, remuneration and commission in COBS 6.4.

By way of guidance, COBS 2.3.11G provides that if a firm enters into an arrangement with another firm under which it makes or receives a payment of commission in excess of the amount disclosed to the client then the firm is likely to have breached the prohibition on inducements. This is unless the increase is attributable to an increase in the premiums or contributions payable by that client.

Additional evidential rules are set out in COBS 2.3.12E and apply in relation to a holding in, or the provision of credit to, a firm which holds itself out as making personal recommendations to retail clients on packaged products.

COBS 2.3.14G and 2.3.15G also provide guidance in relation to certain non-monetary benefits relating to packaged products that would not be prohibited by the inducements rule, called "reasonable non-monetary benefits". This guidance is therefore relevant, but not determinative, in terms of demonstrating compliance with COBS 2.3.1R. The Table in COBS 2.3.15G sets out the types of benefits which the FSA indicates in its guidance in COBS 2.3.14G are capable of enhancing the quality of the service provided to a client and, depending on the circumstances, are capable of being paid without breaching the client's best interests rule in COBS 2.1.1R.

The list of "reasonable non-monetary benefits" includes a product provider who assists an independent intermediary to promote its packaged products where the purpose of the benefits provided by a product company to the intermediary is to enhance the quality of its service to customers. This is also subject to a number of qualifications. The FSA was reluctant to provide a list of permitted and non-permitted "non-monetary" benefits. In the case of packaged products, the FSA did not make any rules or provide guidance and, in other cases, it expressed the view in PS 06/7 that it would be inappropriate to provide a comprehensive list given the diversity of circumstances and benefits that could arise. In other words, it is for firms to assess what is permitted and not permitted under the rules in light of the circumstances of the business.

The list of reasonable indirect benefits, for the purposes of the guidance set out at COBS 2.3.14G, includes 14 such benefits which fall into six categories:

(a) gifts, hospitality and promotional competition prizes;
(b) joint marketing exercises;
(c) seminars and conferences;
(d) technical services and information technology;
(e) training;
(f) travel and accommodation expenses.

Each of the above categories, and the 14 types of reasonable non-monetary benefits that are listed, are subject to a broad range of qualifications. These are set out in detail in the Table at COBS 2.3.15G.

It is worth mentioning that in May 2007 the CESR issued recommendations on inducements under MiFID. The recommendations are designed to foster supervisory convergence across the EU and to ensure consistent implementation and application of the MiFID Implementing Directive.

5.3.9 Record keeping in relation to inducement disclosures

The MiFID Implementing Directive imposes certain record-keeping obligations in Article 51(3) on MiFID firms with regard to the disclosures that they make to clients with respect to inducements. A firm which makes inducement disclosures in relation to its MiFID or equivalent third-country business must, under COBS 2.3.17R(1), make a record of each fee, commission or non-monetary benefit given to another firm that meets the criteria set out in COBS 2.3.1R(2)(b)(ii). In addition, COBS 2.3.17R(2) provides that all firms must make a record of each benefit given to another firm in accordance with COBS 2.3.14G, and must keep that record for at least five years from the date on which the benefit was given.

5.3.10   Agent as client

COBS 2.4.3R sets out rules for determining the "client" in circumstances where a firm is providing services in the course of carrying out designated investment business with or for a person who is acting as agent for another person.

In these circumstances, COBS 2.4.3R(1) provides that if the firm is aware that a person (Client 1) with or for whom it is providing services is acting as agent for another person (Client 2) in relation to those services, it is Client 1, and not Client 2, who is to be regarded by the firm as its client in respect of that business.

However, the rule in COBS 2.4.3R(1) will not apply if the firm has agreed with Client 1 in writing to treat Client 2 as its client. It also will not apply if Client 1 is neither a firm nor an overseas financial services institution and the main purpose of the arrangements between the parties is the avoidance of duties that the firm would otherwise owe to Client 2. If this is the case, then COBS 2.4.3R(2) provides that Client 2, rather than Client 1, is to be regarded as the firm's client for the purposes of COBS.

In addition, where an agreement entered into between the firm and Client 1 provides that Client 1 is to represent more than one Client 2, then the firm will be permitted to discharge its obligations to notify, obtain consent from, or enter into an agreement with each Client 2 by sending to, or receiving from, Client 1 a single communication expressed to cover each Client 2. However, in doing so, each Client 2 will need to receive:

(a)   separate risk warnings required under COBS;
(b)   separate confirmations under the requirements on occasional reporting (COBS 16.3); and
(c)   separate periodic statements.

5.3.11   Reliance on others

The provisions relating to reliance on others apply to firms conducting designated investment business or ancillary activities or, in the case of MiFID or equivalent third-country business, other ancillary activities. The purpose of these rules is to set out the extent to which a firm can rely on others in discharging its regulatory responsibilities. These provisions tie in with Principle 2 of the Principles for Businesses, which requires a firm to conduct its business with due skill, care and diligence. The provisions of COBS 2.4 relate specifically to obtaining, as well as providing, information under COBS. Different rules in COBS 2.4 apply, depending on whether the firm is performing MiFID business. The rules regarding reliance on others were previously found in COB 2.3. The FSA has effectively retained the substance of COB 2.3 and applied it to MiFID and equivalent business. It has achieved this through COBS 2.4.4R (which gives effect to Article 20 of MiFID), and in other situations through COBS 2.4.6R. Both of these rules are discussed below.

COBS 2.4.4R applies where a firm is performing MiFID or equivalent third-country business. If, in the course of performing such business, a firm (Firm 1) receives an instruction to perform an investment or ancillary service on behalf of a client through another firm (Firm 2), then Firm 1 will be entitled to rely upon any information about the client transmitted to it by Firm 2 as well as any recommendations in respect of the service or transaction that have been provided to the client by Firm 2. This is provided, however, that Firm 2 is either a MiFID investment firm or a third-country investment firm, or an investment firm that is authorised in another EEA state and subject to equivalent requirements.

In these circumstances, COBS 2.4.4R(3) provides that Firm 2 will remain responsible for the completeness and accuracy of any information about the client transmitted by it to Firm 1 and the appropriateness for the client of any advice or recommendations provided to the client.

In all other instances, that is business carried on by a firm that falls outside the scope of MiFID or is not equivalent third-country business, the rule in COBS 2.4.6R will apply. This is broadly equivalent to the previous rule in COB 2.3. COBS 2.4.6R(2) provides that a firm will be taken to be in compliance with any rule in COBS that requires it to obtain information to the extent the firm can show it was reasonable for it to rely on information provided to it in writing by another person. The key requirements for being able to rely on this rule are that the party providing the information should not be connected with the firm, and that the person should be competent to provide the information. Guidance on interpretation of this rule, and the evidential provisions relating to it, suggest that reliance on information provided by unconnected authorised persons or professional firms may generally be relied upon. In its Policy Statement on the COB Rules, published in February 2001, the FSA clarified that the evidential provisions relating to the independence of the supplier of information are designed to ensure that the source of the information is not subject to undue influence by the firm concerned. It is similarly acceptable for a firm which is under an obligation to send information to a customer to send the information to another person on the instruction of the customer, as long as the recipient is not connected with the firm.

5.3.12   Other changes in scope of COBS 2

In addition to dealing with the particular regulatory issues set out above, the former Chapter 2 of the Old COB prior to the implementation of MiFID imposed additional obligations on firms with regard to the information barriers, soft commission agreements, and prior and periodic disclosures regarding soft dealing arrangements.

The provisions dealing with information barriers are now more comprehensively dealt with in SYSC 10.1 as part of a firm's overall obligation to have systems in place to identify, manage and avoid conflicts of interest. Provisions regarding soft dealing arrangements and the obligations of investment managers are more completely dealt with in COBS 11.6 which also imposes obligations on investment managers to make adequate prior and periodic disclosure in relation to the execution of trades and the provision of investment research.

5.4   Conclusion

The underlying regulatory purpose of COBS remains the same as that of Old COB, despite the simplification of the obligations in the Chapter and the implementation of relevant MiFID obligations. The comments of the FSA in Consultation Paper 45a are, therefore, arguably still relevant and it would seem that the underlying purpose of COBS continues to be "to set and reinforce business standards for various aspects of firms' relationships with their customers". However, COBS does simplify a number of formerly prescriptive COB rules and simplifies a number of previous COB provisions. The various limitations on the application of COBS reflect the relative needs of different types of clients in terms of ensuring that consumers are treated fairly by firms carrying on regulated activities, and in particular designated investment business which is and is not MiFID or equivalent third-country business. However, many aspects of COBS do not reveal policy shifts or changes in substantive provisions from the Old COB rules, but a modification that is aimed at principles-based regulation in a manner that is consistent with the regulation of investment services and activities across the EU.

Chapter 6

Getting New Customers

Arun Srivastava

Partner
Baker & McKenzie LLP

6.1   Introduction

Client categorisation is the cornerstone of conduct of business regulation. The level of regulatory protections afforded to clients depends on the manner in which the client has been classified. Accordingly, client categorisation is not an end in itself, but is also a means of ensuring that the regulatory obligations that a firm owes to its clients are appropriately calibrated, taking into account the nature and experience of the client. The application of key conduct of business requirements, including matters such as best execution, suitability and appropriateness, depend on the manner in which a client has been classified.

The focus of this Chapter is accordingly on a firm's obligation to correctly categorise its client for regulatory purposes. Client categorisation rules are contained in Chapter 3 of the FSA's Conduct of Business Sourcebook ("COBS" or "the Rules"). The categorisation rules set out in this Chapter are derived from the client categorisation rules contained in the Markets in Financial Instruments Directive (Directive 2004/39/EC) ("MiFID") and the MiFID Implementing Directive (Directive 2006/73/EC). MiFID has had a material impact on FSA client categorisation rules and ensuing conduct of business obligations. Conceptually, the pre-MiFID and post-MiFID rules are similar. However, important substantive changes have been made by MiFID. These changes have been applied in respect of both MiFID business and non-MiFID business, albeit that the rules relating to non-MiFID business apply in modified form.

The FSA's client categorisation rules contained in Chapter 3 of COBS provide for three categories of client:

(a)   retail clients;
(b)   professional clients; and
(c)   eligible counterparties.

These categories are similar to the categories under the pre-MiFID FSA Rules, which also operated a three-tier approach with the categories of private customer, intermediate customer and market counterparty. Under the transitional provisions relating to the implementation of MiFID, firms were able to automatically map many clients from their pre-MiFID to post-MiFID categories. However, as explained below, the changes introduced by MiFID extend beyond mere changes in the terminology used to describe the different categories of client. MiFID shifted the boundaries of the three client categories. In addition to this, the regime for eligible counterparties applies in a different way from the market counterparty regime under the pre-MiFID FSA rules. The eligible counterparty regime only applies in respect of certain types of activities. In this sense under MiFID for many types of business there are effectively only two client categories (retail clients and professional clients) with a distinct eligible counterparty regime covering specified activities. Under this system, a particular client may be treated as a professional client in respect of certain activities and an eligible counterparty in respect of others.

The Rules are designed such that the regulatory requirements for firms are least onerous in relation to those clients who are most experienced with financial products and markets. The Rules endeavour to retain a degree of flexibility, so that clients may be recharacterised (and thereby receive more or less protection, as the case may be), depending on their circumstances. This process is known as "opting down" or "opting up", depending on whether the client is receiving a higher or lower level of protection.

The FSA is of the view that the Rules assist in furthering two of its statutory objectives under the Financial Services and Markets Act 2000 ("FSMA 2000"). These are the objectives of maintaining confidence in the financial system and securing the appropriate degree of protection for consumers. The FSA considers that the Rules satisfy these objectives by tailoring the regulatory protections to suit the needs of individual customers. The Rules are also consistent with the investor protection objective of MiFID. However, MiFID does recognise in Recital 31 that investor protection measures should be adapted to the particularities of each category of investor.

This Chapter examines how the Rules determine a client's categorisation and the consequences that flow from that categorisation. First, however, it provides a brief overview of the prior history of the rules and the changes introduced by MiFID.

6.2   Prior history and MiFID implementation

Unlike many European jurisdictions, the UK has for some time operated a tiered client categorisation system. Client categorisation rules were provided for in the conduct of business rules of the self-regulating organisations established under the Financial Services Act 1986. Thereafter, following N2 and the establishment of the FSA regulatory system, similar client categorisation rules were provided for in Chapter 4 of the FSA's Conduct of Business Sourcebook.

MiFID builds on and is similar in many respects to the pre-MiFID FSA rules contained in Chapter 4 of the FSA's Conduct of Business Sourcebook. However, MiFID has introduced material changes to the client categorisation regime.

The FSA's process of consulting on the implementation of MiFID included detailed consultation on client categorisation issues. The FSA set out indicative proposals on the implementation of MiFID client categorisation rules in its August 2006 Paper on *Implementing MiFID's Client Categorisation Requirements* ("the CC Paper"). This was followed by the consultation in Chapter 7 of CP 06/19 on Reforming Conduct of Business Regulation and later consultations on conduct of business rules, which also covered client categorisation issues. The FSA's Consultation Paper CP 07/9 on Non-MiFID Deferred Matters also dealt with the application of client categorisation requirements to non-MiFID business.

In the CC Paper the FSA identified three broad areas of change under MiFID client categorisation rules. These are as follows.

6.2.1 The boundaries between the three MiFID categories are not the same as those under the former FSA COB boundaries

As explained above, in common with the pre-MiFID client categorisation regime, MiFID operates a three-tier system. While these tiers correspond broadly to the pre-MiFID categories, in the CC Paper the FSA noted that there are material differences between the MiFID and pre-MiFID client category boundaries. Because of this, under MiFID rules a firm may be required to treat a client as falling into a lower level of client category and accordingly provide that client with greater regulatory protections than before.

The CC Paper also referred to the eligible counterparty regime noting that this regime applies only in relation to a limited range of activities. The eligible counterparty categorisation cannot, for example, be used where the service being provided consists of the provision of investment advice.

6.2.2 Changes in criteria and procedures

MiFID also permits movement between different client categories.

A client may choose to be moved or opted up or down from the client's default categorisation. However, the CC Paper noted that the circumstances in which a client may be opted up or down under MiFID differ from the pre-MiFID FSA rules and that different procedures will apply.

The pre-MiFID FSA rules relied to a greater extent on qualitative criteria, whereas MiFID rules require firms to have regard to objective quantitative requirements in assessing whether a client should be moved from the client's default categorisation. Under MiFID rules clients have greater flexibility as to the circumstances in which their client categorisation may be moved up or down. This can, for example, be on a general basis, product basis or trade-by-trade basis. The term "per se" has been used to connote a client who meets the specified requirements for a particular client category, and "elective" is used to connote a client who has opted into a different client category.

MiFID rules also require firms to specifically inform clients that they have a right to request different categorisation and any consequential limitations on the regulatory protections thereby afforded.

6.2.3 More retail clients

The FSA stated in its CC Paper that it expects more clients to be classified as retail clients under MiFID rules than as private customers under pre-MiFID FSA rules. In particular, owing to different quantitative requirements under MiFID, a small corporate which would formerly have been classified as an intermediate customer under pre-MiFID FSA rules (based on size requirements), may need to be classified as a Retail Client for the purposes of MiFID rules. This will, of course, also mean that such clients are entitled to greater regulatory protections.

6.2.4 General approach to implementation

The FSA's general approach to implementation was to replace the pre-MiFID client categorisation provisions with a "copy out" of the relevant MiFID provisions into Chapter 3 of COBS. In other words, the wording in MiFID was inserted into MiFID largely without amendment.

In the course of the consultation on MiFID implementation, the FSA considered the application of the MiFID client categorisation system to non-MiFID business. There are broadly three classes of business:

(a)   business that falls within the scope of MiFID;
(b)   business that falls entirely outside the scope of MiFID; and
(c)   mixed business.

Mixed business covers business that comprises both MiFID and non-MiFID business.

In implementing MiFID the FSA has taken the approach that there should essentially be a single system of client categorisation applying to both MiFID and non-MiFID business. Accordingly, the client categories of retail client, professional client and eligible counterparty apply to all categories of business. However, within this system certain modifications apply depending on whether the business concerned is within or outside MiFID's scope. For business falling outside the scope of MiFID the definition of a professional client is, for example, different from the definition used for MiFID business. In that case the definition used for MiFID business is based on the Directive, whereas the definition used for non-MiFID business incorporates elements of the definition used under the pre-MiFID FSA rules. In relation to mixed scope business, a firm must determine whether to apply MiFID or non-MiFID rules. This depends, essentially, on whether the non-MiFID business is entwined with the MiFID business. Unless the non-MiFID business can be conducted separately from the MiFID business, the business is treated as MiFID business and the rules applying to MiFID business are applicable.

The provisions of MiFID apply to firms who have their head or registered office in the European Economic Area ("EEA"). In principle, therefore, business conducted by a branch of a non-EEA firm (a third-country firm) is outside the scope of MiFID. However, the approach taken by the FSA to the implementation of the client categorisation rules is to treat business conducted by such a third-country firm as MiFID business, provided that the business would otherwise fall within MiFID's scope (i.e., that the business would constitute an investment or ancillary service as defined by MiFID). The client categorisation rules use the term "equivalent third-country business" to cover the position of third-country firms engaged in MiFID business.

6.3 COBS

Pursuant to COBS 3.3.1R a firm must notify a new client of its categorisation as a retail client, professional client or eligible counterparty in accordance with the provisions of Chapter 3 of COBS. This requirement applies only where the firm is conducting designated investment business or, in the case of MiFID or equivalent third-country business, an ancillary service that does not constitute designated investment business. The rule requiring clients to be notified of their categorisation is backed by organisational requirements under which firms are required to implement appropriate written internal policies and procedures to categorise their clients. These organisational requirements are expanded upon in COBS 3.8.

When categorising clients, firms must obtain information to support the categorisation. COBS 3.8.2R(2) includes a specific record-keeping obligation on firms to make a record in relation to each client of the categorisation established for the client which must include sufficient information to support that categorisation.

The obligation to notify clients of their categorisation applies to "new" clients. Under the transitional arrangements explained below, existing clients may be grandfathered into new MiFID categories. This process provides a degree of flexibility for firms since, for example, clients in the intermediate customer category who would not qualify as professional clients may be grandfathered into the professional client category.

Clients may request re-categorisation and must be notified of this prior to any services being provided to them. Accordingly, COBS 3.3.1R provides that before providing services to a client, firms must inform the client in a durable medium about any right that the client has to request a different categorisation and any limitations to the level of client protection that such a different categorisation would entail. Under COBS 3.7.1R a firm must allow a professional client or an eligible counterparty to request re-categorisation as a client that benefits from a higher degree of protection. An eligible counterparty could therefore request re-categorisation as a professional or retail client, and a professional client could request re-categorisation as a retail client.

At the outset of a relationship a firm must therefore notify a client of the categorisation that the firm has decided on and also of the client's entitlement to be re-categorised.

As these requirements only apply in relation to "clients" it is important to understand who is a client for these purposes.

A "client" is a person to whom the firm provides, intends to provide or has provided a service in the course of carrying on a regulated activity or, in the case of MiFID or equivalent third-country business, an ancillary service (COBS 3.2.1R). A client includes a potential client.

The FSA's rules (COBS 2.4.3R) also contain provisions dealing with the position of agents. Where a firm conducts designated investment business or ancillary activities, or in the case of MiFID or equivalent third-country business, other ancillary services with or for a client who it is aware is acting as agent for another person (such other person being the principal), the agent, and not the principal, will be the firm's client unless:

(a) the agent is neither an authorised firm nor an overseas financial services institution and the main purpose of the arrangements between the parties is to avoid duties that the firm would otherwise owe to the principal; or

(b) the firm has agreed with the agent to treat its principal as the firm's client.

COBS 3.2.3R contains the following further provisions as to who the firm's client will be:

(a) in relation to a firm establishing, operating or winding up a personal pension scheme or a stakeholder pension scheme, a member or beneficiary of that scheme will be a client of the firm (COBS 3.2.3R(2));

(b) if a firm which does not fall within the above category provides services to a person acting as the trustee of a trust, the trustee will be the firm's client and not the underlying beneficiaries of the trust (COBS 3.2.3R(3));

(c) in relation to business that is neither MiFID nor equivalent third-country business, if a firm provides services to a collective investment scheme that does not have a separate legal personality, the collective investment scheme will be the firm's client (COBS 3.2.3R(4));

(d) if the firm provides services relating to a contribution to or interest in a Child Trust Fund ("CTF") (except a personal recommendation relating to a contribution to a CTF or in relation to the communication or approval of a financial promotion) the firm's only client is the registered contact (i.e., the person who is capable of giving instructions to the CTF provider with respect to the management of the CTF), if there is one, and otherwise the person to whom the annual statements must be sent in accordance with Regulation 10 of the Child Trust Fund Regulations 2004 (COBS 3.2.3R(5)).

6.4 Retail clients

Retail clients are defined as clients who are neither professional clients nor eligible counterparties. The retail client category is therefore the default category of client categorisation.

The Glossary[1] contains a different definition of a retail client where the firm is providing basic advice on a stakeholder product. In such cases a client is any person who is advised by a firm on the merits of opening or buying a stakeholder product where the advice is given in the course of a business carried on by the firm and is received by a person who is not acting in the course of a business carried on by him.

6.5 Professional client

Professional clients are defined as persons who are either a per se professional client or an elective professional client, as explained below. Professional clients will normally be clients who possess the experience, knowledge and expertise to make their own investment decisions and assess the risks inherent in their decisions.

The definition of a per se professional client is set out below. It is important to note that the definition of a per se professional client depends on the nature of the business to be conducted. The definition of a per se professional client for the purpose of MiFID and equivalent third-country business is based on the definition of a professional client set out in Annex II of MiFID. The definition to be used for other types of business differs as to the types of large undertakings that may be treated as per se professional clients.

Under COBS 3.5.2R the following are per se professional clients unless and to the extent that they are an eligible counterparty or are given a different categorisation under the provisions of Chapter 3 of COBS:

(a) Entities which are required to be authorised and regulated to operate in the financial markets. Annex II to MiFID specifies the

---

[1] This is a reference to the Glossary appearing in the FSA's Handbook of Rules and Guidance.

following under this category: credit institutions, investment firms, other authorised or regulated financial institutions, insurance companies, collective investment schemes and their management companies, pension funds and their management companies, commodity and commodity derivative dealers, locals and other institutional investors. The above include entities authorised in an EEA state or a third country.

(b)   National or regional governments, public bodies that manage public debt, Central Banks, international and supranational institutions such as the World Bank, International Monetary Fund ("IMF"), European Central Bank, the European Investment Bank and other similar international organisations. It should be noted that the FSA takes the view that a local or public authority is not likely to constitute a regional government for these purposes. Accordingly, if a firm wishes to categorise a local or public authority as a professional client it is likely that it will need to do so on the basis that the authority qualifies as a large undertaking, as explained below.

(c)   Other institutional investors whose main activity is to invest in financial instruments (in relation to MiFID or equivalent third-country business) or designated investments (in relation to a firm's other business). This includes entities dedicated to the securitisation of assets or other financing transactions.

As indicated, large undertakings are also treated as per se professional clients. The definition of a large undertaking varies depending on whether the business concerned is MiFID or non-MiFID business.

For MiFID or equivalent third-country business a large undertaking meeting any two of the following size requirements on a company basis is a per se professional client, namely:

(a)   a balance sheet with a total of €20 million;
(b)   net turnover of €40 million; or
(c)   own funds of €2 million.

It should be noted that these quantitative requirements apply on a company as opposed to a group basis. This approach differs from the pre-MiFID FSA rules which took a group approach and under which the size thresholds were in any event lower.

In relation to business that is not MiFID or equivalent third-country business, the FSA has essentially applied the quantitative requirements used for the purpose of the definition of an intermediate customer under the pre-MiFID FSA rules. For the purpose of non-MiFID business a large undertaking meeting the following size requirements is a per se professional client:

(a)   A body corporate (including a limited liability partnership) which has (or any of whose holding companies or subsidiaries has) (or has had at any time during the previous two years) called up share capital or net assets of at least £5 million (or its equivalent in any other currency at the relevant time).

(b)   An undertaking that meets (or any of whose holding companies or subsidiaries meets) two of the following tests:

  (i)   a balance sheet total of €12.5 million;
  (ii)   a net turnover of €25 million;
  (iii) an average number of employees during the year of 250.

(c)   A partnership or unincorporated association which has (or has had at any time during the previous two years) net assets of at least £5 million (or its equivalent in any other currency at the relevant time) and calculated in the case of a limited partnership without deducting loans owing to any of the partners.

(d)   A trustee of a trust (other than an occupational pension scheme, small self-administered scheme ("SSAS"), personal pension scheme or stakeholder pension scheme which has (or has had at any time during the previous two years) assets of at least £10 million (or its equivalent in any other currency at the relevant time) calculated by aggregating the value of the cash and designated investments forming part of the trust's assets, but before deducting its liabilities.

(e)   A trustee of an occupational pension scheme or SSAS or a trustee or operator of a personal pension scheme or stakeholder pension scheme where the scheme has (or has had at any time during the previous two years) at least 50 members and assets under management of at least £10 million (or its equivalent in any other currency at the relevant time).

(f)   A local or public authority.

Although a client may meet the requirements of a per se professional client, the client must be permitted to request treatment as a non-professional client (i.e., a retail client) and the firm may agree to provide a higher level of protection. Clients must be informed that a variation of the agreement with the firm may be sought in order to secure a higher degree of protection. An agreement not to treat a client as a professional client may be limited to particular transactions, services or products so that the client may be treated differently depending on the nature of the business involved.

COBS 3.5.3R provides that a firm may treat a client as an elective professional client where it complies with the requirements of COBS 3.5.3R(1), (2) and (3). This enables firms to treat clients who do not qualify as per se professional clients as elective professional clients. The rules relating to the opting up of clients to elective professional client status set out certain qualitative and quantitative requirements that must be satisfied. In relation to the application of these requirements, a distinction is drawn as to the approach to be taken with MiFID and equivalent third-country business and non-MiFID business. In the former case, both the qualitative and quantitative requirements must be met. In the case of non-MiFID business, only the qualitative requirements must be met. The FSA has taken the decision to switch off the quantitative requirements. In both cases, under COBS 3.5.6R a firm must take all reasonable steps to ensure that the client requesting treatment as an elective professional client satisfies the qualitative and, where applicable, the quantitative requirements.

For both MiFID and non-MiFID business a firm is required under COBS 3.5.3R(1) to carry out an adequate assessment of the expertise, experience and knowledge of the client to obtain a reasonable assurance, in light of the nature of the transactions or services envisaged, that the client is capable of making his own investment decisions and understanding the risks involved. This is the qualitative element of the opting up requirements. Pursuant to COBS 3.5.4R, if the client is an entity, the qualitative test under COBS 3.5.3R(1) must be carried out in relation to the person who is authorised to carry out transactions on the client's behalf.

Additionally, in the case of MiFID and equivalent third-country business, under COBS 3.5.3R(2), a minimum of two of the following criteria must be satisfied in order for a client to be opted up and treated as an elective professional client:

(a)   the client has carried out transactions, in significant size, on the relevant market at an average frequency of 10 per quarter over the previous four quarters;

(b)   the size of the client's financial instruments portfolio, defined as including cash deposits and financial instruments, exceeds €500,000;

(c)   the client works or has worked in the financial sector for at least one year in a professional position, which requires knowledge of the transactions or services envisaged.

For both MiFID and non-MiFID business the following procedure must be followed under COBS 3.5.3(3)R:

(a)   the client must state in writing to the firm that it wishes to be treated as a professional client either generally or in respect of a particular service or transaction or type of transaction or product;

(b)   the firm must give the client a clear written warning of the protections and investor compensation rights the client may lose; and

(c)   the client must state in writing, in a separate document from the contract, that it is aware of the consequences of losing such protections.

Professional clients are responsible for keeping firms informed about any change that could affect their categorisation.

If a firm becomes aware that a client no longer fulfils the initial conditions that made it eligible for categorisation as an elective professional client the firm must take "appropriate action". Where this involves classifying the client as a retail client, the firm must notify the client of its new categorisation.

COBS draws a distinction between the manner in which a per se and an elective professional client should be treated. COBS 3.5.7G states that an elective professional client should be presumed to possess the market knowledge and experience comparable to a per se professional client.

6.6 Eligible counterparty

Where a firm classifies its client as an eligible counterparty, that client will be given comparatively little protection under the FSA's regulatory regime. This reflects the fact that such clients are considered to have sufficient expertise in relation to the financial services sector such that they can to a large extent protect their own position.

The eligible counterparty regime applies only in relation to eligible counterparty business. This is defined as the investment services and activities carried on by a firm which comprise:

(a)   dealing on own account;
(b)   receiving and transmitting orders; and
(c)   execution of orders on behalf of clients.

The eligible counterparty regime also applies to ancillary services directly related to transactions entered into under it. Ancillary services that might be carried on in a manner directly related to the above include corporate finance advice and general recommendations that do not involve the making of any personal recommendation. However, investment advice, as defined under MiFID, falls outside the scope of the eligible counterparty regime, given that the regime only extends to related services that constitute ancillary as opposed to investment services. The eligible counterparty regime is therefore similar to the pre-MiFID interprofessional business regime, save that the concept of interprofessional business extended to transaction specific advice. As indicated, the eligible counterparty regime does not extend to such services.

In respect of business that is not MiFID or equivalent third-country business, the eligible counterparty regime also covers the activity of arranging deals in investments.

The eligible counterparty regime does not apply where the services being provided involve portfolio management, investment advice and underwriting or placing. Accordingly, where a firm is advising a client or providing portfolio management services, the client must be classified either as a retail client or a professional client. The client cannot be categorised as an eligible counterparty in relation to the provision of such services.

Where a person is an eligible counterparty, certain conduct of business rules under MiFID are disapplied both for MiFID and non-MiFID business. In particular, Article 24(1) of MiFID states that investment firms are not obliged to comply with the following requirements where the client is an eligible counterparty:

(a) Article 19 – this covers a range of conduct of business obligations including suitability and appropriateness requirements, requirements relating to marketing communications and the requirement to act honestly, fairly and professionally in accordance with the best interests of the client.
(b) Article 21 – this Article sets out the obligation to execute orders on the terms most favourable to the client (i.e., best execution).
(c) Article 22(1) – this Article relates to client order handling rules.

As eligible counterparties will be clients, other regulatory obligations will continue to apply. Accordingly, firms will need to comply with record keeping, client asset and conflicts of interest obligations, notwithstanding the fact that certain conduct of business obligations have been switched off by virtue of the client's categorisation as an eligible counterparty.

Additionally, it should be noted that while the protections under Articles 19, 21 and 22(1) of MiFID do not apply to business with eligible counterparties, clients who are eligible counterparties can nevertheless agree with firms that some or all of these protections will be provided.

As with the regime for professional clients, certain clients may be per se eligible counterparties, whereas others may be opted up to this status.

Set out below are the categories of persons who are per se eligible counterparties; these categories include equivalent non-EEA entities:

(a) investment firms;
(b) credit institutions;

(c)   insurance companies;

(d)   UCITS and their management companies;

(e)   pension funds and their management companies,

(f)   other financial institutions authorised or regulated under community legislation or the national law of an EEA Member State;

(g)   undertakings exempt from MiFID pursuant to Article 2(1)(k) of MiFID (certain own account dealers in commodities or commodity derivatives);

(h)   national governments or their corresponding offices (including public bodies that deal with public debt);

(i)   central banks; and

(j)   supranational institutions.

While a client may be classified as a per se eligible counterparty on the above basis, the client has the right to request either on a general form or on a trade-by-trade basis, treatment as a client who is subject to Articles 19, 21 and 22(1) of MiFID (i.e., the requirements that are otherwise disapplied from business with eligible counterparties). An eligible counterparty may thereby be classified as either a professional client or a retail client. The default position is that the client who requests higher protections should be regarded as requesting treatment as a professional client unless the client specifically requests treatment as a retail client.

COB 3.6.4R sets out the circumstances in which a client may be treated as an elective eligible counterparty.

For MiFID and equivalent third-country business, a firm may treat an undertaking as an elective eligible counterparty if it is a per se professional client, unless the client is only a per se professional client because it is an institutional investor under COBS 3.5.2R (5)).

In relation to business other than MiFID or equivalent third-country business, an undertaking may be treated as an elective eligible counterparty if it:

(a)   is a body corporate (including a limited liability partnership) which has (or any of whose holding companies or subsidiaries has) called up share capital of at least £10 million (or its equivalent in any other currency at the relevant time);

(b)   meets the criteria in the rule on meeting two quantitative tests (COBS 3.5.2R (3)(b)).

A firm may also treat as an elective eligible counterparty an undertaking that requests such a categorisation and is an elective professional client, but only in respect of the services or transactions for which it could be treated as a professional client.

In relation to MiFID and equivalent third-country business, a firm must obtain the prospective counterparty's express confirmation that it agrees to be treated as an eligible counterparty. This may be in the form of a general agreement or in respect of individual transactions.

6.7   Policies, procedures and records

As explained above, Chapter 3 of COBS imposes organisational requirements on firms in relation to their obligations to appropriately categorise their clients.

Pursuant to COBS 3.8.1R a firm must implement appropriate written internal policies and procedures to categorise its clients.

COBS 3.8.2R imposes various record-keeping requirements. Certain of these requirements relate to obligations to record the form of notices given to or agreements entered into with clients and other obligations relating to the categorisation process.

Under COBS 3.8.2R(1) a firm must make a record of the form of each notice provided and each agreement entered into under COBS Chapter 3. The record is required to be made at the time that the standard form was first used and must be retained for the relevant period after the firm ceased to carry on business with clients who were provided with that form, applicable to the type of business involved. The relevant periods are set out below.

In relation to the categorisation process, a firm must make a record in relation to each client of:

(a)   the categorisation established for the client under COBS Chapter 3 including sufficient information to support the categorisation;

(b) evidence of the despatch to the client of any notice required under COBS Chapter 3, and if such notice differs from the relevant standard form a copy of the actual notice provided; and

(c) a copy of any agreement entered into with the client under COBS Chapter 3.

Accordingly, where standard form notices are used, the firm need only keep evidence of the despatch of the notice and not a copy of the notice itself, unless it differs from the standard form.

The default retention period is three years. The exceptions to this are:

(a) records must be kept indefinitely in relation to a pension transfer, pension opt-out or Free Standing Additional Voluntary Contribution ("FSAVC");

(b) at least five years in relation to a life policy or pension contract; and

(c) five years in relation to MiFID or equivalent third-country business.

In the CC Paper the FSA noted that MiFID would also impose additional monitoring and organisational requirements. In particular Article 19(1) of MiFID imposes an obligation on firms to act honestly, fairly and professionally in accordance with the best interests of its clients and Article 13(2) of MiFID imposes an obligation on firms to establish adequate policies and procedures sufficient to ensure compliance of the firm. The FSA noted that these obligations would be particularly relevant where the firm was opting up a client to a higher categorisation.

On the basis that the FSA has taken the "copy out" approach to MiFID implementation, the FSA have not carried across into COBS the requirement under the pre-MiFID FSA rules for firms to annually review the classification of their expert private customers to ensure that the categorisation remained appropriate. MiFID in fact imposes an obligation on professional clients to keep firms informed of any change which could affect their current categorisation. COBS 3.5.8G therefore states that professional clients are responsible for keeping the firm informed about any change that could affect their current categorisation. Additionally, COBS 3.7.2G provides that it is the responsibility of a professional client or eligible counterparty to ask for a higher level of protection when it deems it is unable to properly assess or manage the risks involved. In the CC Paper, however, the FSA noted that, notwithstanding these provisions, if a firm becomes aware that the client no longer fulfils the initial conditions qualifying them for treatment as a professional client, the firm is also required to take appropriate action. In this regard the FSA went on to state that where the firm obtains information from the client for other business reasons that is also relevant to the client's categorisation, the firm will need to capture this information in order to ensure that the categorisation remains appropriate.

6.8   Transitional provisions

Under transitional arrangements certain clients were automatically grandfathered in the sense that their pre-MiFID FSA rules categorisation was automatically mapped to their categorisation under COBS. In such cases firms did not need formally to review, re-paper or notify the client of its new categorisation. The transitional rules are set out in COBS TP1 and apply indefinitely.

In other cases a transitional grandfathering approach has been taken. Under this a client's categorisation has not automatically mapped from pre-MiFID FSA rules to COBS categories. Firms have been able to use transitional provisions to place these clients into a COBS client category. No re-categorisation exercise has needed to be undertaken. Notifications have been required to be made in certain instances.

In other cases a reviewed grandfathering approach has been taken. In such instances clients have not mapped automatically and nor has the firm been able to use transitional provisions. Firms have had to review these clients.

Individuals categorised as private customers under the pre-MiFID FSA rules map automatically to the retail client category. Undertakings, such as companies, who were private customers do not map automatically to the retail category. They may be treated as retail clients or firms have had to newly categorise them under MiFID rules. Expert private customers have mapped to the professional client category notwithstanding the differences between the pre-MiFID FSA rules and COBS.

Only limited categories of intermediate customers have mapped automatically to professional client status. These include local authorities, special purpose vehicles and regulated collective investment schemes. Under the applicable transitional arrangements, other intermediate customers may be treated as professional clients.

Market counterparties falling within the definition of a per se or elective eligible counterparty may be treated as an eligible counterparty provided that the firm has satisfied itself that the business concerned falls within the scope of eligible counterparty business.

6.9   Consequences of client categorisation

As stated above, the categorisation of clients determines the level of regulatory protection they receive under COBS. This Chapter does not go into detail on each of the protections afforded to retail clients pursuant to COBS. To do so would, in effect, involve a consideration of the whole of COBS. Rather, it is assumed that the reader is familiar with such protections and the Chapter highlights which of these regulatory protections are also provided to professional clients and eligible counterparties.

The final section of this Chapter considers briefly the consequences that may flow from an authorised firm incorrectly classifying a customer, in particular in relation to the rights of action provided for in the FSMA 2000.

6.10   Regulatory protections – eligible counterparties

Where the client is classified as an eligible counterparty, only limited parts of COBS will apply to any transactions between the authorised firm and such client.

Broadly speaking, the consequence of being classified as an eligible counterparty is that various regulatory protections will be "switched off". In particular for eligible counterparty business the following conduct of business rules do not apply:

(a) COBS 2 (other than COBS 2.4) – various conduct of business obligations (duties to act honestly and professionally, inducements and information disclosure before providing services);
(b) COBS 4 (other than COBS 4.4.1R and COBS 4.4.2G) – rules on communicating with clients, including financial promotions;
(c) COBS 6.1 – rules relating to information to be provided about the firm, its services and remuneration;
(d) COBS 8 – requirements relating to client agreements;
(e) COBS 10 – obligations to ensure the appropriateness of transactions;
(f) COBS 11.2, 11.3 and 11.6 – rules imposing obligations regarding best execution, client order handling and use of dealing commissions;
(g) COBS 12.3.1R to 12.3.3R – rules relating to the labelling of non-independent research;
(h) COBS 14.3 – rules relating to the provision of information about designated investments;
(i) COBS 16 – rules in reporting information to clients.

6.11 Consequences of incorrect categorisation

Where an authorised firm incorrectly classifies a client, transactions undertaken by the firm with the client are not voided or made unenforceable. However, Section 150 FSMA 2000 does allow a "private person" who suffers loss as a result of the contravention of a rule to bring an action for damages against the authorised firm. A "private person" has such meaning as may be prescribed (Section 150(5)).

The Financial Services and Markets Act 2000 (Rights of Action) Regulations 2001 (SI 2001/2256) defines a "private person" as:

(a) any individual, unless the loss is suffered in the course of carrying on a regulated activity (or in the course of carrying on any activity which would be a regulated activity apart from any exclusion made by Article 72 (overseas person) or Article 72A (information society service providers) of the Regulated Activities Order); and

(b)   any person who is not an individual, unless he suffers the loss in question in the course of carrying on business of any kind.

Governments, local authorities and international organisations are excluded from the definition of "private person".

Section 150 FSMA 2000 broadly replicates Section 62(1) of its predecessor, the FS Act 1986. Section 62 was considered in a case that highlights the potential pitfalls of client categorisation, *Australia & New Zealand Banking Group Limited* ("ANZ") v *Louis Cattan and Françoise Cattan*.[2] In *Cattan*, the court considered whether ANZ had complied with the relevant Investment Management Regulatory Organisation ("IMRO") client categorisation rules when it reclassified Mr Cattan as a "non-private customer". The relevant IMRO rule was broadly similar to the COB rule allowing an authorised firm to reclassify an expert private customer as an intermediate customer.

The market in which Mr Cattan invested involved instruments in the emerging market debt ("EMD") sector. Prior to his involvement personally, Mr Cattan had formed part of a joint venture with two other people to trade in the EMD sector with ANZ. Mr Cattan had a power of attorney in respect of those dealings. In terms of personal experience, Mr Cattan had worked for a Middle Eastern bank in Paris from the mid-seventies, although it appears that his work experience was not specifically as a banker.

Morison J held that ANZ was correct to classify Mr Cattan as having sufficient understanding and experience in the EMD market to waive the protections provided to private customers by the IMRO rules. The remaining issue was whether ANZ had provided the requisite written warning to Mr Cattan of the protections he would lose should he cease to be classified as a private customer. Mr Cattan had signed and returned the ANZ letter warning him of the consequences of ceasing to be classified as a private customer in late September. However, Morison J found he had already entered into two transactions before he could have reviewed the warning letter.

---

[2] Commercial Court, 2 August 2001 (Lawtel Transcript).

Morison J labelled this breach by IMRO as "technical". Further, he could not see that this technical breach of the rules resulted in any loss on Mr Cattan's part. On this basis, any breach of duty by ANZ did not give rise to the losses claimed by Mr Cattan. However, the case does illustrate the potential exposure of banks to an action by a private person under Section 150 FSMA 2000 for a breach of the Rules.

6.12 Conclusion

Correct client categorisation by firms has always been an important initial (and, in certain circumstances, continuing) task. Firms cannot determine what regulatory protections apply to a client unless that client has been correctly classified. There is a greater flexibility now for clients to be "opted up" or "opted down" between the three categories. However, this flexibility merely reinforces the notion that greater protection should be available to the more vulnerable clients, where the service provider is significantly more experienced than the end user, while ensuring that transactions between market professionals, where the expertise of the provider and end user are more equal, are not subject to unnecessarily burdensome regulation.

Chapter 7

Servicing Clients

James Perry
Partner

Glynn Barwick
Counsel
Ashurst LLP

7.1 Introduction

This Chapter focuses on the heart of the Conduct of Business Sourcebook ("COBS") in the Financial Services Authority's Handbook of Rules and Guidance, namely the chapters that deal with regulated firms carrying on "designated investment business" with or for clients, as follows:

(a) Dealing with clients:

    (i)   information about the firm (COBS 6);
    (ii)   suitability (COBS 9);
    (iii) appropriateness (COBS 10);
    (iv) dealing and managing (best execution, client order handling, limit orders, personal account dealing) (COBS 11);
    (v)   investment research (COBS 12).

(b) Client information:

    (i)   distance communications (COBS 5);
    (ii)   preparing product information (COBS 13);
    (iii) providing product information to the client (COBS 14);
    (iv) cancellation (COBS 15);
    (v)   reporting to clients (COBS 16).

Before reviewing these chapters, some preliminary observations may be useful. Firstly, these chapters in COBS do not seek to regulate the carrying on of all the regulated activities prescribed under the Financial Services and Markets Act 2000 (Regulated Activities) Order 2001 (SI 2001/544) (the "RAO"). Instead, they are mainly deliberately limited to designated investment business. The "designated investments" under COBS are mainly those kinds of instruments and assets which used to be "investments" under the Financial Services Act 1986 ("FS Act 1986"), but now also include rights under stakeholder pension schemes. However, this does not include deposits, general and "pure protection" insurance policies, regulated mortgages or the "Lloyd's investments". Similarly, the designated investment business activities are mostly those activities which used to constitute "investment business" under the FS Act 1986. The conduct of regulated mortgage business and general insurance mediation is governed by special sourcebooks (Mortgages: Conduct of Business Sourcebook ("MCOB") and Insurance: Conduct of Business Sourcebook ("ICOB")).

Second, firms which carry on designated investment business with or for eligible counterparties only will not be concerned with the vast majority of COBS. This is a change to the previous COBS where firms dealing with intermediate customers (the previous term for professional clients) were also largely unconcerned with COB.

Lastly, a word on the scope of what follows. COBS is very lengthy and detailed, and a full review of their provisions would be well beyond the scope of this Guide. Summarised below are the main contents of the COBS chapters listed above.

7.2 Dealing with clients

7.2.1 *Information about the firm (COBS 6)*

Under the COBS rules, firms are required to provide to clients additional information concerning themselves and their services compared to the pre-MiFID COB rules. The information should be provided in good time before the provision of the service[1] and in durable form[2] or

---

[1] COBS 6.1.11(i).
[2] COBS 6.1.13.

via a website (provided that the website conditions[3] are satisfied). The requirement to provide basic information, such as the firm's name and authorised status, has been carried forward, but firms will also have to provide to retail clients the following information:

(a)   details about the languages in which communications between the firm and the client may be conducted;

(b)   the methods of communication between the firm and the client,

(c)   the nature, frequency and timing of the client reporting under COBS 16 (*see* below);

(d)   details of the firm's conflicts of interests policy.[4]

It would seem sensible to disclose this material in the firm's Terms of Business.

In addition, a firm that manages investments for a client (any client, not just a retail client) must also establish for the client an appropriate method of evaluation and comparison such as a meaningful benchmark based on the client's investment objectives[5] and provide details of that benchmark to the client in addition to giving him information about periodic reporting.[6] Again, it would seem sensible to do this in the firm's Terms of Business.

Firms that hold client assets and/or client money also have a reporting obligation[7] to provide information about the assets or money they hold and to provide various risk warnings associated with the business

---

[3] The following conditions:

(a)   the provision of information by means of a website must be appropriate to the context in which the business between the firm and the client is, or is to be, carried on (that is, there is evidence that the client has regular access to the internet, such as the provision by the client of an e-mail address for the purposes of the carrying on of that business);

(b)   the client must specifically consent to the provision of that information in that form;

(c)   the client must be notified electronically of the address of the website, and the place on the website where the information may be accessed;

(d)   the information must be up to date; and

(e)   the information must be accessible continuously by means of that website for such period of time as the client may reasonably need to inspect it.

[4] COBS 6.1.4.

[5] COBS 6.1.6(1).

[6] COBS 6.1.6(2).

[7] COBS 6.1.7.

undertaken with them (such as pooling risk, overseas law risk etc.). In general terms, these reflect the requirements previously required of firms under CASS.

7.2.1.1   *Information about costs and associated charges*

A firm must provide a retail client with information on costs and associated charges, including the price of the investment and all related fees, commissions, charges and expenses and all taxes payable by the firm. The commissions charged by the firm must be itemised separately in each case.[8] The previous COB rule prohibiting excessive charges has not been carried forward, although it is quite possible that the FSA could take action against a firm overcharging clients under the Principles for Businesses.[9]

Finally, a firm carrying on MiFID business must make available to a client who has used or intends to use those services, information necessary for the identification of the compensation scheme or any other investor-compensation scheme of which the firm is a member.[10]

7.2.2   *Suitability (COBS 9.2)*

Firms must ensure that personal recommendations and discretionary trades by investment managers are *suitable* for both retail and professional clients.[11] A personal recommendation is advice on investments that is either presented to the client as suitable or is based on a consideration of the circumstances of that person. Therefore, it is narrower than "advice" as contemplated by Article 53 of the RAO. This is a change to the pre-MiFID regime where the suitability regime applied only to private customers. Firms are also given greater direction by the rules on what they need to consider in making this assessment. Under COBS 9.2.1(2), firms need to obtain information about the client's:

> "(a)   knowledge and experience in the investment field relevant to the specific type of designated investment or service

---

8 COBS 6.1.9.
9 COBS 6.1.11.
10 COBS 6.1.16.
11 COBS 9.2.1(1).

(b)   financial situation

(c)   investment objectives."

Firms must then be able to show that:

"(a)   all relevant advice and discretionary management transactions meet those objectives;

(b)   the client is able financially to bear the relevant risks of
the investment; and

(c)   the client has the necessary experience and knowledge to
understand the risks of the transactions."

In relation to (b) and (c), a firm is entitled to assume that a *per se*
professional client is able to bear the financial risks and that a professional client (elective and *per se*) has the necessary experience and
knowledge without further enquiry.[12]

In assessing a client's knowledge and experience in the investment
field, the firm should have consideration to the nature and extent of
the service to be provided by the firm and the type of product or
transaction envisaged. The firm should also obtain information
regarding:

(a)   the types of service, transaction and designated investment with
which the client is familiar;

(b)   the nature, volume and frequency of the client's transactions in
designated investments and the period over which they have
been carried out; and

(c)   the level of education, profession or relevant former profession
of the client.[13]

It was pointed out to the FSA during the consultation period that a
person's level of education and profession was not a reliable indica-
tor of that person's financial expertise,[14] and firms would probably be
wise to be cautious about not relying too heavily on this aspect of a
person's knowledge.

---

[12] COBS 9.2.8.
[13] COBS 9.2.3.
[14] Paragraph 12.10 PS 07/6.

In a "suitability report", advisers are required to explain to retail clients why the recommended product is suitable for them. This report applies to the same range of packaged products as the pre-MiFID suitability letter, although it is less prescriptive in its contents than the suitability letter. In addition, the pre-MiFID requirement to recommend the "most suitable" packaged product from its range has also been deleted since this would be a requirement additional to the Directive requirements.

7.2.3 *Appropriateness (COBS 10)*

This is a new rule that applies a less stringent suitability-like test for certain execution-only transactions. The obligation is on firms in certain circumstances (*see* below) to warn a client about a transaction it is proposing to enter where the firm does not consider it to be appropriate:

> "If a firm considers, on the basis of information received to enable it to assess appropriateness, that the product or service is not appropriate to the client, the firm must warn the client".[15]

The first question therefore is when does the obligation arise? The appropriateness obligation arises in the following circumstances:

(a) in relation to all MiFID business that a firm undertakes with or for a client; and

(b) where a firm arranges or deals with or for a retail client in relation to a derivative or warrant where the firm is aware, or ought reasonably to be aware, that the business is in response to a direct offer financial promotion except:

   (i) where the firm is providing personal recommendations or providing investment management services (in which case suitability will apply);[16]

   (ii) that the firm may assume that a professional client has the necessary experience and knowledge (and therefore the assessment need not be done, although the FSA Rules are not explicit about this);[17]

---

[15] COBS 10.3.1.
[16] COBS 10.1.1.
[17] COBS 10.2.1(2)(b).

(iii)   where the service is in relation to non-complex instruments and is provided at the initiative of the client.[18]

Therefore, the scope of the new rule causes various problems. First, the definition of a non-complex instrument: Rule 10.4.1(2), provides that the following are non-complex instruments:

(a)   shares listed on regulated markets (or third country equivalent markets);
(b)   money market instruments;
(c)   UCITS.

However, this leaves a large number of other instruments. Rule 10.4.1(3) provides that an instrument not included in COBS 10.4.1(2) is non-complex where (very broadly):

(a)   it is not a derivative or similar instrument;
(b)   there are frequent opportunities to trade the instrument;
(c)   it is not a contingent liability transaction; and
(d)   adequate information is available to allow the investor to make an informed judgment about investing in the product.

Presumably firms will be conservative about what is non-complex if it does not fall in COBS 10.4.1(2)(a)–(c) since the test in COBS 10.4.1(3) will be quite difficult to fulfil.

Secondly, what does "at the initiative of the client" mean? COBS 10.5.1 provides that the service will usually be provided at the initiative of the client unless the client demands it as a result of a personalised communication. For these purposes, "personalised communication" does not include newspaper advertisements or even standardised communications, such as letters, that have been addressed to a particular individual. As the FSA stated in CP06/19:[19] "In most circumstances we believe that it should be clear enough at whose initiative a service is being provided". The authors agree with this comment save that difficulties can arise in circumstances where a service was originally provided at the instigation of the firm. At what

---

[18] COBS 10.4.1.
[19] Paragraph 15.25.

point does a service that is then used at the discretion of the client become at the initiative of the client? This will be a difficult point for firms, and the most helpful guidance is in COBS 10.4.2: "If a client engages in a course of dealing . . . the firm is not required to make a new assessment on the occasion of each separate transaction."

Where a firm considers that a service or product is not appropriate, what should it do? COBS 10.3.1(1) provides that it must warn the client, and COBS 10.3.1(2) provides that the warning may be in a standardised format. This implies (although it is nowhere stated) that it is not necessary to explain to the client in any detail why the firm believes that it is not appropriate. Presumably, though, the firm will be required to explain in at least some detail why it has come to this conclusion, not least because the client is likely to ask why the firm is reluctant to provide the service that the client has requested.

If the warning has been given but the client wishes to continue with the service, what should a firm do? The FSA's guidance,[20] which is not based on any MiFID requirement, is that it is for the firm to consider whether to undertake the service, having regard to the circumstances. This guidance is not particularly forthcoming. The authors suggest that a firm should largely be at liberty to continue with the service where it has given the warning and reasonably believes that the client has understood it but disagreed with it, whereas it would generally be unwise to continue with a service if the firm believes that the client has not fully understood the nature of the service or the warning.

7.2.4 Best execution (COBS 11.2)

The new rule on best execution is significantly wider than the pre-MiFID requirements in COB 7.5. COBS 11.2.1 provides that:

> "A firm must take all reasonable steps to obtain, when executing orders, the best possible result for its clients taking into account the execution factors."

---

[20] COBS 10.3.3.

This rule implements Article 21(1) of MiFID. In assessing the requirements of this rule, it will help to consider each element separately.

7.2.4.1   *Its clients*
The new best execution requirement, unlike the pre-MiFID requirement, will apply to retail and professional clients. The previous opt-out for intermediate customers has been discontinued since it is incompatible with the Directive. However, the rule does not apply to dealings with eligible counterparties unless specifically agreed otherwise by the parties.

7.2.4.2   *Executing orders*
The FSA rules do not define when a firm is *executing* orders and, although in most cases it should be reasonably obvious (such as agency trading and broking), there are some difficult areas. The first point to make is that merely because a firm is dealing with a client as principal that does not mean it is not executing orders.[21] In many derivative markets it is standard practice for firms to execute clients' orders on a back-to-back principal-to-principal basis. Clearly, the duty of best execution applies here. Firms that merely transmit orders rather than executing them are dealt with below.

The situation becomes more difficult when the firm deals on own account rather than just as principal. This particular issue has been put to the European Commission which stated that its view was that the best execution obligation would apply where a dealer is executing an order on behalf of a client in circumstances where the client legitimately relies on the dealer to protect his interests in relation to the pricing and other elements of the transaction.[22] In circumstances where the client is shopping around for various different transaction quotes (such as portfolio manager's dealing desk), it is difficult to say that this test would be fulfilled, and it is therefore unlikely that the duty of best execution would apply.

In addition, whenever there is a specific instruction from a client, the firm must follow that instruction.[23] This, of course, applies only to the

---

[21] COBS 11.2.3.
[22] Commission Paper ESC07/2007.
[23] COBS 11.2.19.

extent of the specific instruction. For example, therefore, if a client instructs a firm to execute a transaction on a particular exchange, it must do so, but, in executing the transaction, the firm must have regard to all the other execution factors in its order execution policy (*see* 7.2.4.4 below).

Firms will need to be careful before concluding that clients' transactions can be dealt with in this way. COBS 11.2.21 provides that firms must not induce clients to deal with them in this way to avoid a best execution duty that would otherwise apply. During the consultation period there was clear dissatisfaction from many on the buy-side of the industry (essentially investment managers) that this approach would leave them vulnerable and without the protection that they believed the rules were intended to provide. It does mean that firms will need to ensure that clients understand clearly the basis on which the firm is dealing with them and the consequences of this.

7.2.4.3 *Best possible result*

Under COBS 7.5, the requirement was simply to obtain the best price, but it is clear that the phrase "best possible result" is wider than that. The firm must consider the effect of each of the "execution factors", which are price, costs, speed, likelihood of execution and settlement, size, nature or any other consideration relevant to the execution of an order. The firm will need to consider the effect of each of these factors for its different client types and instruments traded. Where a firm executes an order on behalf of a retail client, the best possible result must be determined in terms of the total consideration, representing the price of the instrument and the costs related to execution, which must include all expenses incurred by the client which are directly related to the execution of the order.[24] Given the primacy for the role of price for retail clients, this leaves open to firms the issue of the other execution factors. Clearly also the role of price will be important for professional clients, although firms are able to consider, in appropriate circumstances, that other of the execution factors are more important. This could be relevant in circumstances where the implicit costs of executing a large order may be greater than the direct costs.

---

[24] COBS 11.2.7.

7.2.4.4   All reasonable steps

The best execution requirement does not mean that firms must execute and obtain the best result on all occasions but that the firm's procedures are reasonably likely to obtain best execution. This is a "procedures" rather than "outcomes" type requirement.

7.2.4.5   Order execution policy

A firm must establish and implement effective arrangements for complying with the best execution obligation.[25] The order execution policy must include, in respect of each class of financial instruments, information on the different execution venues where the firm executes its client orders and the factors affecting the choice of execution venue.[26] After preparing an execution policy, the firm must provide appropriate information to its clients on the policy.[27] Firms must obtain the prior consent of their clients to the execution policy,[28] and must obtain the prior *express* consent of their clients before proceeding to execute orders outside a regulated market or an MTF.[29]

7.2.4.6   Portfolio managers and receivers and transmitters of orders

By definition, a receiver and transmitter of orders does not execute orders. Also, where an investment manager uses a broker to execute orders on behalf of its underlying client, it does not execute orders either, although managers may execute orders occasionally or more often in relation to certain kinds of financial instruments (*see* below).

Where such firms do not execute transactions they will not specifically owe a duty of best execution under COBS 11.2.1 or Article 21 of MiFID, although they will owe an analogous duty under COBS 11.2.30 and 31 (implementing Article 45 of the MiFID Implementing Directive). The firm must "act in accordance with the best interests of its clients when placing orders with other entities for execution". It is unlikely that "best possible result" in Article 21 and "best interests of its clients" are materially different. Firms will need to prepare an execution policy similar to that applicable to persons executing

---

25 COBS 11.2.14.
26 COBS 11.2.15.
27 COBS 11.2.22.
28 COBS 11.2.25.
29 COBS 11.2.26.

orders, save that there is no requirement to obtain prior consent to the policy from clients.

There is frequently confusion as to who is actually executing orders where there is a chain of firms, such as a manager passing an order to an order transmitter or to a broker through Direct Market Access. In the view of the European Commission:

> "execution of a client order or a decision to deal is always carried out when an investment firm is the last link in the chain of intermediaries between a client order and an execution venue."

In circumstances where the portfolio manager executes transactions (this frequently occurs in bond transactions) then the provisions under Article 21 (above) apply rather than the Article 45 provisions.

7.2.5   Client order handling (COBS 11.3)

The new client order handling rules are largely a continuation of the previous rules on aggregation and allocation. A firm which is authorised to execute orders on behalf of clients must implement procedures and arrangements which provide for the prompt, fair and expeditious execution of client orders relative to other orders or the trading interests of the firm.[30] In general terms, the procedures must ensure that orders executed on behalf of clients are promptly and accurately recorded and allocated and that orders are carried out sequentially and promptly unless the prevailing market conditions make this impractical or the interests of the client require otherwise. Firms must inform retail clients about material difficulties relevant to any proper carrying out of orders promptly upon becoming aware of the difficulty.[31]

The MiFID aggregation rule[32] is the same as the pre-MiFID rules in all material respects: firms must only aggregate orders where it is unlikely that the aggregation will work to the disadvantage of any client, although it must be disclosed to each client whose order is to be aggregated that the effect of aggregation may work to its disadvantage

---

[30] COBS 11.3.1.
[31] COBS 11.3.2.
[32] COBS 11.3.7.

in relation to a particular order. It is usual to make this disclosure in the firm's Terms of Business.

7.2.6 Client limit orders (COBS 11.4)

The provision in relation to client limit orders is a new one under MiFID. In general terms, unless a client expressly instructs otherwise, a firm must, in the case of a client limit order in respect of shares admitted to trading on a regulated market which is not immediately executed under prevailing market conditions, take measures to facilitate the earliest possible execution of that order by making public immediately that client limit order in a manner which is easily accessible to other market participants.[33] A limit order is an order to buy or sell a financial instrument at its specified price limit or better or for a specified size.

In respect of transactions executed between eligible counterparties, the obligation to disclose client limit orders should only apply where the counterparty is explicitly sending a limit order to a firm for its execution.[34]

In general terms, it is likely that a person who has a large order is unlikely to want it to be displayed to the market for execution since the implicit costs of executing a transaction in this manner may be considerable. It is therefore probably usual practice for clients to object to this public disclosure. Under COBS 11.4.5, however, the obligation to make public a limit order will not apply to a limit order that is large in scale compared to normal market size. The FSA gives further guidance in MAR 5.7.10 to 5.7.11 as to when an order may be considered large in scale. Notwithstanding this, many firms dealing with professional clients are likely simply to obtain general instructions (by means of a written form of consent) not to publish unexecuted limit orders except where the client gives a specific instruction to the contrary.

7.2.7 Personal account dealing (COBS 11.7)

A firm that conducts designated investment business must establish, implement and maintain adequate arrangements aimed at preventing

---

[33] COBS 11.4.1.
[34] COBS 11.4.2.

the following activities in the case of any relevant person who is involved in activities that may give rise to a conflict of interest, or who has access to inside information (as defined in the Market Abuse Directive) or to other confidential information relating to clients or transactions with or for clients by virtue of an activity carried out by him on behalf of the firm.[35]

The activities that are prohibited are:

(a) entering into transactions that are prohibited under the market abuse directive;

(b) misusing or improperly disclosing that confidential information;

(c) entering into transactions that conflict with or are likely to conflict with an obligation of the firm to a customer under the regulatory system or any other obligation of the firm under the Directive;[36]

(d) advising or procuring, other than in the proper course of his employment, any other person to enter into a transaction covered by the above restriction;

(e) disclosing other than in the normal course of his employment or contract for services any information or opinion where he knows or reasonably ought to know that as a result of that disclosure the other person will or would be likely to carry on any of the above activities.

The rules contemplate that firms will establish arrangements such that each relevant person is aware of the restrictions and that the firm is informed promptly of any personal transaction entered by that person and that a record is kept of those personal transactions.

These rules are not materially different from the pre-MiFID rules on personal transactions, save that they are more prescriptive regarding the type of transactions that an individual may not carry out and potentially cover a wider scope of prohibited activity.

---

[35] COBS 11.7.1.
[36] COBS 11.7.1(1).

7.2.8 Investment research (COBS 12.2 and 12.3) and research recommendations (COBS 12.4)

The material in COBS 12 in relation to investment research and research recommendations stems from two separate Directives; COBS 12.2 and 12.3 stem from MiFID and therefore operate on a home-state basis. This means that they apply to passported activities carried on by a UK MiFID investment firm from a branch in another EEA state, but do not apply to the UK branch of an EEA MiFID investment firm in relation to its MiFID business.[37] However, COBS 12.4 stems from the Market Abuse Directive (MAD), which operates on a host-state basis. This is a very important point for all firms that are either operating in the UK by way of a branch or which have passported a branch into another Member State.

7.2.8.1 Independent research

"Investment research" is defined in the FSA Rules as, broadly, research or other information recommending or suggesting an investment strategy, explicitly or implicitly, concerning one or several financial instruments including any opinion as to the present or future value or price of such instruments in relation to which the following conditions are met:

(a) it is labelled or described as investment research or in similar terms, or is otherwise presented as an objective or independent explanation of the matters contained in the recommendation;

(b) if the recommendation in question were to be made by an investment firm to a client, it would not constitute the provision of a personal recommendation.

Firms which provide "investment research" must ensure their conflict of interests policy under SYSC 10.1.11R properly covers the conflicts faced by analysts and other relevant persons involved in the production of investment research.[38] In summary, the firm must ensure that the following conditions are satisfied:

---

[37] COBS 12.1.3.
[38] COBS 12.2.3.

(a) if a financial analyst or other relevant person has knowledge of the likely timing or content of investment research which is not publicly available, that person must not undertake personal transactions or trade on behalf of another person including the firm until the recipients of the research have had the opportunity to act on it. This is the prohibition on front running;

(b) in circumstances not covered by (a) above, the relevant person must not undertake personal transactions to which the investment research relates contrary to current recommendations, except in exceptional circumstances and with the prior approval of the firm's legal or compliance function;

(c) the firm itself, financial analysts and other relevant persons involved in the production of investment research must not accept inducements from those with a material interest in the subject matter of the research;

(d) the firm itself, financial analysts and other relevant persons involved in the production of the research must not promise issuers favourable research coverage;

(e) issuers, relevant persons other than financial analysts and any other persons must not, before the dissemination of investment research, be permitted to review a draft of the research for the purpose of verifying the accuracy of factual statements made in that investment research or for any other purpose other than verifying compliance with the firm's legal obligations, if the draft includes a recommendation or a target price.

The FSA has carried over its non-MiFID rule in COBS 12.2.9 that financial analysts involved in the preparation of research should not participate in other aspects of investment banking business such as corporate finance business, underwriting, participating in pitches for new business or roadshows for new issues of financial instruments or being otherwise involved in the preparation of issuer marketing.

The FSA rules require a firm in preparing its conflict of interests policy to provide internal guidance on the publication and distribution to its clients of the research in an appropriate manner.[39] For example, the FSA considers it will be appropriate for a firm to take

---

[39] COBS 12.2.11.

reasonable steps to ensure that its investment research is published or distributed only through its usual distribution channels and inappropriate for an employee (whether or not a financial analyst) to communicate the substance of any investment research except as set out in the firm's conflict of interests policy.

It is worth pointing out that the concept of dissemination of investment research to clients or to the public is not intended to include dissemination exclusively to persons within the group or the firm.[40] Also, because the definition of "investment research" stems from the MAD definition of a "research recommendation", it incorporates the exclusion (in the MAD definition) of informal short-term buy or sell recommendations issued by sales or trading teams.

7.2.8.2   Non-independent research

Where a firm is not able or does not wish to comply with the above requirements in relation to independent research, it may issue non-independent research under COBS 12.3. In these circumstances it will not be treated as research but as a marketing communication. The firm must ensure that it is clearly identified as such and contains a clear and prominent statement that it has not been produced in accordance with the legal requirements designed to promote the independence of investment research. Notwithstanding this exemption, firms will still be required to manage conflicts of interest in accordance with SYSC 10 even where they are producing non-independent research.[41]

7.2.8.3   Research recommendations

In very general terms, a research recommendation is defined in the FSA rules as research or other information concerning one or more financial instruments admitted to trading on a regulated market which explicitly or implicitly recommends or suggests an investment strategy or directly or indirectly expresses a particular investment recommendation or expresses an opinion as to the present or future value or price of such investments.

The disclosures that must be made by firms producing research recommendations provided under the Market Abuse Directive are

---

[40] COBS 12.2.2.
[41] COBS 12.3.4.

regarding the identity of the producers of the research,[42] the general standard for the fair presentation of recommendations,[43] the disclosure of conflicts of interest.[44] These requirements have been carried forward from the previous COB regime.

7.3   Information for clients

Most of COBS 13, 14 and 15 apply to firms which carry on a regulated activity in relation to "packaged products" with retail clients. "Packaged products" are life policies, units in regulated collective investment schemes, investment trust savings schemes, ISAs, PEPs or Child Trust Funds ("CTFs") containing any of the above investments, stakeholder pension schemes and personal pension schemes. As discussed below, however, the application and requirements have been significantly altered by the implementation of the Distance Marketing Directive in the UK. The information requirements now apply to "distance contracts" to accept deposits (as well as cash-deposit ISAs); and the cancellation requirements will apply to a much broader range of designated investment business. Separately, the requirements for "simplified prospectuses" under the UCITS Directive mean that, in the case of regulated schemes, product disclosure will be required for subscribers whether or not they are retail clients.

In the main, the rules give details about the type of information which retail clients must be given about a product on offer and its potential risks and returns (in some cases in the form of "key features") and about customers' rights to cancel or withdraw from a contract if they change their mind.

7.3.1   *Distance Marketing Directive ("DMD") (COBS 5)*

The DMD, implemented in the UK with effect from 9 October 2004, affects firms which enter into "distance contracts" with "consumers". Article 2 of the DMD defines a "distance contract" as:

---

[42] COBS 12.4.5.
[43] COBS 12.4.6, 12.4.7.
[44] COBS 12.4.9, 12.4.10.

"any contract concerning financial services concluded between a supplier and a consumer under an organised distance sales or service provision scheme run by the supplier who, for the purpose of that contract, makes exclusive use of one or more means of distance communication up to and including the time at which the contract is concluded".

"Means of distance communication" include media used for distance marketing without the simultaneous physical presence of the supplier and the consumer, such as fax, telephone and the internet. "Consumers" are natural persons acting for purposes outside their trade, business or profession. The definition of a consumer for the purposes of the DMD is both broader and narrower than the FSA's definition of a retail client. For example, individual elective professional clients will still be "consumers" entitled to the DMD's protections, while some small corporations and partnerships will be retail clients but fall outside the "consumer" definition.

The broader application of the DMD and the key definitional issues are dealt with elsewhere in this Guide. As far as the product information chapters are concerned, the important changes required by the DMD relate to:

(a) the pre-contract information required to be given to consumers in relation to packaged products sold at a distance, which have necessitated disclosures relating to the information contained in, and the timing and means of communication of, key features documents;

(b) requirements for pre-contract information relating to deposits when they are sold at a distance (since a deposit is a financial service covered by the DMD); and

(c) significant changes to the previous regime for cancellation rights (COBS 15.2), including new cancellation rights for consumers where investment services other than packaged products are sold to the customer (including investment management, advisory or stockbroking services).

These changes are discussed below. Both in relation to the provision of key features and the offering of cancellation rights, it is important that the DMD allows its requirements to apply only to an "initial service agreement" where that agreement is followed by "successive operations or a series of separate operations of the same nature performed over time", provided the position is made clear in the original agreement.[45] If there is no explicit initial service agreement but there is a further operation of the same nature between the two parties, the firm need not provide further pre-contract information as long as there is less than 12 months between the operations – but the customer will apparently retain the right to cancel the "successive operation".[46] Firms will find these provisions particularly useful in the context of longer-term customer relationships – such as investment management – where the information and rights provided at the outset should be sufficient.

7.3.2 Key features and other product information (COBS 13 and 14)

COBS 13 and 14 provide the rules on the preparation and provision respectively of product information.

7.3.2.1 Preparation

Key features documents were initially introduced by the self-regulating organisations ("SROs") in order to explain the main details of packaged products in a clear and comprehensible manner, and to assist customers to compare competing products. To some extent, key features were designed to compensate for the highly technical nature of most contractual documents under which life policies and personal pensions have traditionally been sold, which are unlikely to be easily understood by most consumers.

The headline rule is that a firm must prepare a key features document for each packaged product, cash deposit ISA and cash deposit CTF it produces, in good time before that document has to be provided (COBS 13.1.1). It is not required to provide a key features document for:

(a) units in simplified prospectus schemes;
(b) units in an EEA simplified prospectus scheme;

---

[45] COBS 5.1.8.
[46] COBS 5.1.9.

(c)   units in a key features scheme if it prepares a simplified prospectus or the information appears with due prominence in another document instead or

(d)   units is a stakeholder pension scheme or personal pension scheme that is not a personal pension policy if the information appears with due prominence in another document.[47]

In preparing key features documents, firms should consider the requirements of COBS 13.2.2 that sets out the general requirement as to the appearance of the document, and that sets out specific requirements about the information that needs to be contained in it.[48]

7.3.2.2   Provision

A firm that sells various types of products will need to supply the investor with the documents provided in accordance with the above requirements. These will be:

(a)   a key features document to a retail client in relation to a packaged product;

(b)   the Consolidated Life Directive information to a client in relation to a life policy;

(c)   sufficient information to a retail client regarding the variation of a life policy or personal pension scheme;

(d)   the key features document to a retail client for a cash ISA or cash deposit CTF;

(e)   the simplified prospectus to a client in relation to a unit in a simplified prospectus scheme; and

(f)   a simplified prospectus to a client in relation to an EEA simplified prospectus scheme.[49]

There are various exceptions to the above requirements in COBS 14.2.5 and 14.2.7. In very general terms these exemptions are intended to ensure that firms are not required to supply information that is supplied by other persons or that has already been supplied in another format.

---

[47]   COBS 13.1.3.
[48]   COBS 13.3.1.
[49]   COBS 14.2.1.

7.3.3   Information about designated investments (COBS 14.3)

Under the old COB rules where a firm made a personal recommendation, acted as a discretionary investment manager, arranged or executed a deal in a warrant or derivative or engaged in stock lending activity, it was required to give a private customer certain risk warnings and was not able to effect the transaction unless it had taken reasonable steps to ensure that the customer understood the nature of the risks involved.[50] COB 5.4 and COB 5 Annex 1 contained standard risk warnings to be given to private customers.

It was always questionable how effective these risk warnings were since they were in standard form and often given by firms to customers in circumstances that were not relevant since firms often included the whole warning rather than tailoring it to the relevant circumstances. The new COBS regime does not require the giving of specific risk warnings (save in the context of appropriateness above) but it does require firms to give tailored descriptions to clients explaining the nature of the specific type of designated investment concerned, as well as the risks particular to that investment.[51] This description needs to include the risks associated with the investment, the volatility of the price and any limitations on the available market for such investments, the fact that the investor might assume as a result of transactions in the investments financial commitments and other obligations additional to the cost of investments and to provide information about any margin requirements.[52] In some respects, therefore, the scope of this requirement is broader than the old COB 5.4.

7.3.4   Cancellation and withdrawal (COBS 15)

The cancellation period begins either from the day of the conclusion of the contract (except in respect of contracts relating to life policies where the time limit will begin from the time when the consumer is informed that the contract has been concluded), or, if later, from the day on which the consumer receives the contractual terms and conditions and any

---

[50] COB 5.4.3 and 5.4.4.
[51] COBS 14.3.2.
[52] COBS 14.3.2.

other pre-contractual information required under the COBS.[53] The firm must disclose to the consumer in good time before or, if that is not possible, immediately after the consumer is bound by a contract, that it attracts a right to cancel or withdraw and in a durable medium,[54] the existence of the right to cancel or withdraw, its duration and the conditions for exercising it including information on the amount which the consumer may be required to pay.

The effect of a cancellation is that the consumer withdraws from the contract, and the contract is terminated. Of course, it is quite possible that there has been market movement in the price of the investment since the contract was initially concluded up to the date of termination. COBS 15.4.3 provides that the firm may require the consumer to pay for any loss under a contract caused by market movements, that the firm would reasonably incur in cancelling it. The period for calculating the loss shall end on the day on which the firm receives the notification of cancellation. It should be noted, however, that the rule does not apply for a distance contract or for a contract established on a regular or recurring premium or payment basis; and it only applies if the firm has complied with the obligations to disclose information concerning the right to cancel.

A summary of the new rules for cancellable agreements in brief, tabular form is reproduced in Table 7.1, though reference should be made in all cases to the detailed rules and guidance in the Handbook.

7.3.5 Reporting information to clients (COBS 16)

The client reporting requirements divide into occasional reporting (trade confirmations/contract notes etc.) and periodic reporting (statements), a distinction which mirrors the pre-MiFID rules.

7.3.5.1 Occasional reporting
Where a firm has carried out an order for a client in designated investment business (note, not just MiFID business), it must promptly provide the client with the essential details of the transaction.[55] There are some variations to this provision:

---

[53] COBS 15.2.3.
[54] COBS 15.2.5.
[55] COBS 16.2.1(1)(a).

Table 7.1   *Rules for cancellable agreements*

Cancellable contract	Cancellation period	Supplementary provisions
Life pensions		
A life policy (including a pension annuity, a pension policy or within a wrapper) A contract to join a personal pension scheme or a stakeholder pension scheme A pension contract A contract for a pension transfer A contract to vary an existing personal pension scheme or stakeholder pension scheme by exercising, for the first time, an option to make income withdrawals	30 calendar days	For a life policy effected when opening or transferring a wrapper, the 30-calendar-day right to cancel applies to the entire arrangement. For a contract to buy a unit in a regulated collective investment scheme within a pension wrapper, the cancellation right for "non-life/pensions (advised but not at a distance)" below may apply Exemptions may apply (*see* COBS 15 Annex 1)
Cash deposit ISAs		
A contract for a cash deposit ISA	14 calendar days	Exemptions may apply (*see* COBS 15 Annex 1)
Non-life/pensions (advised but not at a distance): a non-distance contract		
To buy a unit in a regulated collective investment scheme (including within a wrapper or pension wrapper) To open or transfer a child trust fund To open or transfer an ISA or PEP For an Enterprise Investment Scheme	14 calendar days	These rights arise only following a personal recommendation of the contract (by the firm or any other person). For a unit bought when opening or transferring a wrapper or pension wrapper, the 14-calendar-day right to cancel applies to the entire arrangement. Exemptions may apply (*see* COBS 15 Annex 1)
Non-life/pensions (at a distance): a distance contract, relating to . . .		
Accepting deposits Designated investment business	14 calendar days	Exemptions may apply (*see* COBS 15 Annex 1)

(a)   where the client is a retail client, the confirmation must include
      the information required by COBS 16, Annex 1 and be sent no
      later than the business day following execution or following
      receipt if the confirmation is sent to it by a third party.[56] For
      professional clients, there is no specific time period;

(b)   the requirement does not apply to a firm managing investments;[57]

(c)   where the business is not MiFID business or "third country
      equivalent business", the firm may agree with the client (in writ-
      ing if it is a retail client) that confirmations need not be
      prepared.[58] Where it is MiFID business or third country equiva-
      lent business, there is no such opt-out;

(d)   there is also a limited exclusion for transactions in relation to
      units or shares in collective investment undertakings executed
      periodically as part of a series of orders.[59]

7.3.5.2   *Periodic reporting*

Where a firm is managing investments, it must provide the client
with a periodic statement unless that statement is provided by a third
party.[60] In particular:

(a)   where the client is a retail client, the statement must include the
      information required by COBS 16 Annex 2;

(b)   for retail clients, the statement must be sent every six months,
      although the client may request one every three months,[61] and
      the firm must inform him of this right.[62] There are two excep-
      tions to this: where the client receives information on transac-
      tions on a transaction-by-transaction basis, the statement need
      be sent only every 12 months;[63] where the portfolio is leveraged,
      the statement must be sent at least once a month;[64]

(c)   where the business is not MiFID business or equivalent third
      country business, the firm need not send a statement to a client

---

[56] COBS 16.2.1(1)(b).
[57] COBS 16.2.1(2).
[58] COBS 16.2.6.
[59] COBS 16.2.1(5).
[60] COBS 16.3.1(1).
[61] COBS 16.3.2(1)(a).
[62] COBS 16.3.2(2).
[63] COBS 16.3.2(1)(5).
[64] COBS 16.3.2(1)(C).

habitually resident outside the UK if the firm has taken reasonable steps to establish that he does not wish to receive it.[65]

In addition to the above, a firm holding client money or client investments must send a statement at least once a year detailing the money and investments it holds.[66]

---

[65] COBS 16.3.10(1).
[66] COBS 16.4.1.

Chapter 8

The Client Asset Regime

Dick Frase

Partner
Dechert LLP

8.1 Overview

The Financial Services and Markets Act 2000 (Regulated Activities) Order 2001 (SI 2001/544) ("RAO") defines custody[1] as:

(a) the safeguarding of assets belonging to another coupled with the administration of those assets; or

(b) arranging for another person to carry on that activity (where the assets consist of or include designated investments).[2]

The provision of a safekeeping function (in the very narrow sense of merely holding assets for a client) is thus not enough to qualify as custody within the scope of the RAO. The firm must also be providing administrative services in support of that function. Administration for this purpose would include settlement of sale transactions, dealing with income arising from an investment, and carrying out corporate actions such as voting. The nature of the administration services must be such that there is no (material) discretion; otherwise the activity is likely to constitute the management of investments.[3]

This activity is regulated under the FSA's client asset regime, which is set out in the Client Assets sourcebook ("CASS"). CASS applies generally to activities carried on by a firm from an establishment in

---

[1] RAO Article 40.

[2] Or where the assets may consist of or include designated investments and either they have done so at any time since 1 June 1997 or the arrangements have at any time been held out as ones under which designated investments would be safeguarded or administered.

[3] PERG 2.7.9.

the UK, and also to passported activities carried on by it from a branch in another EEA state.[4] It does not apply to a non-UK firm based elsewhere in the EEA and passporting into the UK under the Markets in Financial Instruments Directive ("MiFID"). For such a firm the client asset rules of its home state will apply.[5]

CASS is split into a number of parts including rules[6] for the regulated activity of insurance mediation. This is outside the designated investments regime and is not discussed further in this Chapter. Following the introduction of MiFID the main CASS regime applicable to designated investment business is split between CASS 2 to 4 for non-MiFID business and CASS 6 and 7 for MiFID business. CASS 2–4 are the original pre-MiFID FSA client money rules which are still in force for certain purposes. However, where a MiFID firm holds financial instruments belonging to a client in the course of its MiFID business, this is subject to the new MiFID-based rules in CASS 6 and 7.

A firm which carries out both MiFID and non-MiFID business is thus faced with having to operate two separate regimes for essentially the same activity. However, CASS does include provisions which allow a firm in this position to elect to operate solely under the MiFID rules. While this is likely to be the preferred option for most firms, there is still potential for providing such services under the old regime.

The MiFID rules are broadly similar to the non-MiFID rules, but because they apply pursuant to the MiFID directives, which address client asset requirements only in general outline, they tend to be less detailed than the non-MiFID rules.[7] In a number of cases the FSA has addressed this by including detail from the old regime in the MiFID rules as guidance illustrative of general principles, rather than as specific rules as such. There are also new rules allowing firms to place client money in qualifying money market funds instead of in a client money bank account.

---

[4] CASS 1.3.2–3.
[5] CASS 1.2.3(2).
[6] CASS 5.
[7] *See* generally CP06/14 "Implementing MiFID" paragraphs 10.1–10.35.

Probably the most substantive difference is that the MiFID client money rules do not permit an opt-out from client money protection. However, they do allow firms which hold a client's money as security for liabilities owed by the client to the firm to treat this as collateral held on a full transfer of ownership basis. This concept is aimed primarily at securities, and reads rather oddly in a money context, since money does not normally posses the same proprietary characteristics as securities. Nevertheless the result allows MiFID firms to continue to hold money on what is effectively an opted out basis in most circumstances.

Despite the many similarities between the MiFID and non-MiFID rules, the FSA has evidently concluded that it is more practical to set out each regime separately and in full rather than establishing a single set of rules with variations. The rest of this Chapter follows this FSA sequence, beginning with the non-MiFID rules.

8.2 The non-MiFID rules – introduction

The non-MiFID rules will prima facie apply to the following activities:

(a) safe-keeping of securities and the holding of client money by way of custody, when not carried out as an ancillary activity to a MiFID investment service;
(b) stock lending activity with or for customers;[8]
(c) corporate finance business;[9]
(d) oil market activity;[10]
(e) depositaries;[11]
(f) trustee firms which are not depositaries.[12]

---

[8] CASS 1.4.2.
[9] CASS 1.4.3.
[10] CASS 1.4.4.
[11] With some modifications. *See* CASS 1.4.6–7.
[12] But only CASS 4.5. *See* CASS 1.4.8.

8.3 The non-MiFID custody rules

8.3.1 *The scope of the non-MiFID custody regime*

The FSA's non-MiFID custody regime is contained primarily in CASS 2. Its main focus is on "safe custody investments", which are defined as designated investments, which are not the property of the firm but for which the firm or the firm's nominee is accountable, which have been paid for in full by the client, and which cease to be a safe custody investment when the firm disposes of them in accordance with a valid instruction.

This is a little narrower than the conventional common law custodianship where the custodian as trustee would normally have, for instance, a trustee's duty to get in the trust assets. However, the rules are also applied to a somewhat broader category of assets which do not quite come within the scope of the RAO designated investment regime but which a firm holds in conjunction with a designated investment held for or on behalf of the same client. These are known as "custody assets".

In a number of situations, the application of CASS 2 is altered or qualified:

(a) Eligible counterparties: custody protection is not available to eligible counterparties, but then eligible counterparty status only applies to execution services in any event.[13]

(b) Arrangers: although arranging client asset protection is regulated by the RAO and CASS, a firm such as an investment manager, which does no more than arrange for a client to receive custody services from another, has very limited duties. It must risk assess the custodian, make adequate risk disclosures and maintain records of the arrangements made.[14] A similar risk assessment duty will also apply to a firm which merely recommends a custodian if the recommendation is made to a retail client. Arranging custody services does not include a mere introduction.[15] These

---

[13] CASS 1.2.8.

[14] CASS 2.1.21–2.1.22.

[15] CASS 2.1.5; RAO Article 42. The distinction being drawn between introducing and arranging in the custody context is often less than clear.

are obvious common law duties anyway, and though there is a degree of uncertainty as to what is intended by the distinction between arrangers and introducers, nothing very material appears to turn on this.

(c) Affiliates: the custody rules do not protect designated investments of the firm's affiliates unless the affiliate notifies the firm that such designated investments belong to the affiliate's client(s), or the affiliate can itself be properly classified as a bona fide arms'-length customer.[16] This approach seeks to ensure that client assets are protected when an affiliate "fails" and the failed affiliate would, if treated as a client, expose other unrelated clients to the risks inherent in the entire group. For instance, if a group's proprietary trading division was treated as a client and sustained disastrous losses, trying to meet those losses out of the client assets might drain the resources of the other clients, in turn causing a shortfall in the client assets which the group lacked the resources to make good.

(d) Delivery Versus Payment ("DVP") Settlement: under this concession a firm settling a trade through a third-party commercial settlement system, where settlement is due to take place within one day, is allowed up to three days to rectify a failed trade before it is obliged to segregate the designated investments concerned.[17]

(e) Temporary custody: the rules do not apply[18] where a personal investment firm holds a designated investment (other than a bearer instrument) belonging to a client only on a strictly temporary basis, as where, following a purchase by an executing broker, the broker sends the share certificates to the personal investment firm for onward transmission to the personal investment firm's client. To benefit from this concession the personal investment firm must take reasonable care of the designated investment, retain it for no longer than is necessary, and keep a record of the action it has taken.

(f) Depository receipts: an adjusted regime applies to firms which are issuers of depository receipts, reflecting the fact that holders of receipts including a firm who have purchased them in the

---

[16] CASS 2.1.9 (1).
[17] CASS 2.1.13 *See also* CASS 4.1.15 for equivalent client money provisions.
[18] CASS 2.1.9(3).

secondary market will not stand in a client relationship with that firm.[19]

(g) Nominees: a firm's responsibilities to its client will include accepting responsibility for any nominee company which the firm controls.[20]

(h) Depositaries: the client money rules are disapplied in relation to scheme deposits and references to a "client" are to be construed as references to the trustee, trust or scheme.[21]

(i) Recognised Collective Investment Schemes: CASS is disapplied in relation to open-ended investment companies ("OEICs") and other Undertakings for Collective Investment in Transferable Securities ("UCITS") funds, and from a regulated collective investment scheme operator acting as such.[22]

(j) Trustees and depositories: a trustee or depositary acts as custodian of a formally constituted trust or collective investment scheme, it is subject only to certain limited aspects of the custody rules provided the trust or scheme is established by a written instrument which together with relevant trust law provides equivalent protection to that contained in the custody rules.[23] This provision seems to be written with collective investment schemes in mind, though as drafted it will apply to other trust-based custody as well. Since many custodians are reluctant to draw attention to the trust-based nature of their services, there may be limited interest in using this qualification to restructure normal custody services.

(k) Occupational pension scheme ("OPS") firms: firms authorised as operators of occupational pension schemes are to treat the OPS or welfare trust as their customer for custody purposes with the scheme trustees taking the operative role of the customer for information and decision-making purposes.[24]

(l) Authorised professional firms: such firms are not subject to CASS in relation to their non-mainstream regulated activities, and are not subject to CASS 5 (insurance mediation) if their

---

[19] CASS 2.1.23–2.1.26.
[20] CASS 2.1.11.
[21] CASS 1.4.6–1.4.7.
[22] CASS 1.2.3; 2.1.9(2).
[23] CASS 2.1.16–2.1.20.
[24] CASS 1.4.1.

designated professional body operates an approved alternative regime to which they are subject, such as the solicitors' or accountants' client money rules.[25]

8.3.2   Specific requirements of the custody rules

8.3.2.1   The general approach
The FSA says that the custody rules are intended to codify basic principles of segregation, restrict the commingling of house and client assets, prevent a client's safe custody assets from being used by the firm without the client's consent or being treated as the firm's assets on insolvency.[26] The MiFID custody rules include a very similar statement.[27]

8.3.2.2   Segregation
A firm which provides safe custody must segregate safe custody investments from its own designated investments.[28] Where the assets are held in an account with the firm itself (i.e. the account is contained in the firm's own records), the title of the account must make it clear that the assets belong to a client and are segregated.[29] Where they are credited to an account with a third-party custodian the firm must ensure that the title of the account makes it clear that the safe custody investments belong to client(s) of the firm.[30] Designated investments of affiliated companies must be kept separate from safe custody investments of arms'-length clients.[31]

8.3.2.3   Protecting the client's proprietary interest
The custody rules set out separate provisions for the protection of registrable (intangible) securities and bearer (tangible) securities. It may be noted that in an immobilised depository system such as Euroclear, a bearer security held in the depository's vaults may be bought and sold by the depository debiting and crediting its members' accounts without the underlying bearer document ever

---

[25] CASS 1.2.4–1.2.5.
[26] CASS 2.1.12.
[27] CASS 6.1.23.
[28] CASS 2.2.3.
[29] CASS 2.2.5–2.2.6.
[30] CASS 2.2.7.
[31] CASS 2.2.8.

physically moving. In such an immobilised system it may well be that what is being bought and sold is not the underlying bearer security but the enforceable right against the depository to delivery of the bearer security. This puts tangible and intangible securities in very much the same position for custody and settlement purposes. As a result a truly tangible security is a rarity, and both dematerialised and immobilised securities usually constitute a form of chose in action – a book entry "entitlement" with proprietary characteristics.

8.3.2.4 Registration of intangibles

A firm must, as far as practical, register legal title to a safe custody investment in the name of:[32]

(a)   the client (or, if the client is itself an authorised firm acting for a client, in the name of the underlying client);
(b)   a nominee company (i.e. a bare trustee) controlled by the firm, an affiliate, a recognised investment exchange or designated investment exchange, or by a custodian;
(c)   a custodian, if the investment is subject to the law or market practice of an overseas jurisdiction and the firm has taken reasonable steps to ensure that:

    (i)   it is in the client's best interests to register or record it in that way, or
    (ii)   it is not feasible to do otherwise because of the nature of the local law or market;

and the firm has given written notice to the client of this;
(d)   the firm itself, if the investment is subject to the law or market practice of an overseas jurisdiction and the firm has taken reasonable steps to ensure that:

    (i)   it is in the client's best interests to register or record it in that way, or
    (ii)   it is not feasible to do otherwise because of the nature of the local law or market and the firm has notified the client and (if he is a retail client) obtained his prior written consent.

---

[32] CASS 2.2.10.

In this situation the firm may, subject to certain restrictions, register legal title to its and its client's investments in the same name;

(e) any other person provided this is in accordance with the client's specific written instruction, the firm has made appropriate risk disclosures under CASS 2.3.11 and (in the case of a retail client) the other person is not the firm's associate. The firm may choose to add some additional disclaimer of liability in such circumstances.

If (c) or (d) are relied on the firm must demonstrate that adequate investigations have been made of the market concerned by reference to local sources which may include appropriate legal opinion.[33]

Generally speaking registration in the client's own name gives rise to dealing and settlement difficulties, and a stockbroker or professional custodian providing a domestic custody service would be expected to register securities in the name of its nominee company (or perhaps a professional third-party custodian). The same arrangement would apply for overseas custody arrangements as well. However, where the firm does not have a local presence it will need to appoint a local "correspondent" to provide the custody service, commonly referred to as a sub-custodian. The sub-custodian would need to qualify as a "custodian" in terms of the custody rules and would conventionally be expected to hold through a nominee or special purpose custodian entity.

In a limited number of jurisdictions it is not possible to operate separate custody arrangements and (d) above is designed to address these situations.

8.3.2.5 *Bailment of tangibles*
A document of title such as a bearer security must be held:[34]

(a) in the physical possession of the firm or, for a retail client, with a custodian in a client safe custody account;
(b) for an eligible counterparty or professional in an account designated for clients' safe custody investments;

---

[33] CASS 2.2.12.
[34] CASS 2.2.15.

(c)   with any person that the firm reasonably believes provides appropriate safe custody services; or

(d)   in accordance with the eligible counterparty's or professional client's specific written instructions. Where a firm holds its own bearer instruments it must keep them separately from its clients' bearer instruments.[35]

Note that references to eligible counterparty may be an error in the rules since eligible counterparties are not within the CASS regime.

8.3.2.6   Appointing and monitoring sub-custodians

CASS 2.2.18–2.2.23 lay down the principles by which a firm should identify suitable custody arrangements for holding safe custody investments. This is described as a risk assessment.

There are various requirements for a firm to take reasonable care to ensure that any custodian it appoints is suitable for the job in hand. For a conventional custodian (as distinct from someone who merely arranges custody services) these and other similar requirements will apply primarily where it delegates its custody functions to a sub-custodian.

The firm must carry out a risk assessment of any custodian before it uses that custodian or recommends it to a private customer.[36] The risk assessment should take account of[37] all relevant circumstances including legal requirements and custodial practices in the relevant jurisdiction. Relevant factors include the expertise and market reputation of the custodian, its performance of its services to the firm, its arrangements for holding and safeguarding an investment, the obtaining by the firm of a legal opinion on the standard of protection of custody assets held by the custodian on its insolvency, current industry standard reports, whether the custodian is regulated and by whom, the custodian's financial resources, its credit rating, and any other activities undertaken by the custodian or its affiliates.

---

[35] CASS 2.2.17.
[36] CASS 2.2.18–2.2.23.
[37] CASS 2.2.21–2.2.22.

The firm must establish and maintain a system for assessing the appropriateness of its selection of the custodian and periodically assess the continued appointment of the custodian as often as is reasonable in the relevant market, bearing in mind the current legal requirements and custodial practices in that jurisdiction. The firm must maintain records evidencing this.[38]

A firm must accept the same liability for nominees controlled by the firm or its affiliates as for itself[39] and may not disclaim liability for losses arising from its fraud, wilful default or negligence.[40]

The general effect of these provisions is that a firm is responsible to the FSA (though not necessarily to the client itself) for using reasonable care and skill in appointing and maintaining a sub-custodian, unless the custodian is a member of the same group, in which case it must accept full responsibility.

8.3.2.7 Client agreement
Detailed client agreement provisions are set out in CASS 2.3.1–2.3.16.

Before providing any safe custody service to a client the firm must notify the client[41] of the terms and conditions which apply to that service including where applicable the following matters:[42]

(a) how investments will be registered if they will not be registered in the client's own name;
(b) the extent of the firm's liability on the default of a custodian (essentially this refers to a custodian firm's liability for its sub-custodians – the client agreement rules do not apply to mere custody arrangers);
(c) the circumstances in which the firm may realise a safe custody investment held as collateral to meet the client's liabilities;
(d) arrangements for claiming and receiving dividends, interest and other entitlements;

---

[38] CASS 2.2.20 and SYSC 3.2.20.
[39] CASS 2.3.2(2).
[40] CASS 2.3.2(2).
[41] Cass 2.3.2. As drafted this provision does not say that the notification must be in writing. However, it is presumed that the FSA does not have in mind a purely oral notification.
[42] CASS 2.3.2(1)–(10).

(e)   arrangements for dealing with takeovers, voting rights, conversion and subscription rights;

(f)   arrangements for distribution of entitlements and benefits arising from corporate events where client balances are pooled;

(g)   arrangements for provision of information on safe custody investments held by the firm/its nominee;

(h)   frequency of account statements and basis of valuation of assets in the statement;

(i)   fees and costs of safe custody services;

(j)   notification of any pooling arrangements for safe custody investment holdings of clients and, in the case of a private customer, an explanation of the effect. The firm should advise[43] a private customer that, as a result of pooling, individual entitlements may not be identifiable by separate certificates, other physical documents or equivalent electronic records, and in the event of an irreconcilable shortfall after the failure of a custodian, clients may share in the shortfall in proportion to their original share of the assets in the pool.

Other matters which need notifying to the client and may be contained in the client agreement include:

(a)   written notice to the client if the firm intends to hold his assets with a custodian in the same group;[44]

(b)   notice (written agreement in the case of a private customer) of arrangements for giving and receiving instructions, including any arrangement under which the client authorises another person to give such instructions;[45]

(c)   notice (written agreement in the case of a private customer) of any lien or security interest over the safe custody assets in favour of the firm or a third party other than those relating to administration and safekeeping;[46]

(d)   a risk warning to customers about different practices in overseas jurisdictions;[47]

---

[43] CASS 2.3.3.
[44] CASS 2.2.23. *See* also the equivalent client money provision in CASS 4.3.46(2).
[45] CASS 2.3.4(1).
[46] CASS 2.3.4(2).
[47] CASS 2.3.7.

(e) notice (prior consent in the case of a private client) that an investment may be registered in the firm's name (if this is the case). As a result it may not be segregated from the firm's investments and subsequently on a failure of the firm the client's assets may not be as well protected;[48]

(f) where the client instructs the firm how investments should be held under CASS 2.2.10(5) (registration of intangibles) or CASS 2.2.15(2)(c) (bailment of tangibles) a notice that the consequences of this are at the client's own risk (unless the firm has agreed otherwise).[49]

Certain modifications apply to these requirements where the firm does not intend to provide a custody service and unintentionally finds itself holding assets in circumstances which were not reasonably foreseeable,[50] or the client is resident outside the UK and does not wish to execute an agreement.[51]

8.3.2.8 Account statements

Account statements[52] must be provided at least annually[53] and despatched within 25 days[54] of the statement's record date unless the client is resident outside the UK and has previously agreed in writing that he does not wish to receive statements.[55] The relevant statement must be provided if the firm has held custody assets at any time during the firm's financial year, even if the account balance is nil at the date of the statement, unless the account has been formally closed and the client has been sent a closing statement.

The statement must:

(a) list[56] all custody assets held for the client;

(b) identify assets registered in the client's own name separately from other assets;

---

[48] CASS 2.3.10.
[49] CASS 2.3.11.
[50] CASS 2.3.5.
[51] CASS 2.3.6.
[52] CASS 2.3.12–2.3.21.
[53] CASS 2.3.12.
[54] CASS 2.3.13.
[55] CASS 2.3.13–2.3.15.
[56] CASS 2.3.17.

(c)   distinguish from other assets those that are being used as collateral;

(d)   show the market value of any collateral held;

(e)   in the case of a private customer base the statement on either trade date or settlement date information and give notice of which basis is being used.

8.3.2.9   *Sub-custody agreements*[57]

Before a principal or "master" custodian holds its clients' investments with a (sub-) custodian it must agree written terms with the custodian including:[58]

(a)   the title to the account must indicate that investments credited to the account do not belong to the firm or an affiliate;

(b)   that the custodian will record investments belonging to the firm's clients separately from investments belonging to the firm or the custodian;

(c)   the date on which statements will be delivered describing the investments credited to the account;

(d)   that the custodian will not claim any lien, right of retention or sale over any investment credited to such account except with the client's written consent or in respect of charges relating to administration and safe keeping;

(e)   how investments will be registered, if not in the client's own name;

(f)   that the custodian is not permitted to withdraw any investments from the account except for delivery to or to the order of the firm;

(g)   procedures for giving instructions;

(h)   procedures for claiming and receiving dividends, interest and other entitlements;

(i)   the extent of the custodian's liability on the loss of an investment due to the fraud, wilful default or negligence of the custodian or an agent appointed by it.

While the principal (or master) custodian firm is expected to include all of these requirements in its agreement with the sub-custodian, it

---

[57] CASS 2.4.
[58] CASS 2.4.2 (1)–(9).

need not do so if this is impossible because, for instance, of legal requirements or custodial practice imposed by depositories or clearance systems.[59]

8.3.2.10 *Use of safe custody investments and stock lending*[60]
A firm may only:

(a)   use a client's investments for its own account; or
(b)   use a customer's investments for the account of another client,

if the client/customer has been notified (and in the case of a private customer given his written consent).[61] This is commonly referred to as a right of "use" or "rehypothecation" and is discussed further at 8.4 below in the context of the FSA's collateral rules. It is essentially a form of stock borrowing by a leverage provider such as a prime broker as a quid pro quo for its provision of leverage to a client. (Stock lending is in contrast an activity which is undertaken by investors with relatively static, unlevered portfolios, who are looking to generate some income from that portfolio.)

The firm may also "use" its clients' assets by lending them out to third parties. This is distinguished from rehypothecation by the fact that the "use" of the securities is not a perk for the financier but an added-value service for the client.

A firm may only engage in stock lending for a customer (note that this restriction does not apply to stock loans on behalf of a market counterparty) if it has the customer's consent and the activity is carried out on appropriate terms and conditions.[62] The model terms and guidance of bodies such as the International Stock Lending Association are relevant here.

Where stock lending is carried out for a private client the firm must ensure that relevant collateral is provided by the borrower in favour of the customer, the value of the collateral is monitored

---

[59] CASS 2.4.4.
[60] CASS 2.5.
[61] CASS 2.5.2.
[62] CASS 2.5.4.

daily, and the firm (unless agreed otherwise with the private customer) provides collateral to make up any shortfall.[63] Where several customers' investments are pooled, none of them may be used for stock lending unless all the pooled customers have consented, or the firm has systems which are adequate to ensure that only investments of the pooled customers who have consented are so used.[64] Cash or custody assets (i.e. this rule includes assets over and above safe custody assets) held for a customer for stock lending must be held in accordance with the client money or custody rules.[65]

8.3.2.11   Reconciliations

Where custody assets are held by a third party there is a risk that the firm's own records may fall out of line with the third party's records. To guard against this, the rules require a firm to reconcile its records of safe custody investments which it does not itself hold[66] with the records of the custodian who does hold them as often as necessary, and in any case not less than every 25 business days. In the case of dematerialised investments held by someone other than a custodian, it must reconcile its records with those of the person who maintains the record of legal entitlement. The sorts of person the FSA has in mind regarding this last provision are depositories such as CREST and the Central Gilts Office ("CGO").

Firms whose clients have investments in collective investment schemes may be unable to obtain statements on a monthly basis. In many cases it is a matter for the investment scheme as to just how often it produces its statements. In recognition of this, the rules allow firms dealing with such schemes to carry out reconciliations when statements are actually received, save that in any event a reconciliation must take place at least once every six months.[67]

A firm must as often as necessary, and no less than once every six months, carry out a count of all the safe custody investments it physically holds for clients, and reconcile this with its records of such

---

[63] CASS 2.5.8.
[64] CASS 2.5.9.
[65] CASS 2.5.10.
[66] CASS 2.6.2.
[67] CASS 2.6.4.

holdings.[68] Any discrepancies revealed must be promptly corrected and any shortfall made good.[69] The firm must promptly notify the FSA if it is unable to carry out such reconciliations in any material respect, or to make good any errors or deficiencies identified.[70]

The FSA regards the total count method, under which all safe custody investments are counted and reconciled as at the same date, as the best reconciliation method. However, it acknowledges that some firms find this impractical. Firms using other methods such as the rolling stock method, may apply this subject to certain requirements, including confirmation from the firm's auditors that the firm has adequate systems and controls to operate the alternative method.[71]

8.4 Collateral

There are two main ways of taking security. The first, traditional method, is to take a security interest, usually in the form of a first fixed mortgage, or perhaps a floating charge, over assets held in custody by the mortgagee. A charge of this sort operates as a first claim on the asset concerned. The chargeholder is entitled to indemnify itself out of the charged assets, but once it has done so it holds the remainder on trust for the charge giver. This residual proprietary interest is described, in mortgage terms, as the charge giver's equity of redemption.

Investment banks, custodians and broker-dealers often include a charging clause of this sort in their standard terms on a purely precautionary basis. But in cases where the firm is providing significant leverage or financing to its client, such as cash or securities loans, or by acting as a derivatives counterparty, the firm's security interest is much more important. If the client defaults on its liabilities to the firm the security interest provides the means by which the firm can enforce its rights against the client's property. Such a security will often be coupled with an arrangement whereby the client is required

---

[68] CASS 2.6.6.
[69] CASS 2.6.11.
[70] CASS 2.6.14.
[71] CASS 2.6.10.

to make available whatever level of property the firm requires by way of collateral or margin cover for the client's liabilities.

A firm providing this sort of service will often also require a right to re-charge or otherwise dispose of the client's collateral (and thus dispose of the client's proprietary interest in such property) to a third party. This is commonly described as a right of rehypothecation.[72] The firm may deposit the rehypothecated assets with a third party financier to obtain cheaper funding, lending the assets to another client, or simply use them as a "perk" for its own proprietary trading purposes.

When collateral has been rehypothecated, the firm's duty to return the original asset to the client is replaced by a personal (non-custodial) obligation on the part of the firm to return an equivalent asset, as and when required. Rehypothecation is thus predominantly part of the arm's-length counterparty function of lending and taking security rather than the fiduciary-type custodian function. However, it is also associated with a residual custodial function, and the firm's obligation to return the assets is potentially within the scope of its custody of the client's property.

The other main way of taking collateral is by full "transfer of ownership" such that the client does not retain any proprietary interest or equity of redemption in the collateral. The collateral becomes the sole property of the firm, subject to the firm's personal obligation to return equivalent assets (to the extent that these are not required as cover for its loans to the client). The effect is the same as a right of rehypothecation *which has been exercised*. In the FSA's terminology, the firm is being given the title and associated rights to the asset obtained. The arrangement does not involve a custody element but will be subject to the collateral rules.[73]

---

[72] Strictly speaking, hypothecation describes the taking of security without any physical deposit of the secured property (in contrast to a pledge) and rehypothecation is the recharging to a third party of the property originally charged in favour of the firm. In the London market the term "rehypothecation" tends to be treated as a generic term covering any recharging, resale or other right to "use" the asset concerned.

[73] *See* CASS 3.1.6 citing the International Swaps and Derivatives Association ("ISDA") English law Credit Support Annex and FSA Consultative Paper 45a paragraph 13.51 citing English law repo agreements.

The FSA's collateral rules apply[74] when the firm receives assets in connection with an arrangement to secure the obligations of a client in the course of or in connection with its designated investment business on terms that the firm is entitled to use the assets as its own – either through a right of rehypothecation or because full legal ownership of the collateral has been transferred to the firm by way of security.

The collateral regime potentially encompasses assets held as collateral in the course of investment business which are not themselves investments. CASS 3.1.5G says that the regime will apply where the firm is given a right to use the asset and treats the asset as if legal title and associated rights to that asset had been transferred to the firm subject only to an obligation to return equivalent assets upon satisfaction of the client's obligation to the firm.

This wording may have been written with ISDA-type margining arrangements in mind. It is more problematic where the client's whole portfolio has been collateralised, where the requirement that obligations must be satisfied before assets are returned would technically require the client to be completely unleveraged. In practice, if a client wishes to sell securities which the firm has rehypothecated or received on a transfer of title basis the firm is expected to make available equivalent securities in time for delivery to the buyer on the settlement date, subject to the overall level of collateral available remaining adequate.

The collateral rules, then, apply to transfer of ownership collateral and to assets subject to a security interest in respect of which a right of rehypothecation has been exercised.[75] In such situations the firm must ensure that it maintains adequate records to enable it to meet any future obligations including the obligation to return equivalent assets to the client.[76]

The rules make it clear that the mere taking of a security charge over a portfolio does not give a firm carte blanche to ignore the custody rules. The collateral rules do not apply where the security only gives

---

[74] CASS 3.1.1.
[75] CASS 3.1.7 says that the firm "exercises its right to treat the assets as its own".
[76] CASS 3.2.2.

the firm a right to realise assets on the client's default and there is no associated right of rehypothecation. In such a situation the firm must hold the assets either as client money or a safe custody investment, unless and until it can exercise the right to realise it.[77] This equates with the situation where the client retains an equity of redemption or similar proprietary interest in collateralised assets.[78] The FSA described this as a "bare security interest" and confirms that in such cases the firm must comply with the custody and client money rules where appropriate.[79]

Similarly, where there is a right of rehypothecation, the custody and client money rules will still apply to assets in respect of which the right of rehypothecation has not yet been exercised.[80]

8.5 The non-MiFID client money regime

8.5.1 Introduction

Money, like other intangibles, is a chose in action. However, to a very large extent it is regarded as a unique form of property with its own characteristics. At a strict level, money means physical cash – notes and coins – and it is a basic legal principle that a seller is always entitled to insist on cash payment. The point of this (insofar as it does have a point) is that the seller is not under any obligation to accept a mere promise to pay. He could insist if he wished on payment in coins and notes. In practice an intention not to insist upon payment in coins and notes is almost automatically inferred.

Leaving aside this theoretical legal point, money means "bank money", a credit into an account with a commercial bank, normally paid not in the form of coins and notes, but by debiting the payer's

---

[77] Consultative Paper 45a; COB Sourcebook paragraph 13.49.
[78] Though theoretically it would be possible to exercise a right of rehypothecation, say by recharging the client's securities in favour of a third party, in such a way that the client's proprietary interest could still be traced through to the securities in the hands of the third party. In practice it seems fairly unlikely that the securities would be sufficiently identifiable to achieve this. Many rehypothecation clauses provide specifically that title in the securities will automatically pass on rehypothecation.
[79] CASS 3.1.3.
[80] CASS 3.1.7; 3.2.3.

bank account and crediting the receiver's bank account with the transferred value. Its existence is dependent on the ability of the paying bank to pay. If the bank or banking system collapses the "money" disappears.

Where a bank customer[81] pays money to a firm the firm may pay it into a bank account in the name of the customer. On the principle that bank money is the same as money, the money (more precisely the right to the payment of the money owed by the bank to the customer) remains the property of the customer (not the firm) and can be enforced as a debt immediately due and payable by the bank to the customer. The right to that payment can also be assigned, as a piece of property, to third parties.[82]

Where, however, a firm such as a broker-dealer takes its client's money and pays it into an account in the firm's name, the money becomes the property of the firm and not the client. The bank's obligation to pay the money is owed to the firm, not the client, and the client is left with a purely personal claim against the firm for compensation.

Under a third option the firm pays the money into an account in its name so that legal title to the money belongs to the firm, but holds it on trust for its client(s), so that the underlying beneficial ownership stays with the client. This is known as a Quistclose trust, from the first case in which the principle was established.[83] The trust, if properly established, is proof against any claim by the firm's creditors. In particular the bank where the money is held, if it is on notice of the trust, will be in breach of trust if it purports to pay amounts owing to it by deduction from the trust assets.

The client money rules took this Quistclose principle and developed it by creating a statutory trust based on the same principles. The statutory trust applies automatically on the back of the client money

---

[81] In banking law depositors and borrowers are normally referred to as customers to indicate the arm's-length counterparty nature of the relationship, and the absence of client relationship duties on the part of the bank as service provider.

[82] Section 136 Law of Property Act 1925 and also in equity generally.

[83] *Barclays Bank plc* v *Quistclose Investments Ltd* [1968] 3 All ER 651.

rules. Prior to the introduction of this regime, it was common for stockbrokers to use client money deposited with them as working capital. Another advantage, where settlement or futures margining was involved, was that the broker could use one client's money to finance the positions of another client (known historically as "the broker's advantage").[84]

8.5.2 Scope of the non-MiFID client money rules

Client money is defined by the FSA as money which in the course of carrying on designated investment business a firm holds in respect of any investment agreement entered into or to be entered into with or for a client, or which a firm voluntarily treats as client money in accordance with the client money rules.[85]

Money ceases to be client money,[86] and the firm's trust duties are terminated, when the money is paid:

(a) to the client;

(b) to the client's duly authorised representative;

(c) to a third party on the instructions of the client (unless it is being transferred to an exchange clearing house or intermediate broker in the course of effecting a transaction in accordance with CASS);

(d) into a bank account in the name of the client which is not also in the name of the firm;

(e) to the firm itself when due and payable to it,

or where it represents an excess on the client bank account.

---

[84] Arguably the brokers and indeed the investment banks who did this were only following the practice of commercial banks, where clients' money is used not just as working capital, but as a springboard to leverage and risk-taking.

[85] This last point is quite significant. Where the firm creates an excess in the client account by topping up with its own money, there was historically concern that the resulting commingling might call into question the purity of the client money trust and allow the firm's liquidator to have recourse against it. The passage of time and the increasingly statutory-based nature of the trust has evidently convinced everyone that topping up of this sort is not a problem.

[86] CASS 4.3.98–4.3.102.

8.5.2.1 *Money due and payable*

Money due and payable to the firm for its own account is not client money.[87] In normal language, a debt is due or due and payable (the phrase "due and payable" is a convention, and the word "due" on its own would usually have the same legal effect) when the obligation to pay is immediate and not fixed at a point of time (whether determined or yet to be determined) in the future. By way of an example, a bank overdraft is due and payable when the bank demands repayment. In contrast, a term loan is not due and payable until the expiry of the term (or if earlier on the acceleration of the obligation to reply following an event of default).

The FSA rules contain their own paraphrase of this expression. A firm's own fees and commission charges may be treated as due and payable by its customers where:

(a) they have been agreed by the client either precisely or according to a precise formula; or

(b) five business days have elapsed since a statement showing the charges was sent to the customer.

Money due and payable to the client from the firm must within one business day after it becomes due be paid either into the client money account or to the order of the client.[88] A firm whose business permission does not allow it to hold client money must ensure that monies due and payable to the client, such as a commission rebate, are paid to the client as soon as they become due and payable.

8.5.2.2 *Banks*

A firm which is an approved bank may hold client money either as a trustee under the client money rules or as a banker. If it holds as banker, crediting the money to a bank account in its own books, it must notify the client that the money is held as a bank deposit and is not protected by the client money rules.[89]

---

[87] CASS 4.1.19.
[88] CASS 4.3.24.
[89] CASS 4.1.2(3).

If a bank holds money for a client with a third party such as an agent or broker, typically for settlement purposes, the bank is not holding the money as banker and the client money rules apply. However, if the bank deposits its own money with the other bank or third party broker, and retains the client's money in the bank's own deposit account, the related debt to the client will continue to be owed by the bank and the client money rules will not apply.[90]

8.5.2.3 *Opting out of the client money regime*
Money held by the firm on behalf of or received from a market counterparty or intermediate customer is not client money if the firm obtains a written acknowledgement from that counterparty or customer that:

(a)   the money will not be held as client money;
(b)   it will not be segregated from the firm's money; and
(c)   the person will rank only as a general creditor on an insolvency of the firm.[91]

8.5.2.4 *DVP*
As in the custody rules there is special treatment for DVP transactions.[92] Money used to settle DVP transactions through a commercial settlement system is excluded on similar terms to those applicable to safe custody (settlement within one day with a three-day window for errors). Money used to settle an issue or redemption of collective investment scheme units need not be treated as client money if (broadly) it is received by the firm in the course of issuing such units and the issue price will be determined within one business day, or it is held for the purposes of redeeming units, and the redemption price will be paid within the timeframe required by the Collective Investment Scheme rules.

8.5.2.5 *Affiliates*
It is FSA policy that the proprietors of a firm should not be better off than their clients if their firm becomes insolvent. Because of this,

---

[90] It would also appear from this that money merely treated as a trading debt by the bank, as distinct from money credited to a formally established banking account, would not necessarily be covered by the bank account exemption and still be potentially subject to the client money rules. Some banks appear to take a different view.
[91] CASS 4.1.8–4.1.9.
[92] CASS 4.1.15–4.1.16.

money belonging to clients which are affiliates is not subject to client money protection[93] unless:

(a) the firm has been notified by the affiliate that the money belongs to a client of the affiliate;
(b) the affiliate is an arm's-length client; or
(c) the affiliate is an occupational pension scheme or overseas company, the money is given to the firm to carry on designated investment business for clients of the affiliate, and the firm has notified the affiliate that it will treat the money as client money.

8.5.2.6 Solicitors
FSA authorised solicitors are subject to the client money rules of the Law Society – that is, the Solicitors Accounts Rules 1998 and similar legislation – and are not required to comply with FSA client money rules.[94]

8.5.2.7 Trustee firms
As with custody there is a special limited regime for trustee firms who must hold client monies separate from their own money at all times but otherwise are subject to a lighter regime.[95] The assumption is that, where there is already an express trust over the money, it is not necessary also to impose the full statutory trust, which may indeed contradict the particular terms of the express trust.

8.5.2.8 Unclaimed client money balances
The new FSA regime introduces a provision under which a firm may cease to treat any unclaimed client money balance as client money where the clients concerned have over a period of time become untraceable.[96] The firm must show that it has taken reasonable steps to trace the client concerned and return the balance. Reasonable steps should include a written agreement under which the client agrees to the firm releasing after a period of no less than six years any client money balances, writing to the client at his last known address, keeping records of all balances released and undertaking to make good

---

[93] CASS 4.1.17–4.1.18.
[94] CASS 4.1.25–4.1.26.
[95] CASS 4.1.27–4.1.29.
[96] CASS 4.3.103–4.3.106.

any valid claim against released balances. This provision does not apply to a firm which is being wound up or where it is unable to allocate amounts to a particular client. Nor does it apply to unclaimed balances existing prior to December 2001 (the date when the FSA rules came into effect).

8.5.2.9 Part 30 futures firms

A futures firm with a Part 30 exemption under the US Commodity Exchange Act must treat the money of any US resident investor received in respect of investment on non-US exchanges as client money.[97] The Part 30 exemption provides an exemption from the general US ban on futures business taking place other than on US futures exchanges. It permits UK futures firms to do business with US customers on non-US exchanges subject to certain standards being maintained, of which this is one.

8.5.3 The Client Money Trust

CASS 4.2[98] sets out the statutory trust on which the client money regime is based. Under this provision, a firm receives and holds client money as trustee on trust:

(a) for the purposes of the client money rules;
(b) for the clients for whom the money is held, on the failure of the firm;
(c) for the payment of costs properly attributable to the distribution of the client money in accordance with (b); and
(d) after all claims under (b) and (c) have been met, for the firm itself.

This tracks the common law/equitable duties of a trustee in a client money context.

The original 1987 rules[99] divided client money into separate pools reflecting different levels of risk. Where client money is used for transaction settlement or margin payments it is often very difficult to

---

[97] CASS 4.3.107–4.3.110.
[98] Based on Section 139(1) FSMA 2000.
[99] The Financial Services (Clients Money) Regulations 1987.

identify cash movements by reference to individual clients. In practice the broker usually makes a block payment in respect of all its clients' settlement and margin obligations. To the extent that there is not time to call for the necessary money from individual clients (or the clients do not pay in time), the short-term effect is that the client money of one client is financing another client's liabilities. Under the 1987 rules there was an obligation on the broker in this situation to "top up" the account on a daily basis. This in turn gave rise to a concern that such topping up might spoil the purity of the client trust, leaving it open to attack by the firm's receiver or liquidator. Reflecting these concerns, the original client money regimes (formulated by the Securities Association and the Association of Futures Brokers and Dealers) provided for settlement and margin money to be held in pools (i.e. accounts) which were separated from each other and from the ordinary "free money".

These separate accounts were also divided between sterling and foreign currency transactions (since foreign currency transactions usually took longer to settle and were therefore more likely to generate inter-client borrowing). In the event of a default by the firm, clients had a right of recourse against the pool into which their money had been paid,[100] for the amount of that money. The only clients exposed to the higher risk settlement and margin accounts were (in theory) those who chose to be involved in such transactions. In practice, however, the regulators came to the conclusion that the costs and complexity of maintaining the separate pools outweighed the benefits they were designed to achieve. It was particularly evident that, not only would a defaulting firm's records often prove inadequate to identify individual entitlements, but it would also often have raided one pool to fund another pool as a stop-gap measure.

In the 1991 rewrite of the client money rules,[101] where a firm defaulted, all client money was pooled and distributed pro rata to clients according to their claims to such assets. While this exposed low-risk consumers to the risks involved in activities such as margin

---

[100] The point being (in this context) not that the client's claim was better than everyone else's but that it was made against a small specifically identified pool shared with clients who were less likely to make difficult demands on it.

[101] The Financial Services (Client Money) Regulations 1991 Part 3 (Default Regulations), which came into force on 1 January 1992.

trading, it also made the system much easier to operate. It was also argued that sharing the risk across a wider client base was more likely to generate a large number of relatively small claims which could be more easily met by the Investors Compensation Scheme. However, firms were still required[102] to operate settlement bank accounts and margined transaction accounts unless they were able to settle transactions without using one client's money to discharge another client's liability.

The FSA has continued the pooling of all client money on default. It considers that, because of this ultimate pooling, there is no need to require firms to continue to operate segregated pools. The FSA approach (involving the daily calculation of all pluses and minuses, followed by a daily top-up) is now extended to former Personal Investment Authority and Investment Management Regulatory Organisation firms. The result (in the FSA's view) is that there is less risk of the money being allocated to the wrong account and therefore records are more likely to be accurate and up to date. No one class of clients is treated more favourably than the other.

8.5.3.1 Operation of the Trust

The FSA rules require the firm to hold client money separate from its own money.[103] Where the money is held in a different currency from the currency it is received in, this must be adjusted each day to ensure that it remains equal in value to the amount originally deposited.[104] If a firm pays its own money into the client money account, this will itself become client money.[105]

Client money must be segregated in one of two ways:

(a) Either by the normal approach:[106] under this the firm must pay the money into a client bank account as soon as possible and no later than the next day. Automated transfers must either be received directly into the client money account or, if received in

---

[102] Under the Financial Services (Client Money) Supplementary Regulations 1991 or analogous provisions in the SRO rules.
[103] CASS 4.3.3.
[104] CASS 4.3.4.
[105] CASS 4.3.6.
[106] CASS 4.3.8.

the firm's account, they must be transferred to the client account within one business day.

(b) Or by the alternative approach:[107] this is designed for firms operating in a multi-product multi-currency environment where the normal approach would be unduly burdensome. It allows the firm to receive money into and pay it out of its own account, provided it can monitor the client money flows accurately and ensure that an equivalent amount is segregated elsewhere in a client money account. The firm must carry out the segregation calculation for client money and make sure that an equivalent amount is credited each day to its client money account.

Where a firm receives a remittance which is a mixture of client and non-client money[108] the whole sum must be paid first into the client money account to ensure that it is impressed as soon as possible with the statutory trust. The non-client money surplus must then be paid out within one day of the date on which the original remittance would normally be cleared. This is designed to address standard concerns that if money is first received by the firm on an indeterminate basis it may subsequently be difficult to class as subject to a trust in favour of a third party. In practice, the client money regime seems now to be well enough established to obviate these concerns.

8.5.3.2 Representatives and agents
A firm must ensure that client money received by its appointed representatives or other agents[109] is kept separate from any other money, and is either paid into the firm's client money account or sent to the firm so as to be received by it within three days.

8.5.3.3 Client entitlements
Client entitlements,[110] such as dividends or interest payments, must be paid into a client money account if received in the UK, or into an appropriate account if received overseas. The firm should ensure that it is notified of the receipt of such payments by the relevant

---

[107] CASS 4.3.10.
[108] CASS 4.3.13–4.3.14.
[109] CASS 4.3.15–4.3.18.
[110] CASS 4.3.19–4.3.23.

depository or payer, and that they are allocated to individual clients within a reasonable time after notice of receipt. A new evidential provision provides that allocation within 10 business days is evidence of compliance with this requirement.

8.5.3.4 *Interest on client monies*
All interest earned on a private customer's client money must be paid to the customer unless the firm notifies him to the contrary. In the case of intermediate customers and counterparties the payment of interest is a matter for negotiation. Interest due to a client is itself client money.[111]

8.5.3.5 *Passing client money to third parties*
Under some circumstances the payment of client money to a third party will mean that it ceases to be client money (*see* 8.3.2 above). However, a firm may also pass client money to an exchange or its clearing house, or to an intermediate broker, to effect settlement,[112] or to meet margin calls. Thus, UK futures clearing firms regularly pay client money to the London Clearing House to meet margin calls in respect of the positions they hold for their customers. In such circumstances the firm remains responsible for the client's equity balance held at the third party. The rules only allow the firm to make such a transfer for the purpose of a transaction for the client through or with that third party, or to meet the client's obligation to provide collateral for such a transaction. A private customer must be notified if his client money may be transferred to another person in this way.

Where a futures broker (or any firm carrying out a similar function) passes client money to an exchange clearing house, intermediate broker or over-the-counter ("OTC") counterparty, the recipient must acknowledge in writing that the money must be paid into the firm's client transaction account which may not be combined with or set off against any other account.[113]

---

[111] CASS 4.3.26–4.3.28.
[112] CASS 4.3.30–4.3.32. Some markets involve free money transfers. And even a DVP market involves an element of time delay.
[113] CASS 4.3.48–4.3.55.

If a third party with whom client money is held becomes insolvent, the firm must notify the FSA of this and also whether it intends to make good any shortfall.[114]

8.5.3.6 *Distribution of client money on a default*
CASS 4.4 sets out detailed provisions for the handling of client money on the insolvency or failure of the firm which holds the money. The general principle is that client money in the client money account is treated as pooled and must be distributed so that each client receives a proportionate entitlement, with any shortfall being shared on the same basis. Similar provisions apply where the shortfall is due to the failure of an intermediate broker, settlement agent or OTC counterparty.

8.5.4 *Structure of client money bank accounts*

The general rule is that client money must be held in a client bank account with an approved bank. The firm may have as many such accounts as it wishes. A trustee firm must maintain separate client money bank accounts for each trust.[115]

The firm must take reasonable steps to establish that the bank it uses is appropriate to the firm's purposes. It should take account of the bank's capital and credit rating, the amount of client money placed with it as a proportion of its capital and deposits, and (to the extent information is available) the level of risk in the lending and investment activities of the bank and its group.[116] The bank must acknowledge in writing that money credited to the account is held by the firm as trustee and the bank is not entitled to set it off against any money owed to it by the firm; and the title of the account must clearly distinguish the client money account from the firm's other proprietary accounts.[117] A different form of acknowledgement is required from exchanges, clearing houses and intermediate brokers.[118]

---

[114] CASS 4.3.64.
[115] CASS 4.3.33–4.3.34.
[116] CASS 4.3.41–4.3.45.
[117] CASS 4.3.48–4.3.51.
[118] CASS 4.3.52.

8.5.4.1 Designated accounts

A client may agree with the firm that his money should be held in a client bank account with a particular bank – X bank. Another client may not mind too much which bank holds his money so long as it is not Y bank. Under the original client money rules all client bank accounts were pooled to determine clients' entitlement to that money so that a client who had specified that his money should be held by X bank, or not held by Y bank, would still be disadvantaged if the firm had a client money account with Y bank, Y bank became insolvent, and there was a shortfall in the Y bank client money account. Since 1991, however, firms have been able to set up special bank accounts to deal with this issue. If Y bank goes into default, clients who have agreed with the firm that their money will be held at X bank should be entitled to the actual money in the X bank client bank account unaffected by Y bank's collapse.

The accounts chosen in this way by the client are termed "designated accounts"[119] and are divided into two types:

(a) those which contain the money of one client only (a designated client bank account);

(b) those which contain a "designated fund", that is, money of two or more clients (a designated fund account).

The designated fund may be held in more than one designated fund account at different banks. If one such designated fund bank were to become insolvent, the designated fund clients would still be entitled to the money held at the remaining designated fund banks.

8.5.4.2 Non-approved banks

Under the original rules there were no exceptions to the use of approved banks. The new FSA regime acknowledges that some firms may wish to carry on business in jurisdictions where approved banks are not readily available. Under the new concession, a firm (other than a trustee firm) may hold client money at a bank which is not an approved bank if it is used for transaction settlement or income distribution in an overseas jurisdiction and, because of local law or

---

[119] CASS 4.35–4.3.39.

market practice, it is not possible to hold the money in a client bank account with an approved bank. All counterparties and customers must give written consent (in an FSA prescribed form) to such an arrangement.[120]

8.5.4.3 *Group accounts*

Under the original client money regime there was no restriction on a firm depositing client money with a bank in the same group. On the collapse of the British and Commonwealth Group in 1989 it became apparent that, where a regulated firm defaulted, any bank in the same group was likely to collapse at the same time. While at one time the FSA considered prohibiting deposits at affiliated banks, the approach that has been taken since 1991 is to treat this primarily as a matter for disclosure. Under the current rules, if a firm holds client money with a bank in the same group it must review the bank's suitability to at least the same standard as an unconnected bank and warn the client that it intends to hold money at a bank in the same group and identify the bank(s) concerned. If the client does not wish his money to be held with a group bank the firm must either place it with an unconnected bank or return it to the customer.[121]

8.5.4.4 *Overseas accounts*

A firm may only hold client money in an account outside the UK if it has disclosed this to the client, warning him in writing that the legal and regulatory regime may be different and (if such is the case) that a particular bank has not accepted that it has no right of set-off against the money in respect of sums owed to it by the firm.[122]

A firm may only undertake a transaction which involves client money being passed to an intermediate broker, settlement agent or OTC counterparty outside the UK if it has warned the client in writing that the legal and regulatory regime may be different, and on a failure of such person the money may be treated differently from the way it would be in the UK.[123]

---

[120] CASS 4.3.40.
[121] CASS 4.3.46–4.3.47.
[122] CASS 4.3.56.
[123] CASS 4.3.61.

If the client, before entering into a transaction, notifies the firm that his money is not to be held in a particular jurisdiction, or that his money is not to be passed to an intermediate broker, settlement agent, or OTC counterparty in a particular jurisdiction, the firm must either act in accordance with that instruction or return the money to the client.[124]

8.5.5 The client money calculation[125]

The daily client money calculation is designed to ensure, *inter alia,* that firms do not use the money of one client to finance the liabilities of a different client. Segregation must be carried out on a gross rather than a net basis so that firms must top up any temporary client money shortfall with their own money. The main areas where this is an issue are settlement and margin accounts. The Financial Services and Markets Act 2000 ("FSMA 2000") extended this requirement to personal investment firms and investment managers. As they are not normally involved in running settlement and margin accounts, the FSA considers that the imposition on them of this top-up requirement ought not in practice to amount to much more than a daily check that the money recorded in the bank ledger is the same as the total for client balances.

The FSA also considers that applying the daily calculation requirement to all firms will improve the quality of record-keeping in circumstances where a firm is about to fail, and the ease and accuracy of any subsequent client money distribution.

Under CASS a firm must carry out the daily client money calculation based on the balances as at the close of the previous business day. The calculation is designed to ensure that the firm has at all times enough money segregated in its client money accounts to pay out the relevant client in full. In FSA terminology, the calculation is the measure for ensuring that the client money resource matches the client money requirement.[126] In the case of the "normal approach" this is designed to see that the amount of client money segregated

---

[124] CASS 4.3.63.
[125] CASS 4.3.65–4.3.97.
[126] CASS 4.3.66.

with banks and third parties is sufficient to meet the firm's obligations to its clients on a daily basis. If there is a shortfall the firm must top the account up with its own money. In the case of the "alternative approach" the firm is calculating the amount of its own money which it needs to segregate to meet such obligations, and no shortfall should arise.

The Client Money Requirement[127] is made up of:

(a) Individual *client balances* excluding client balances which are in deficit;
    plus
(b) the *clients' equity balances* plus the total *margined transaction requirement*.

Individual client balances[128] are:

(a) free money (i.e. money not earmarked for trades) and sale proceeds due to the client;
    less
(b) money owed by the client on client purchases where payment has not been made but the investments have been delivered; plus proceeds paid to the client on sales where the client has not delivered the investments.

The client's equity balance[129] is the amount the firm would be liable to pay the client (ignoring any non-cash collateral) if all his open positions were liquidated at current market prices.

The total margined transaction requirement[130] is the sum of:

(a) the clients' equity balances (excluding negative balances);
    less
(b) the part of any individual negative client equity balances which are secured by collateral and the net aggregate of the firm's

---

[127] CASS 4.3.71.
[128] CASS 4.3.72–4.3.74.
[129] CASS 4.3.79.
[130] CASS 4.3.81.

equity balance (negative balances being deducted) on transaction accounts with exchanges, intermediate brokers and OTC counterparties.[131]

To reduce the amount requiring segregation,[132] where a client:

(a) has a positive individual client balance and a negative client equity balance, the firm may offset these so as to reduce the individual client balance;

(b) has a negative individual client balance and a positive client equity balance the firm may offset these so as to reduce the client equity balance for that client.

The firm must notify the FSA immediately if it is unable to perform the calculation or identifies a shortfall which it may not be able to make good on the day it was identified.[133]

Client money balances must be reconciled[134] as often as necessary to ensure the accuracy of the records, and in any event no less than every 25 business days. Reconciliation involves comparing the firm's own records of client bank accounts and client transaction accounts with the statements issued by the bank holding the money or the person with whom the transaction account is held.

8.6 The MiFID custody rules

8.6.1 Scope of the MiFID custody rules

The MiFID custody and client money rules apply to a MiFID investment firm that holds financial instruments belonging to a client in the course of its MiFID business or which opts in to the MiFID custody rules.[135]

---

[131] Under the new FSA scheme, client money held with third parties is treated as part of client money resources. The Firm's Equity Balance is the amount it would have to pay exchanges, intermediate brokers and OTC counterparties (or vice versa) in respect of the firm's margined transactions if all open positions were liquidated at current prices. *See* CASS 4.3.80.

[132] CASS 4.3.85–4.3.86.

[133] CASS 4.3.97–4.3.88.

[134] CASS 4.3.89–4.3.97.

[135] CASS 6.1.1.

MiFID business means investment services and activities and, where relevant, ancillary services carried on by a MiFID investment firm.

A MiFID investment firm is a firm to which MiFID applies. Generally speaking, MiFID applies to firms which carry on any of the investment services and activities set out in Annex 1 to MiFID in relation to MiFID instruments. The main MiFID services and activities are the reception and transmission of orders, the execution of orders on behalf of clients, portfolio management, the giving of investment advice, underwriting and placing, and the operation of multilateral trading facilities. Ancillary services are specified in Section B and include custody, the financing of transactions in financial instruments where the firm is involved in the transaction, advice on capital structure, corporate strategy and mergers and acquisitions, foreign exchange services related to investment services, investment research, and services related to underwriting and to the underlying of a derivative. MiFID instruments are those specified in Section C of Annex 1, broadly consisting of transferable securities, money market instruments and most derivatives.

If a firm carries on ancillary services but does not carry on any MiFID investment service it will not be a MiFID investment firm and will not come within the MiFID custody or client money rules though it may still come within the scope of the non-MiFID rules described above.

Also outside the scope of the MiFID custody rules is a firm which simply arranges or recommends custody services but does not provide them itself,[136] and a firm which acts as the issuer of depository receipts, both of which will be subject to the non-MiFID rules.

Where a firm is involved in both MiFID and non-MiFID business it may opt to comply with the MiFID rules in respect of all of its custody business. This opt-in does not extend to arranging custody and depositary receipt business where the non-MiFID rules provide specialised regimes which are outside the scope of the MiFID rules.[137] Nor is a firm which only carries on non-MiFID custody entitled to opt into the MiFID custody rules.

---

[136] CASS 6.1.12–14.
[137] CASS 6.1.17–18.

The reference in CASS 6.1.1 to holding instruments belonging to a client should be sufficient to exclude any obviously non-custody arrangements. However, MiFID goes on specifically to create certain exemptions when title to assets is held by or transferred to the firm.[138] In cases of this sort it should be apparent that the firm is not "holding instruments belonging to a client" because the client retained no proprietary interest in the instrument. However, the position may be less clear under legal systems which do not have the proprietary interest concept.

The rules do not apply:

(a) Where a firm carries on business in its name but on behalf of a client where that is required by the very nature of the transaction and the client is in agreement. An example of this is where the firm borrows financial instruments as principal from a client under a stock-lending arrangement.[139]

(b) Where the client transfers full ownership of a financial instrument to a firm for the purposes of securing or otherwise covering present, future, actual, contingent or prospective obligations.[140]

(c) To delivery versus payment transactions through a third-party commercial settlement system, where settlement is due to take place within one day. The firm is allowed up to three days to rectify a failed trade before it is obliged to segregate the designated investments concerned.[141]

(d) To the arranging of the registration of a financial instrument or the recommendation to a retail client of a custodian. In such circumstances the firm must, however, comply with the rules applicable to arrangers in CASS 2.1.21–22.[142]

(e) To the temporary handling of financial instruments belonging to a client, provided this takes no longer than is reasonably necessary. In most cases this would be no longer than one business day. The firm is still expected to comply with Principle 10 (Client Assets) of the FSA's Principles for Businesses.[143]

---

[138] CASS 6.1.5–6; MiFID recitals 26 and 27.
[139] CASS 6.1.4–5.
[140] CASS 6.1.6–7.
[141] CASS 6.1.12.
[142] CASS 6.1.13–14.
[143] CASS 6.1.15–16.

The fact that a client is the firm's affiliate does not affect the operation of the custody rules.[144] Note the contrast with CASS 2.1.9 which provides a more restricted application of the non-MiFID custody rules to affiliates.

The rules cease to apply to an instrument which has been disposed of in accordance with a valid client instruction.[145] It is presumed that instruction can be given a fairly wide interpretation for these purposes – for example, an instruction in the client agreement entitling the firm to liquidate client assets in order to pay its fees.

8.6.2 Specific requirements of the custody rules

8.6.2.1 The general approach
The purpose of the rules is stated in very similar terms to the non-MiFID rules – restrict the commingling of house and client assets and minimise the risk of the client's assets being used by the firm without the client's consent or being treated as the firm's assets on insolvency.[146]

8.6.2.2 Protecting the client's proprietary interest
The MiFID rules are rather less detailed on the principles of protection than the equivalent provisions on segregation in the non-MiFID rule (CASS 2.2). They lay down a general duty to make adequate arrangements to safeguard client ownership rights, especially on the firm's insolvency, and to prevent the use of the assets without the client's express consent.[147] The detailed requirements for safeguarding title to the clients' assets track CASS 2.2.10. A firm must, to the extent practicable, effect appropriate registration or recording of legal title to a financial instrument in the name of:[148]

(a) the client (or, if the client is itself an authorised firm acting for a client, in the name of the underlying client);

(b) a nominee company (i.e. a bare trustee) controlled by the firm, an affiliate, a recognised investment exchange or designated

---

[144] CASS 6.1.10.
[145] CASS 6.1.21.
[146] CASS 6.1.23.
[147] CASS 6.2.1.
[148] CASS 6.2.3.

investment exchange, or by a third party (custodian) with whom financial instruments are deposited under CASS 6.3;

(c)   any other third party, if the instrument is subject to the law or market practice of an overseas jurisdiction and the firm has taken reasonable steps to ensure that:

(i)   it is in the client's best interests to register or record it in that way; or

(ii) it is not feasible to do otherwise because of the nature of the local law or market;

and the firm has given written notice to the client of this;

(d)   the firm itself, if the instrument is subject to the law or market practice of an overseas jurisdiction and the firm has taken reasonable steps to ensure that:

(i)   it is in the client's best interests to register or record it in that way; or

(ii) it is not feasible to do otherwise because of the nature of the local law or market and the firm has notified the client and (if he is a retail client) obtained his prior written consent.

If (c) or (d) are relied on, the firm must demonstrate that adequate investigations have been made of the market concerned by reference to local sources which may include appropriate legal opinion.[149]

Unlike non-MiFID rule 2.2.10(5), the MiFID rules do not state that the instruments can be held with any other person if specifically instructed by the client. It is unclear whether this is because it is considered unnecessary or because of a perceived MiFID scope problem.

The equivalent requirements for bearer instruments consist only of a brief statement that bearer instruments belonging to clients must be kept separately from bearer instruments belonging to the firm.[150] Contrast non-MiFID rule 2.2.15–17.

---

[149] CASS 6.2.6.
[150] CASS 6.2.7.

The requirement to accept responsibility for nominee companies controlled by the firm is slightly narrower than the non-MiFID rule as it does not include nominees controlled by the firm's affiliates.[151]

As in non-MiFID rule 2.2.13, there is a specific rule on commingling house and client assets. A firm may record title to its own instruments in the same name as that in which clients' instruments are recorded but only if the firm's instruments are separately identified in the firm's own records and title to the instrument is recorded in accordance with CASS 6.3.3(4) – that is, it is doing so because the asset is held outside the UK, it is in the client's best interest to do so and the client has been notified or, in the case of a retail client, has consented.[152]

The firm should maintain records which enable it to distinguish the instruments of any one client from instruments belonging to another client or to the firm, and it should keep these for five years (as opposed to the three years specified in the non-MiFID rules).[153]

There is no MiFID equivalent of the detailed client agreement and client statement requirements contained in non-MiFID rule 2.3.

8.6.2.3 *Appointing and monitoring sub-custodians*
The criteria for sub-custody specified in CASS 6.3 are different in form, though very similar to, the equivalent non-MiFID requirements in CASS 2.18–23.[154]

Where the firm deposits instruments it holds with a third party (i.e. a sub-custodian) it must:[155]

(a) exercise skill, care and diligence in the selection, appointment and periodic review of the third party and the arrangements for the holding and safekeeping of those instruments;

(b) ensure that those instruments are identifiable separately from the financial instruments belonging to the firm and instruments

---

[151] CASS 6.2.4.
[152] CASS 6.2.5.
[153] CASS 6.5.2–3; MiFID second level Article 16(1)(b).
[154] MiFID Level 2 Articles 16(1)(d) and 17.
[155] CASS 6.3.1.

of the sub-custodian by means of differently titled accounts on the books of the sub-custodian or other equivalent measures that achieve the same level of protection;

(c)   take into account the expertise and market reputation of the sub-custodian, and any legal requirements or market practices relating to the holding of those instruments that could adversely affect clients' rights; and

(d)   make a record of the grounds on which it is satisfied as to the appropriateness of the selection of the sub-custodian at the date it makes the selection, which must be kept until five years after it ceases to use the sub-custodian concerned.

In discharging its obligations the firm should also consider the following together with any other relevant matters:[156]

(a)   once an instrument has been lodged with the sub-custodian, the sub-custodian's performance of its services to the firm;

(b)   the arrangements the sub-custodian has for holding and safeguarding the instrument;

(c)   current industry standard reports, such as the Financial Reporting and Audit Group (FRAG) 21 report or equivalent;

(d)   the capital, financial resources and credit rating of the sub-custodian and the other activities undertaken by the sub-custodian or, if relevant, its affiliates.

The firm should carefully consider the terms of its agreement with the sub-custodian[157] including:

(a)   whether the title of the account indicates that any financial instrument credited to the account does not belong to the sub-custodian;

(b)   whether the sub-custodian will hold or record the firm's clients' instruments separately from instruments belonging to the firm or the third party;

(c)   the arrangements for registering or recording the instrument if it will not be registered in the client's name;

---

[156] CASS 6.3.2.
[157] CASS 6.3.3.

(d) the restrictions over the sub-custodian's right to claim a lien, right of retention or sale over the instruments;

(e) the restrictions on the circumstances in which the sub-custodian may withdraw assets from the account;

(f) the procedures and authorities for passing instructions to or by the firm;

(g) procedures for claiming and receiving dividends, interest payments and other entitlements; and

(h) provisions dealing with the extent of the sub-custodian's liability on the loss of an instrument due to the fraud, wilful default or negligence of the sub-custodian or an agent appointed by it.

These provisions are a close match for the client agreement content requirements in non-MiFID rule 2.4.2.

8.6.2.4 *Authorisation and jurisdictional requirements*[158]

There are some distinctive MiFID jurisdictional requirements which reflect a certain mistrust of non-EEA based service providers as well as the marginal value attached to the firm making its own assessment of their capabilities. Where the sub-custodian is in a jurisdiction which specifically regulates and supervises custody services, the sub-custodian must be subject to that regulation. Where the sub-custodian is based in a country outside the EEA which does not regulate custody, it must only be used if the nature of the instruments concerned requires them to be deposited with such a person, or the firm is acting for a professional client who has requested the firm to deposit them with a sub-custodian in such a third country. This requirement does not apply to non-MiFID activities which have been opted into CASS 6, but certain minimum custody standards will still apply.

8.6.2.5 *Use of instruments (stock lending, repos and rehypothecation)*[159]

A firm must not enter into security financing transactions in respect of client instruments or use such instruments for its own account or the account of another client of the firm unless the client has given express prior consent and the rehypothecation or use of the instruments is restricted to the specified terms consented to.

---

[158] CASS 6.3.4. Based on Article 17(2)–(3) of the second level Directive.
[159] CASS 6.4.1. Based on MiFID second level Directive Article 19.

In addition, where the firm enters into financing arrangements or rehypothecates or uses client instruments held in an omnibus account with a third party, either each client must have given express prior consent or the firm must have in place systems to ensure that only the instruments of clients who have so consented may be used in this way. This is similar to non-MiFID rules 2.5.2–4 and 2.5.8–9.

Certain non-MiFID requirements for stock lending from CASS 2.5.8 are added into the MiFID rules in the form of guidance. Pursuant to the "best interests rule" in MiFID first level Directive Article 18(1), where stock lending is carried out for a retail client, the firm should ensure that relevant collateral is provided by the borrower in favour of the customer, the value of the collateral is monitored daily, and the firm (unless agreed otherwise with the retail client) provides collateral to make up any shortfall.[160] Proper records must be kept of such transactions to enable the correct allocation of any loss.[161]

8.6.2.6   Reconciliations

The MiFID reconciliation requirements are rather more generalised than those in the non-MiFID rules, and couched mostly in the form of guidance.

A firm should perform internal reconciliations of the instruments held for each client with the reconciliations held for the firm as often as necessary and as soon as reasonably practicable after the date to which the reconciliation relates, using the total count method or the rolling stock method. No period is specified within which this should be done.[162]

External reconciliations, between the firm's records of instruments it does not itself hold and the records of the custodian who does hold them, should also be conducted on a regular basis. The firm should obtain statements from its sub-custodians for this purpose and perform such reconciliations as often as necessary and as soon as reasonably practicable after the date to which the reconciliation relates.[163]

---

[160] CASS 6.4.2.
[161] CASS 6.4.2.
[162] CASS 6.5.4–5.
[163] CASS 6.5.6–6.5.8.

The firm should correct any discrepancies revealed as a result of such reconciliations and make good any shortfall which is the fault of the firm.[164]

Non-MiFID rule 2.6 contains similar provisions but prescribes the periods within which such internal and external reconciliations must take place.

8.7 The MiFID client money rules

8.7.1 Scope of the MiFID client money rules

The MiFID client money rules apply to a MiFID investment firm that holds client money or opts into the client money rules. The opt-in applies to money which falls within the scope of the non-MiFID client money rules.[165] MiFID client money is held subject to a similar statutory trust to that contained in CASS 4.2.2 of the non-MiFID rules.[166]

Client money in this MiFID context means any money a firm receives or holds for or on behalf of a client in the course of or in connection with its MiFID business,[167] save that money is not MiFID client money:

(a) Where it consists of coins held not as money but for the intrinsic value of the metal.[168]
(b) Where the firm carries on business in its own name on behalf of the client where this is required by the very nature of the transaction and the client is in agreement.[169]
(c) Where the client transfers full ownership of money to the firm by way of collateral or a transfer pursuant to a right of rehypothecation or similar right of use.[170] A retail client most be notified

---

[164] CASS 6.5.1.
[165] CASS 7.1.1, 7.1.3.
[166] CASS 7.7; CPO6/14 paragraphs 10.17–18. For a description of MiFID business *see* paragraph 8.6.1 above.
[167] CASS 7.2.1.
[168] CASS 7.1.14. .
[169] CASS 7.2.2.
[170] CASS 7.2.4. This is to be distinguished from the taking of a security interest where the client retains a proprietary interest in the money and full ownership accordingly does not pass to the firm. *See* CASS 7.2.5.

that full ownership has been transferred, the client no longer has a proprietary claim over the money and the firm can deal with it in its own right; the transfer is to secure or cover the client's obligations, an equivalent transfer will be made back to the client if the provision of collateral to the client is no longer necessary, and there is a reasonable link between the timing and the amount of the collateral transfer and the obligation that the client owes or is likely to owe to the firm.[171]

Firms relying on transfer of ownership by way of collateral as an alternative to the old client money opt out should thus ensure that the money is genuinely held as security, otherwise there is a risk they may be carrying on deposit-taking which would require a full banking licence. The FSA has stated that while such a collateral arrangement may be used for retail clients, it would expect this only to be done in very limited circumstances, for example stock lending, or arrangements for the retention of commission rebates in the personal investment market (i.e. sales commissions repayable to the client which are retained as security by the personal investment firm who has agreed to rebate them).[172]

(d) Where the money is employed in a delivery versus payment transaction through a commercial settlement system, if the money is due to or from the client within one business day after performance of the non-cash side of the transaction, unless delivery or payment by the firm has not occurred within three days of payment or delivery by the client.[173]

(e) Where money is due and payable to the firm for its own account. This will depend on the business and contractual arrangements between the firm and its clients, but typical examples are where fees are due to the firm which it is entitled to deduct from the client's account, where the firm is entitled to be reimbursed for a payment made on the client's behalf, or the firm enforces a security right over the client money (but any excess of the amount owed should be promptly recredited to the client money account).[174]

---

[171] CASS 7.2.7.
[172] FSA Policy Statement 07/02 paragraph 8.5.
[173] CASS 7.2.8.
[174] CASS 7.2.9–7.2.11.

(f) Where a commission rebate is to be paid to the client, but that rebate has not yet become due and payable. Once due and payable, a rebate should be treated as client money unless an arrangement for the full transfer of ownership by way of collateral has been agreed.[175]

The firm must pay a retail client all interest earned on client money unless there is a written agreement to the contrary. The interest will itself be client money.[176]

Money ceases to be client money if paid:

(a) to the client or its authorised representative;
(b) to a third party on instructions from the client or in the course of effecting a transaction;
(c) into a bank account in the client's name;
(d) to the firm itself where due and payable to the firm; or
(e) to the firm to reconcile an accounting discrepancy.[177]

Where a firm is transferring its business it must transfer any client money in a way which meets its obligations under the client money rules.[178]

If the firm draws a cheque or other payment order to discharge its obligations to the client this must continue to be treated as client money until presented and paid by the bank.[179]

A firm may cease to treat money as client money if it can demonstrate that it has taken reasonable steps to trace the client and return the balance. This includes:

(a) obtaining the client's initial written consent to such a release;
(b) determining that there has been no movement in the client's balance for at least six years;
(c) writing to the client at the client's last known address;

---

[175] CASS 7.2.12–13.
[176] CASS 7.2.14.
[177] CASS 7.2.15.
[178] CASS 7.2.16.
[179] CASS 7.2.17.

(d)   keeping records of all balances so released;

(e)   undertaking to make good any valid claim against released balances.[180]

8.7.2   *Organisational requirements*

The firm must make adequate arrangements to safeguard client money against misuse, fraud, poor administration, inadequate record keeping or negligence.[181]

8.7.3   *Segregation*

Client money must be placed in a client money account with a central bank, a credit institution recognised as such under the Second Banking Directive, a bank authorised in a third country, or a qualifying money market fund.[182]

The ability to use a "money market" or "liquidity" fund as an alternative to a cash deposit is specifically addressed by MiFID, though the practice has existed in the wholesale markets for some time, where it has depended more on the ability of the custodian to manage the logistics of a daily cash sweep from the client's account rather than any particular regulatory concession. Although now addressed in the FSA MiFID client money rather than the custody rules, it actually involves substituting securities for cash, and thus moving the clients' asset out of the client money regime and into the custody regime. Arguably it offers better protection than client money since a money market fund, unlike a bank, should have a perfect 100 per cent matched cover for its liabilities to its investors. Although the arrangement is addressed as such only in MiFID rules, it appears to be equally compatible with the non-MiFID rules.[183]

Where money is placed with a credit institution, other authorised bank or money market fund, the firm must exercise due skill, care and

---

[180] CASS 7.2.19–21. Similar to CASS 4.3.103–106.
[181] CASS 7.3.1–2.
[182] CASS 7.4.1–2.
[183] CPO6/14 paragraphs 10.11–16.

diligence in selecting, appointing and reviewing periodically the bank or fund concerned and its arrangements for holding the money. In doing this the firm should have regard to the expertise and market reputation of the party concerned, and any legal requirements or market practices that could adversely affect the clients' rights. It should also consider:

(a)   the need for diversification of risk;
(b)   the capital and credit rating of any credit institution or bank and, to the extent information is available, the level of risk in it and its affiliates' investment and loan activities;
(c)   the amount of client money placed as a proportion of the credit institution or bank's capital and deposits.[184]

In the case of a money market fund, the fund must be an approved money market fund, the firm must consider any limits placed by the fund on the volume of redemptions permitted in any period, and the units in the fund must be held in accordance with the custody rules. If the firm is subject to requirements to disclose information, before providing services it must notify the client that the money will be held in a qualifying money market fund under the custody rather than the client money rules.[185]

The firm must make a record of the grounds on which it has satisfied itself as to the appropriateness of the credit institution, bank or money market fund and give the client a right to oppose this arrangement.[186]

8.7.4   Client bank accounts

The firm should ensure that the money is deposited in an account or accounts which are separately identified from any accounts that hold money belonging to the firm itself. A similar principle applies to a "deposit" in a money market fund.[187]

---

[184] CASS 7.4.7–9.
[185] CASS 7.4.3–6, 7.4.9(3).
[186] CASS 7.4.10.
[187] CASS 7.4.11.

The account may be established as a general bank account, designated client bank account or designated client fund account. The same concepts are used in the non-MiFID rules. *See* 8.5.4 above.

The firm may hold MiFID client money according to either the normal approach or (where it operates in a multi-product, multi-currency environment where the normal approach would be unduly burdensome) the alternative approach. This is the same principle described in CASS 4.3.8–9. Either the firm pays the money into a client bank account (the normal approach) or the firm receives payments in a single currency of account, such as US dollars, and reconciles this with its client money obligations in sterling, euros etc.[188] Where the firm segregates money in a different currency from that of receipt it must adjust the amount held each day to allow for variations in exchange rates.[189] If the client instructs the firm to hold the money in a particular currency this instruction will take precedence over other arrangements.[190]

A firm operating the normal approach:

(a) which receives client money in the form of automated transfers should use reasonable efforts to ensure that this is received directly into the client account or if received into the firm's own account that it is transferred by the next business day. A payment which mixes client money and non-client money should be paid in full into the client account and the non-client element should then be transferred out again within one business day;[191]

(b) should ensure that any money received by its appointed representatives, field representatives or other agents is either paid direct into its client money account or forwarded to the firm itself within one business day, and that until then its representatives or agents keep the client money separately identifiable from any other money. Small branches may be treated in the same way as appointed representatives;[192]

---

[188] CASS 7.4.14–19. Compare non-MiFID CASS 4.3.8–9.
[189] CASS 7.4.30.
[190] CASS 7.4.31.
[191] CASS 7.4.22–23.
[192] CASS 7.4.24–26.

(c) which receives client entitlements such as dividends or interest payments on behalf of clients outside the UK should pay any client money element into a client bank account within five business days. Client entitlements should be allocated to the individual clients within 10 business days;[193]

(d) should pay any money due and payable to the client within one business day.[194]

Any money other than client money deposited in a client bank account should be promptly paid out unless it is a minimum sum required to keep the account open. If it is prudent to do so to ensure the money is protected, the firm may pay in its own money, which then becomes client money.[195]

8.7.5 Passing client money to third parties

The firm may transfer client money to a third party such as an exchange, clearing house or intermediate broker only for the purpose of a transaction or to meet an obligation to provide collateral; and if the client is a retail client he/she must be notified of this.[196] *See* 8.5.3.5 above.

8.8 Records, accounts, reconciliations and defaults

The MiFID record-keeping and accounting requirements are couched in more general terms than the equivalent non-MiFID obligations.[197] The firm has a general obligation to keep such records and accounts as are necessary to enable it to distinguish money held for one client from money held for another client and from its own money, and any client money received in the form of a client entitlement must be promptly identified. Records must be kept for five years.[198]

---

[193] CASS 7.4.27–28.
[194] CASS 7.4.29.
[195] CASS 7.4.20–21.
[196] CASS 7.5.2.
[197] CASS 7.6.
[198] CASS 7.6.1–5.

The firm should perform internal reconciliations as often as necessary and as soon as reasonably practicable after the date to which the reconciliation relates. A firm which is not using the standard method must ensure that its records show that the method of reconciliation used gives an equivalent degree of protection to the standard method and enables the firm to comply with the client money distribution rules.[199]

External reconciliations between the firm's records and the records of any third party with whom client money is held should also be conducted on a regular basis. The firm should perform such reconciliations as often as necessary and as soon as reasonably practicable after the date to which the reconciliation relates.[200]

The firm should correct any discrepancies revealed as a result of such reconciliations and make good any shortfall with its own money until the matter is resolved.[201]

8.9 Distribution of client money on a default

CASS 7.9 (equivalent to non-MiFID rule 4.4) sets out detailed provisions for the distribution of MiFID client money on the insolvency or failure of the firm holding the money.

8.10 The mandate rules

CASS 8 deals with "mandates" and corresponds to the rules on mandates formerly contained in CASS 4.5. The term "mandate" appears to be used in roughly the same sense as a bank mandate, where a bank customer gives a third party a mandate to draw on his bank account. Examples given by the FSA[202] are an authority over a client bank account, a firm's authority over a safe custody account or over a bank or building society account including direct debits in favour of the firm, and the holding of a client's credit card details.

---

[199] CASS 7.6.6–8.
[200] CASS 7.6.9–11.
[201] CASS 7.6.13–15.
[202] CASS 8.1.2.

This should be borne in mind when looking at CASS 8, because the literal wording appears to go much wider. CASS 8.1.1 says that the mandate rules apply to a firm:

> "in respect of any written authority from a client under which the firm may control a client's assets or liabilities in the course of, or in connection with, the firm's designated investment business".

In ordinary language the term "mandate" is also capable of going beyond a mere authority to give a direction to a third party to dispose of a client's assets. In an investment business context a mandate commonly refers to the scope of the services to be provided by a broker, investment manager, corporate finance adviser or personal investment firm to its client, in particular the scope of the discretion granted to the firm by its client to act on the client's behalf. Thus, a discretionary investment manager will make an investment decision on behalf of its client, instruct a broker to execute a trade, and then instruct the client's custodian to pay the purchase price and take delivery of the securities (or as the case may be, deliver the securities and take payment of the purchase price) when the trade is settled. The instructions to the custodian are clearly within the FSA's concept of a mandate. It is not clear whether the instructions to the broker are also within this concept, but on a purposive construction CASS 8 is presumably directed at the handling of a client's property and not exercising a discretion on a client's behalf.

Under the mandates rules, a firm that holds written authority from a client under which it may control the client's assets or liabilities in the course of or in connection with the firm's designated investment business must establish and maintain adequate records and controls[203] including:

(a)   an up-to-date list of the client's authorities and any conditions placed on their use;
(b)   a record of all transactions entered into using that authority and internal controls to ensure that they are within the scope of the firm's authority;

---

[203] CASS 8.1.5.

(c)   details of the procedures and authorities for giving and receiving instructions under the authority; and

(d)   where the firm holds a passbook or similar documents belonging to the client, internal controls for safeguarding the same.

As with the custody client agreement provisions discussed at 8.3.2.7 above, these requirements extend beyond ordinary client relationships to include counterparty relationships. However, it is extremely difficult to envisage a situation where a firm exercising a discretion of this sort would ever be able to treat the recipient of such a service as anything other than a client (in ordinary language terms) though perhaps not always a customer (in FSA terms).

Chapter 9

Specialist Regimes

Kirstene Baillie

Partner
Head of Financial Services and Funds Group
Field Fisher Waterhouse LLP

9.1   Introduction

This Chapter is concerned with the Financial Services Authority's "special" conduct of business provisions in Chapter 18 of the FSA's Conduct of Business Rules ("COBS") for the regulation of:

(a)   Collective investment schemes and trusts:

    (i)   operators and depositaries of collective investment schemes;

    (ii)   trustee firms (other than depositaries);

    (iii) occupational pension scheme ("OPS") firms; and

(b)   Particular regulated activities:

    (i)   corporate finance business; and

    (ii)   energy market activity and oil related activity;

    (iii) stock lending activity.

Paragraphs 9.2–9.15 explain the regime for collective investment schemes, trustee firms and OPS firms. Paragraphs 9.16–9.18 concern corporate finance business. Paragraphs 9.19–21 comment on energy market activity and oil market activity. Paragraph 19.22 comments on the special regime for stock lending activity.

We do not here consider COBS 19 (Pension – supplementary provisions) nor COBS 20 (with profits business) given that this work is intended as a general guide and these chapters are highly technical and product specific. On a similar basis, the provisions in COBS 18 for Lloyd's firms and authorised professional firms are regarded as outside the scope of this Guide.

9.1.1 Understanding the context

These provisions for specialist regimes look innocent enough. They are quite short, specific and of limited relevance. However, for business concerned with such areas, they are important – and background knowledge is required in order for them to be understood.

Following the style of the FSA's Handbook generally, the provisions contain much helpful guidance. Hopefully this Chapter of the Guide will further expand on this guidance for these particular types of business generally, and explain some of the relevant jargon, so that it becomes clear where the Handbook provisions fit in, before then summarising the rules, and commenting on their implications.

In order to make the Chapter more readable, the detail of the various rules is covered within a series of questions which might be asked by a newcomer to the area. The answers give some of the background to the issues as well as a summary of the relevant rules.

9.1.2 Recent changes

The conduct of business provisions have recently been revised pursuant to implementation of the EU Markets in Financial Instruments Directive ("MiFID") and the FSA's broader review of the conduct of business regime and general move towards more principles-based regulation. The provisions for non-MiFID specialist regimes are due to come into effect from 1 May 2008.

9.2 Why is there a special regime for collective investment schemes and trusts?

For collective investment schemes trustee firms and OPS firms, the COBS rules are only part of a larger picture.

Investment funds are intermediate structures interposed between investors and investments – they may be corporate, trust or contract-based. Trusts, including OPSs, are again interposed as an intermediate arrangement and are constituted by a trust document of some description. Each of these has its own legal basis and particular requirements – which are particularly extensive, for example, in the case of authorised funds and OPSs.

These requirements are not replaced or qualified by COBS, although, in some instances, the terms of the scheme may incorporate, by reference, certain FSA Handbook provisions, such as the trust deed of an authorised unit trust incorporating the COLL Sourcebook by reference. Generally COBS are in addition to the basic law provisions that apply to a particular intermediate structure.

Each FSA authorised firm's role in respect of a specific collective investment scheme or trust should be considered only as one relevant aspect to consider in connection with that collective investment scheme or trust's legal and regulatory position.

9.3   What is a collective investment scheme?

9.3.1   *Collective investment scheme definition*

Chapters 18.5 and 18.7 of COBS set out the regulations for operators and depositaries of collective investment schemes. The first hurdle, prior to understanding these regulations for operators and depositaries, is to look at what constitutes a "collective investment scheme" and the respective roles of its operator and depositary.

The term "collective investment scheme" encompasses various types of intermediate structures which can be interposed between a number of investors and a pool of investments. The UK definition of a collective investment scheme, which is in Sections 235–237 of the Financial Services and Markets Act 2000 ("FSMA 2000"), is particularly wide. A collective investment scheme means any:

> "arrangements with respect to property of any description, including money, the purpose or effect of which is to enable persons taking part in the arrangements (whether by becoming owners of the property or any part of it or otherwise) to participate in or receive profits or income arising from the acquisition, holding, management or disposal of the property or sums paid out of such profits or income".

The criteria which these arrangements must demonstrate in order to be a collective investment scheme under FSMA 2000 are as follows:

(a) participants do not have day-to-day control over the management of the property, whether or not they have the right to be consulted or to give directions; and

(b) either or both of the following characteristics must be present:

(i) the contributions of the participants and the profits or income out of which payments are to be made to the participants are pooled; and/or

(ii) the property is managed as a whole by and on behalf of the operator of the scheme.

Note that the property in which the scheme invests can be any property, not just securities and other investments regulated under FSMA 2000.

9.3.2 Open-ended investment company definition

No body corporate ("BC") other than an open-ended investment company ("OEIC") comes within the definition of a collective investment scheme. An OEIC is a collective investment scheme which satisfies both:

(a) the property condition, which is that the property belongs beneficially to and is managed by and on behalf of a BC having as its purpose the investment of its funds with the aim of:

(i) spreading the investment risk; and

(ii) giving its members the benefit of the results of the management of those funds by or on behalf of such body; and

(b) the investment condition, which is that, in relation to BC, a reasonable investor would, if he were to participate in the scheme:

(i) expect that he would be able to realise, within a period appearing to him to be reasonable, his investment in the scheme (represented, at any time, by the value of shares in, or securities of, BC held by him as a participant in the scheme); and

(ii) be satisfied that his investment would be realised on a basis calculated wholly or mainly by reference to the value of property in respect of which the scheme makes arrangements.

Although a closed-ended investment company does not constitute a collective investment scheme, a closed-ended entity set up as another legal form (e.g. as a unit trust or limited partnership) can constitute a collective investment scheme.

9.3.3 Exemptions

There are various exemptions to the scope of the definition of a collective investment scheme set out in the Financial Services and Markets Act 2000 (Collective Investment Schemes) Order 2001 (SI 2001/1062). These include exemptions for individual investment management arrangements, schemes not operated by way of business, certain employee share schemes, occupational and personal pension schemes and group arrangements.

Even so, the above-mentioned collective investment scheme definition covers a very wide range of pooled investment arrangements.

9.3.4 FSA guidance

The FSA's Perimeter Guidance Manual contains some guidance on the boundaries of the collective investment scheme regime, and in particular the OEIC definition.

9.4 What are the different types of schemes?

9.4.1 UK authorised funds

In practice, the most common investment funds which a UK business will encounter, and the funds to which Chapters 18.5 and 18.7 of COBS are most relevant, will be UK authorised funds. These may be:

(a) Authorised unit trusts: the long-established option for a UK retail fund is an authorised unit trust. A unit trust is constituted by a trust deed made between a unit trust manager and a trustee. It is authorised by the FSA and is subject to the FSA's Collective Investment Schemes Sourcebook ("COLL Sourcebook"[1]).

(b) ICVCs: the corporate version of a UK authorised unit trust is an ICVC – an investment company with variable capital. An ICVC is a special form of company, and is an OEIC. (UK authorised OEICS are now termed ICVCs in order to differentiate them from OEICS generally.) Introduced in 1997, ICVCs are subject to a special corporate code made under Treasury regulations (the Open-Ended Investment Companies Regulations 2001). An ICVC is governed by the terms of its instrument of incorporation. It is authorised by the FSA and is subject to the FSA's COLL Sourcebook. An ICVC must have an authorised corporate director ("ACD"), which has a similar role to a unit trust manager, and an appointed "depositary", which has a similar role to the trustee of a unit trust.

The COLL Sourcebook provides for three categories of scheme – UCITS schemes, non-UCITS retail schemes and qualified investor schemes.

The introduction of qualified investor schemes was intended to facilitate innovative developments for UK authorised funds. There are few specific restrictions which apply for these schemes. However there has been a slow take up of these because of particular tax issues. Note that these schemes should not be confused with unregulated collective investment schemes. They are authorised funds which are subject to less restrictive FSA rules than those applicable to the two categories of retail schemes. They may not however be promoted to the general public – effectively they are non-retail schemes.[2] They are not treated as packaged products with a consequent need for compliance with the FSA's rules on disclosure at point of sale.

---

[1] The COLL Sourcebook came into effect on 1 April 2004 and was introduced over a transitional period extending to February 2007.

[2] Note the revision of the qualified investor scheme rules: *see* FSA Policy Statement 07/18, commenting on the removal of the restriction on the promotion of qualified investor schemes in favour of relying on the restriction on issuing or transferring units to restricted categories of purchaser.

In relation to retail schemes, key features or simplified prospectus disclosure is required at point of sale in accordance with COBS 14.2. Simplified prospectus rules apply to "a simplified prospectus scheme" which includes UCITS schemes other than Section 264 recognised schemes (*see* 9.4.2 below) and any scheme where the manager has elected to produce a simplified prospectus instead of a key features document. For funds classified as UCITS schemes and for those others for which the managers make an appropriate election, the simplified prospectus should follow the terms set out in the EU Recommendation on the Simplified Prospectus. Note that the EU Commission has acknowledged that the simplified prospectus provisions have not proved effective and a revised Recommendation on the regime is expected to codify enhanced risk, cost and performance disclosures, with subsequent amendments to the UCITS Directive expected to follow.[3] For schemes other than simplified prospectus schemes, the FSA is pursuing its established key features approach. The FSA has confirmed it still considers the requirement to provide retail clients with either a simplified prospectus or a key features document as the most appropriate means of achieving the outcomes sought.[4]

9.4.2 Recognised schemes

UK authorised funds, together with "recognised schemes", comprise "regulated schemes" which can be promoted to the general public. Recognised schemes cover:

(a) Section 264 Undertaking for Collective Investment in Transferable Securities ("UCITS") schemes;
(b) Section 270 designated territory schemes; and
(c) Section 272 individually recognised schemes.

Recognised schemes are packaged products and are therefore, as mentioned above, subject to the product disclosure regime (COBS 13

---

[3] European Commission White Paper on enhancing the Single Market Framework for Investment Funds: 15 November 2006 and *see* European Commission Exposure Draft: Initial orientations for discussion on possible adjustments to the UCITS directive Part 5: Simplified prospectus – investor disclosure regime (part of a working document of DG Market Services published for discussion purposes). Also *see* CESR Consultation Paper on content and form of Key Investor Information disclosures for UCITS, October 2007.
[4] FSA Policy Statement 07/14, paragraph 6.

and 14). As a caveat to this however a Section 264 recognised UCITS scheme need only comply with its home state's simplified prospectus requirements, which is only to offer the simplified prospectus document.

9.4.3 Unregulated collective investment schemes

Schemes which are not UK authorised or recognised schemes are called "unregulated schemes". The title "unregulated" is indicative of the approach taken by the FSA in the Conduct of Business rules in respect of unregulated schemes. Subject to the requirements mentioned below, they are unregulated by the FSA (although of course an unregulated fund set up in an offshore jurisdiction may well be regulated in that jurisdiction to some greater or lesser extent). They are not within the packaged products regime. They cannot, however, be promoted to the general public. Unregulated schemes include unauthorised unit trusts and other pooled investment structures, such as limited partnerships.

9.5 Who operates a collective investment scheme?

The operator's identity and role is not fully defined in FSMA 2000. However, for most UK authorised funds, their identity and role is clear.

9.5.1 Unit trusts

For UK authorised or unauthorised unit trusts (where there is a separate trustee), the operator is the unit trust manager. For an authorised fund, the manager's role is set out in the COLL Sourcebook and, to some extent, in the fund's trust deed and prospectus; for an unauthorised fund, it is set out in the fund's trust deed.

9.5.2 ICVCs

For an ICVC, for FSMA 2000 purposes, the operator is the ICVC itself. However, for the purposes of the COBS rules, it is the ICVC or, if applicable, the ACD.

Note that the ICVC itself, although an authorised person under FSMA as well as being a form of collective investment scheme, is not subject to the COBS rules (except in relation to financial promotion rules which apply to an ICVC).[5]

The focus for conduct of business regulation is on the ACD. The ACD's role is set out in the Open-Ended Investment Company Regulations 2001, the COLL Sourcebook, and, to some extent, in the fund's instrument of incorporation and prospectus.

9.5.3 Unregulated schemes

For unregulated schemes, the position may well be similar but, for certain unregulated structures such as limited partnerships, it is not obvious, and there could, in theory, be more than one operator. The question is who is operating the collective investment scheme in terms of issuing and redeeming units, pricing units, dealing in investments, distributing income and reporting to investors. Note that the FSA Handbook Glossary definition of an operator refers to any person who, under the constitution or founding arrangements of the scheme, is responsible for the management of the property held for or within the scheme.

9.6 What is "scheme management activity"?

Operators of collective investment schemes, such as unit trust managers, have a variety of responsibilities.

"Scheme management activity" is defined for the purposes of the FSA rules in the Glossary as:

> "the management by an operator of the property held for or within the scheme of which it is the operator, excluding the receiving and holding of client money and safeguarding and administering investments."

In other words it encompasses asset management activities for collective investment schemes.

---

[5] Pursuant to the Conduct of MiFID Sourcebook (MiFID Transposition) Instrument 2007, with effect from 1 November 2007, an ICVC is brought within the financial promotion rules.

For scheme management activities, the modifications to the conduct of business rules explained in the following Sections apply. For an operator's other activities, the conduct of business rules in other Chapters apply as normal.

COBS continues with the established general approach to regulation of scheme management activity, although the FSA is making some amendments (as explained below). There is an exemption from MiFID for operators of collective investment schemes which applies in respect of any investment services or activities they may carry on in that capacity. There should therefore be no major impact resulting for collective investment scheme operators which are non-MiFID firms. To the extent that an operator also provides investment services or performs investment activities in a different capacity, these services and activities fall outside the scope of the exemption and the MiFID scope provisions of COBS apply.

9.7 What modifications apply to the COBS rules for operators?

9.7.1 General approach to modification

The relevant provisions for operators of collective investment schemes in COBS are short. They set out modifications to COBS provisions in relation to an operator's scheme management activities by cross-referencing other provisions of the COBS rules.

For a regulated scheme, detailed regulation of the operator of the scheme in relation to its operation of the scheme under the FSA's conduct of business regime is unnecessary. There is detailed regulation which is applicable to the scheme itself and, with that regulation, the role of the operator in respect of it, under the COLL Sourcebook and other documents.

(a) An authorised unit trust scheme is subject to Sections 242–261 FSMA 2000 and to the detailed rules in the COLL Sourcebook.
(b) An ICVC is subject to the Treasury's Open-Ended Investment Companies Regulations 2001 and to the detailed rules in the COLL Sourcebook.

(c) A recognised scheme is subject to regulation in the jurisdiction of its establishment and, in addition, will have to provide scheme facilities (i.e. redemption facilities and arrangements for inspection of documents) under the COLL Sourcebook.

For an unregulated scheme, no comparable prescribed terms exist in rules and regulations, but the scheme has its constitutional document. Also, as the range of their participants is limited, the retail investor protection concerns are not normally apparent.

Subject to the further particular regulations mentioned in 9.8 and 9.9 below, the modifications to the conduct of business requirements in respect of scheme management activities are therefore the same for regulated and unregulated schemes.

9.7.2 *Disapplication and modification of the conduct of business regime*

COBS 18.5.2 disapplies the COBS rules in respect of scheme management activity except as identified (and modified) as follows:

(a) application (COBS 1);
(b) acting honestly, fairly and professionally (COBS 2.1.1);
(c) inducements (COBS 2.3);
(d) agent as client and reliance on others (COBS 2.4);
(e) fair, clear and not misleading communications (COBS 4.2.1 to COBS 4.2.4);
(f) e-commerce (COBS 5.2);
(g) best execution – for a regulated scheme as if the scheme were a retail client (although, for client classification purposes, under COBS 3.5.2 a regulated scheme is classified as a professional client) and, for an unregulated scheme, see 9.7.2 below (COBS 11.2); Note that, on best execution, it is proposed that collective investment scheme operators are subject to the MiFID-based rules but the old exemption for an unregulated scheme (explained in 9.8 below) is retained. The parts of the new best execution rules likely to be of most relevance to CIS operators are expected to be those which apply to portfolio managers in COBS 11.2.30 and 11.2.32 to 11.2.34 (explained elsewhere in this Guide).
(h) client order handling (COBS 11.3);

265

(i)　　record keeping, client orders and decisions to deal (COBS 11.5);

(j)　　use of dealing commission (COBS 11.6); and

(k)　　operators of collective investment schemes (COBS 18.5).

Effectively therefore there are COBS equivalents of most of the previous COB 10 provisions to be applied, but some COB rules that are no longer thought necessary are removed.

9.7.3　General modifications

General modifications are also made under COBS 18.5 so that other conduct of business rules apply appropriately:

(a)　　references to "customer" are references to the "scheme" concerned;

(b)　　in relation to an unregulated scheme, references to terms of business or client agreements are references to the scheme documents of the unregulated scheme;

(c)　　also in relation to an unregulated scheme, where the operator is required to provide information to, and/or obtain consent from, a customer, the "customer" is the participant or potential participant in the scheme. In other words, the operator's customers are the investors.

Under COBS 3.6.2, a collective investment scheme authorised under the UCITS Directive or its management company is a per se eligible counterparty although it is expected that most schemes will in practice be categorised as professional clients. Other collective investment schemes and the management company of a scheme are per se professional clients. Note that, under COBS 3.2.3R(4) in relation to non-MiFID business if a firm provides services to a collective investment scheme which does not have separate legal personality, that collective investment scheme will be the firm's client. However, care should be taken in applying these provisions as, in many cases, a firm such as an investment manager carries on activities with or for an operator of the scheme rather than with or for a scheme itself.

9.7.4　Other applicable rules

Operators must comply with relevant provisions of the Handbook generally, for example:

(a)   the Principles for Businesses;
(b)   Senior Management Arrangements, Systems and Controls ("SYSC"); and
(c)   client money, if holding client money otherwise than as trustee of an unregulated collective investment scheme (Client Assets Sourcebook).

As mentioned above, UK authorised and recognised schemes (regulated schemes) are packaged products and COBS 13 and 14 contain particular provisions which relate to product disclosure and the customer's right to cancel or withdraw in respect of transactions in relation to such products.

9.8   Are there any additional rules for unregulated schemes?

For unregulated schemes, in addition to the modified COBS rules which are described in 9.7 above, there is one particular conduct of business rule to consider.

There is an exception to the requirement to offer best execution under COBS 11.2 in relation to an unregulated collective investment scheme whose scheme documents include a statement that best execution does not apply in relation to the scheme and in which:

(a)   no participant is a retail client; or
(b)   no current participant in the scheme was a retail client on joining the scheme as a participant.

9.9   If unregulated schemes are not subject to the COLL Sourcebook, what provisions govern them and what information is to be given about these?

Unregulated schemes are, as the name suggests, "unregulated" as to the nature of their constitution and the terms of that constitution. Under COBS 18.5, there are limited provisions relating to two aspects of the regulation of the documentation, and information provided to participants/investors.

9.9.1   Scheme documents

The first point to note is that scheme documents can consist of a number of documents, as long as it is clear that they constitute collectively the scheme documents and provided that the use of various documents in no way diminishes the significance of any of the statements which are required to be given to a potential participant.

The relevant rule is that an operator of an unregulated collective investment scheme must not accept a retail client as a participant in the scheme unless it has taken reasonable steps to offer and, if requested, provide scheme documents which adequately describe how the operation of the scheme is governed to the potential participant.

For those unregulated schemes which are not made available to retail clients, and this is the case with most, for example unauthorised unit trusts in order that they are tax effective, there may be no cause for concern. In other cases, COBS 18.5.10 should be considered. It is an evidential provision listing the matters about which scheme documents should include provision, as follows:

(a)   status disclosure by the operator where appropriate (for example for a UK operator that it is authorised and regulated by the Financial Services Authority);

(b)   the nature of the services that the operator will provide in relation to the scheme;

(c)   details of payments for services;

(d)   commencement;

(e)   accounting for transactions effected;

(f)   how the appointment of the operator may be terminated;

(g)   complaints procedure;

(h)   whether or not compensation may be available from the Financial Services Compensation Scheme or any other applicable compensation scheme, with relevant details;

(i)   the investment objectives for the portfolio of the scheme;

(j)   details of investment restrictions;

(k)   details regarding holding of scheme assets, cash and related matters, such as accounting for income received and the exercise of voting rights in respect of investments;

(l)   whether any scheme money may be held in a client bank account outside the UK;

(m) disclosure of the stabilised investments and exchange rate risk warnings;

(n) disclosure of conflict of interest and material interests;

(o) disclosure of use of dealing commission;

(p) disclosure as to whether the operator may act as principal in a transaction with the scheme;

(q) whether the scheme may enter into stock lending transactions;

(r) details of any possible contingent liability investment;

(s) periodic statements (*see* Section 9.9.2 below) and whether those statements will include some measure of performance and, if so, on what basis;

(t) valuation arrangements;

(u) borrowing parameters;

(v) whether there will be any underwriting commitments;

(w) whether there will be investment in other collective investment schemes operated or advised by the operator or an associate or a collective investment scheme which is not a regulated scheme; and

(x) whether any of the investments in securities are underwritten by the operator.

The above list is very similar to the usual list of contents one expects to see in a terms of a business letter.

The point to notice is that there is an additional disclosure point under COBS 18.5.8 where the scheme is an unregulated collective investment scheme and no current participant in the scheme was a retail client on joining the scheme as a participant. In such a case, the scheme documents must include a statement that explains that:

(a) if a participant is reclassified as a retail client subsequent to join-ing the scheme as a participant, then the operator may continue to treat all participants in the scheme as though they were not retail clients;

(b) if a participant is reclassified as a retail client subsequent to join-ing the scheme as a participant, then COBS 18.5.4 modification of best execution requirements (*see* 9.7.2 above) will continue to apply to that scheme; and

(c) in the event of a reclassification described in (a) the operator will not be required to provide best execution under COBS 11.2 in relation to the scheme.

However, the operator still has to comply with other conduct of business provisions as a result of reclassification of a participant as a retail client, for example the requirement under COBS 18.5.11 to provide periodic statements to participants who are private customers in an unregulated collective investment scheme (*see* 9.9.2 below).

Guidance in COBS 18.5.7 makes it clear that COBS 18.5.8 is not designed to require that scheme documents must be produced for an unregulated scheme. However, if they do exist, they must make it clear that, if a participant is reclassified as a retail client, this reclassification will not affect certain scheme management activities of the operator of the scheme.

9.9.2 Periodic statements

The general section on periodic statements in COBS 16.3 is modified so as to take account of the way in which the results for an unregulated scheme are reported to its investors.

Under COBS 18.5.11 an operator of an unregulated scheme must, promptly and at suitable intervals, provide to participants in the scheme a written statement which contains adequate information on the value and composition of the portfolio of the scheme at the beginning and end of the period of the statement, subject to the exceptions from the requirement to provide a periodic statement in COBS 18.5.13. Operators must keep records of periodic statements for a minimum period of three years.

There is an evidential provision (COBS 18.5.14E) setting out the details regarding periodic statements, that is:

(a) statements should be provided at least:

(i)   six monthly; or
(ii) once in any other period (not exceeding 12 months) which has been mutually agreed between the operator and the participants in the scheme;

(b) the information should be that set out in COBS 18.5.17E and COBS 18.5.18E if appropriate, or such information as a participant who is a retail client ordinarily resident outside the UK (or, if the operator is an outgoing electronic commerce activity ("ECA") provider, outside the EEA) or who is a professional client has, on his own initiative, agreed with the operator as adequate.

9.9.3 *Effect on existing schemes*

Imposition of these rules should not impose a great burden as compared with the standard practice. The rules are designed to enforce best commercial practice. Firms normally volunteer documentation which contains most of the required information for the contents of scheme documents set out in the above list of provisions, irrespective of the rules. In practice, the issues which will arise will be in drafting scheme documents for any unregulated schemes which may have participants who are retail clients.

9.10 What is a depositary?

For conduct of business purposes, the term "depositary" is defined in relation to the various types of schemes:

(a) ICVCs: for an ICVC, the depositary is the appointed depositary for the purposes of regulation 5 of the Treasury's Open-Ended Investment Companies Regulations 2001, to whom is entrusted the safekeeping of all the scheme property.
(b) Authorised unit trusts: for an authorised unit trust, the depositary is the trustee.
(c) Other unit trust schemes: for any other unit trust scheme (i.e. any other collective investment scheme whose property is held on trust), the depositary is the person holding the property on trust for the participants.
(d) Other collective investment schemes: for any other collective investment scheme, the depositary is any person to whom the property which is subject to the scheme is entrusted for safekeeping.

9.11 What modifications apply to trustee firms who are depositaries?

9.11.1 General approach

The definition of scheme management activity (which is the area of activity covered by COBS 18.5) specifically excludes the receiving and holding of client money and safeguarding and administering investments. The depositary's role is centred on the safekeeping of scheme assets and this is the area covered by COBS 18.7.

For a regulated collective investment scheme, the depositary, like the unit trust manager or ACD, is subject to the COLL Sourcebook rules and, for ICVCs, in addition, the Treasury's Open-Ended Investment Companies Regulations 2001, which apply to the scheme.

For an unregulated collective investment scheme, the scheme documents set out the depositary's role.

Again, the task is to consider the appropriate modifications to the general conduct of business regime. The modifications are explained in the following sections.

9.11.2 Specific modifications

The tables for the conduct of business modifications for depositaries in COBS cover depositaries of both regulated and unregulated collective investment schemes in one table.

The conduct of business rules are basically disapplied except for those specified, as set out below:

(a) acting honestly, fairly and professionally (COBS 2.1);
(b) inducements (COBS 2.3, except COBS 2.3.1R(2)(b) and 2.3.2R so a prohibition on inducements remains but the elements of the new provision whereby, in relation to MiFID business, the fee or commission must be designed to enhance the quality of service to the client and be disclosed, are not applied). Depositaries may be unlikely to make or receive inducements but applying this provision is intended to ensure that there are no loopholes in the rules;

(c)　communicating with clients, including financial promotions (COBS 4), but only in relation to communicating or approving a financial promotion (i.e. not the wider general communication rule); and

(d)　personal account dealing (COBS 11.7).

The Client Assets Sourcebook specifically refers to custody matters for collective investment schemes. CASS 4.1–4.4 do not apply to a depositary when acting as such. In other respects, it applies generally so that references to the "client" refer to the trustee, trust or collective investment scheme as appropriate or, in the case of mandates, to the trustee, collective investment scheme or collective investment scheme instrument as appropriate.

9.11.3　*General modifications*

Note that, in applying the modified rules for depositaries, the depositary's "client" is the collective investment scheme. As mentioned in 9.7.3 above, however, it is possible for a scheme to be re-classified under COBS 3. (Care should, however, be taken in applying this provision as a custodian or other party may carry on activities with or for the depositary of the scheme rather than with or for the scheme).

9.11.4　*Other applicable rules*

Depositaries must also comply with other parts of the FSA's Handbook, in particular:

(a)　the Principles for Businesses; and

(b)　SYSC.

9.12　What are trustee firms?

Special provisions apply not only to depositaries (as described in 9.10 and 9.11 above) but also to trustee firms which are not depositaries, and this section is concerned with such firms.

Generally trustees, nominees and personal representatives are exempt from the requirement to be authorised, under Article 66 of the

Financial Services and Markets Act 2000 (Regulated Activities) Order 2001 (SI 2001/544). This exemption covers:

(a) a bare trustee, in Scotland, or nominee (X) entering into transactions which involve dealing in investments, in Scotland, as principal when acting on Y's instructions, providing that X does not hold himself out as providing a service of buying and selling regulated investments; and

(b) if a trustee or personal representative is not remunerated, other than as a trustee or personal representative, the following activities of that person:

    (i)   arranging deals in investments;
    (ii)   managing investments, unless he holds himself out as providing such a service, or he is managing OPS assets and he is treated as carrying on that activity by way of business;
    (iii) assisting in the administration and performance of a contract of insurance unless he holds himself out as providing such a service;
    (iv)   safeguarding and administering investments, unless he holds himself out as providing such a service;
    (v)   sending dematerialised instructions; or
    (vi)   giving advice to fellow trustees or personal representatives or beneficiaries.

However, this exemption will not be available in all circumstances. In such circumstances (and if no other exemption is available), a trustee or personal representative may require authorisation and become a "trustee firm".

The rules explained in 9.13 below concern such trustee firms.

9.13 What special rules apply to trustee firms that are not depositaries?

9.13.1 General approach

There are particular modifications to COBS for trustee firms which are not depositaries. The trusts which are relevant to such trustee firms often do not have applicable detailed rules and regulations (outside the conduct of business rules) similar to those that govern collective investment schemes. Consequently, the application of COBS is more extensive for such trustee firms than for depositaries.

9.13.2 *Effect of MiFID*

With the implementation of MiFID, the regime for trustees was revised. Trustee firms carrying on MiFID investment services or activities on a professional basis as trustee fall within the scope of MiFID. (The article 2(1)(h) exemption from MiFID which applies for depositaries is not relevant).

The FSA indicated that it wished to apply COBS to MiFID scope trustee firms only to the extent required to implement MiFID. Certain MiFID business related disapplications and concessions under the pre-MiFID regime had to be discontinued.

MiFID does not deal specifically with the treatment of trustee firms. The questions of who is the trustee's client (whether it is, for example, the beneficiary, another trustee or the trust) is therefore not addressed by MiFID. Where a trustee firm owes a duty to a client under an applicable rule in COBS, the trustee firm is required to consider who, in the context of that rule and having regard to the particular arrangement, is the most appropriate person to treat as its client (COBS 18.1.6G).

9.13.3 *Disapplications for MiFID business*

In relation to MiFID business carried on by a trustee firm (other than as a depositary or the trustee of a personal pension scheme or stakeholder pension scheme), the following COBS provisions do not apply:

(a) describing the breadth of a firm's advice on investments (COBS 6.2);
(b) disclosing information about services, fees and commission – packaged products (COBS 6.3);
(c) disclosure of charges, remuneration and commission (COBS 6.4);
(d) suitability reports (COBS 9.4);
(e) special rules for providing basic advice on a stakeholder product (COBS 9.6);

(f)   guidance on contingent liability transaction (COBS 16.3.9);
(g)   quotations for surrender values (COBS 16.5);
(h)   life insurance contracts – communications to clients (COBS 16.6); and
(i)   information to be provided in accordance with COBS 16.2.1 R and 16.3 (COBS 16 Annex 1 R(1)14).

The following provisions of COBS are unlikely to be relevant:

(a)   distance communications (COBS 5);
(b)   preparing product information (COBS 13);
(c)   providing product information (COBS 14.2);
(d)   cancellation (COBS 15);
(e)   claims handling for long-term care insurance (COBS 17);
(f)   energy market activity and oil market activity (COBS 18.2);
(g)   corporate finance business (COBS 18.3);
(h)   stock lending activity (COBS 18.4);
(i)   pensions – supplementary provisions (COBS 19); and
(j)   with profits (COBS 20).

9.13.4   Other applicable rules

Trustee firms must also comply with other parts of the Handbook, in particular:

(a)   the Principles for Businesses; and
(b)   SYSC.

9.14   When must a trustee firm obtain proper advice?

COBS does not carry forward the COB 11.8 provisions for a trustee firm to obtain and consider proper advice whenever it intends to exercise a power of investment, except where there are reasonable grounds for not doing so. More reliance will therefore now fall back on the requirement to obtain proper advice which is implicit in trust law at common law – and indeed is explicit in Section 5 Trustee Act 2000.

9.15 What regulation applies to an occupational pension scheme firm?

9.15.1 *Position for an occupational pension scheme*

An OPS is not an investment for the purposes of the FSMA 2000, and so it does not require an authorised "operator". The activities of a trustee of an OPS are usually excluded from being regulated activities under the FSMA 2000 unless the trustee holds himself out as providing a service of managing investments by way of business or he takes day-to-day decisions relating to the management of the scheme's investments (*see* Article 66 of the Financial Services and Markets Act 2000 (Regulated Activities) Order 2001 (SI 2001/544) (and in particular paragraph (3) of that Article) and Article 4 of the Financial Services and Markets Act 2000 (Carrying on Regulated Activities by Way of Business) Order 2001 (SI 2001/1177) as amended. Note Chapter 10 of the FSA's Perimeter Guidance Manual on activities relating to pension schemes.

For certain entities such as trustees involved with OPSs, however, an authorisation issue may arise and an OPS firm may be authorised.

9.15.2 *Occupational pension scheme firms*

An OPS firm is a firm which:

(a)   carries on OPS activity (*see* 9.15.3 below); and
(b)   is one or more of the following:

    (i)   a trustee of the OPS in question;
    (ii)   a company owned by the trustees of the OPS in question;
    (iii)   a company which is:

- an employer in relation to the OPS in question in respect of its employees or former employees or their dependants; or
- a company within the group which includes such an employer; or
- an administering authority subject to the Local Government Superannuation Regulations 1986,

or a firm which has satisfied these requirements at any time during the past 12 months but is no longer able to comply with those requirements because of a change in the control or ownership of the employer referred to above during that period.

9.15.3 Occupational pension scheme activity

OPS activity is:

(a) managing investments in a case where the assets managed are:

    (i) held for the purposes of an OPS; or

    (ii) held for the purposes of welfare trust established by a person who is, or has at any time during the past 12 months been, an associate of the OPS firm; or

    (iii) assets of a collective investment scheme the contributions to which consist entirely of assets held for an OPS;

(b) any one or more of the following activities undertaken in the course of, or incidental to, the operation of such an OPS, welfare trust or collective investment scheme:

    (i) dealing in investments as principal;

    (ii) dealing in investments as agent;

    (iii) arranging (bringing about) deals in investments;

    (iv) making arrangements with a view to transactions in investments;

    (v) safeguarding and administering investments;

    (vi) advising on investments; and

    (vii) receiving or holding client money.

9.15.4 Occupational pension scheme firm regulation

For any OPS activity undertaken by an OPS firm, COBS applies with the following modifications:

(a) references to "client" are to the relevant OPS or welfare trust in respect of which the OPS firm acts;

(b) where an OPS firm is required by any rule in COBS to provide information to, or to obtain consent from, a client, that firm must ensure that the information is provided to, or consent obtained from, each of the trustees of the relevant OPS or welfare trust in respect of which that firm acts, unless the context requires otherwise; and

(c) COBS is modified, notably to modify the context of periodic statements, and COBS 8 does not apply so an OPS firm that is also the trustee of the scheme will not be required to send terms of business to itself.

Note that any OPS firm wishing to obtain best execution will have to request best execution.[6]

9.16 How is corporate finance business regulated?

Corporate finance business has, in the past, either been outside the scope of regulation or, where within the scope of regulation, subject to a light touch regime with only certain of the old Conduct of Business Rules applying.

The corporate finance business which comes within the scope of FSA regulation is designated investment business (principally arranging deals in investments and advising on investments) where it comes within the scope of the corporate finance business definition in the Glossary to the FSA Handbook. This can encompass advice to issuers of investments; advice to certain entities on terms on which business activities or undertakings are to be financed, structured, managed, controlled, regulated or reported upon; merger, de-mergers, reorganisations or reconstructions involving investments issued by the relevant person; and being involved in negotiations or decisions relating to the commercial financial or strategic intentions or requirements of a business or prospective business.

With the implementation of MiFID, those firms which are regulated for corporate finance business will fall into one of two categories – either subject to the COBS generally because the corporate finance business is MiFID business or a concessionary regime similar to the

---

[6] *See* for further details Section 9 of FSA Consultation Paper 07/09 May 2007 paragraphs 9.7–9.12 and Section 9 of FSA Policy Statement 07/18 of October 2007 at paragraph 9.5.

old light touch regime for corporate finance business which is non-MiFID business under COBS 18.3.3.

9.17 What COBS rules apply for corporate finance business which is MiFID business?

Most corporate finance business is undertaken by firms which are within the scope of MiFID and therefore it is not possible for the FSA to apply a concessionary regime in respect of such firms. All relevant COBS rules implementing MiFID apply to the MiFID business of such firms.

COBS 18.3.1 states that the provisions of COBS do not apply in respect of corporate finance business carried on by a firm which is MiFID business as follows:

(a) describing the breadth of a firm's advice on investments (COBS 6.2);
(b) disclosing information about services fees and commissions – packaged products (COBS 6.3);
(c) disclosure of charges for remuneration and commission (COBS 6.4);
(d) suitability report (COBS 9.4);
(e) special rules for providing basic advice on a stakeholder product (COBS 9.6);
(f) use of dealing commission (COBS 11.6);
(g) guidance on contingent liability transaction (COBS 16.3.9);
(h) quotations for surrender values (COBS 16.5);
(i) life insurance contracts – communications to clients (COBS 16.6); and
(j) information to be provided in accordance with COBS 16.2.1R and 16.3 regarding occasional reporting and periodic reporting (COBS 16 Annex 1R(1)14).

The following provisions in COBS are unlikely to be relevant to any corporate finance business carried on a firm which is MiFID business:

(a) distance communications except in relation to distance contracts concluded with consumers (COBS 5);

(b) insurance mediation (COBS 7);
(c) preparing product information (COBS 13);
(d) providing product information (COBS 14.2);
(e) cancellation except cancellation of withdrawal rights in relation to distance contracts concluded with consumers (COBS 15);
(f) claims handling for long-term care insurance (COBS 17);
(g) trustee firms regime (COBS 18.1);
(h) energy market activity and oil market activity (COBS 18.2);
(i) stock lending activity (COBS 18.4);
(j) supplementary provisions (COBS 19); and
(k) with profits (COBS 20).

9.18 What COBS rules apply for corporate finance business which is non-MiFID business?

It is possible however for some firms to carry on corporate finance business which is non-MiFID business. They may, for example, fall within the Article 2(1)(c) exemption for professional firms who carry on an investment service which is incidental to professional activity or the Article 3 exemption which exempts firms who do not hold client funds or securities; only receive and transmit orders and/or provide investment advice in relation to transferable securities and units in collective investment undertakings; and only transmit orders to a limited range of other firms.

For such firms, the only provisions of COBS which apply are as follows (and note that they apply as they apply for other types of non-MiFID business – particular COBS rules can apply differently to MiFID and non-MiFID business, notably for example, inducements):

(a) application (COBS 1);
(b) acting honestly, fairly and professionally (COBS 2.1.1);
(c) inducements (COBS 2.3);
(d) agent as client and reliance of others (COBS 2.4);
(e) client categorisation (COBS 3);
(f) communications to clients including financial promotions, except COBS 4.5–4.11 (COBS 4);
(g) the information or the requirements of the distance marketing directive but only in relation to distance contracts concluded with consumers (COBS 5.1);

(h)   e-commerce (COBS 5.2);
(i)   personal account dealing (COBS 11.7);
(j)   investment research (COBS 12); and
(k)   cancellation but only in relation to distance contracts completed with consumers. Cancellation is unlikely to be particularly relevant to a corporate finance business because distance contracts concluded with consumers in the course of corporate finance business will be exempt from COBS 15 if the price of the financial service is dependent on fluctuations in the financial market outside the firm's control (COBS 15).

Note that the disapplications applied under the old Conduct of Business Sourcebook have under this regime been extended to provisions covering consumers understanding of risk, information about the firm, suitability, and customer order and execution records. This additional disapplication of certain rules is intended by the FSA to give corporate finance business firms slightly more flexibility about the information they give to their clients. The FSA's rationale is that, because the consumers of these services are experienced corporate entities, there should be no prejudice to the investor protection objective.

9.19   What is energy market activity and oil market activity?

COBS 18.2 relates to energy market activity and oil market activity. Energy market activity is defined in the FSA Handbook Glossary and covers:

(a)   any regulated activity in relation to an energy investment or to energy which is the executing of own account transactions on a recognised investment exchange or designated investment exchange or, if it is not performing the executing of transactions on such exchanges, it is performed in connection with or for persons who are not retail clients; and
(b)   establishing, operating or winding up of a collective investment scheme which is an energy collective investment scheme in which retail clients do not participate.

Oil market activity is defined in the FSA Glossary Handbook as any regulated activity in relation to an oil investment on a similar basis.

As explained in paragraph 9.17 relating to corporate finance business, the FSA has, with the COBS rules on implementation of MiFID, had to disapply various previous concessionary provisions from the conduct of business regime. All relevant COBS rules implementing MiFID will apply to the specialist regime activities where they constitute MiFID business of the firm concerned.

9.20 What rules apply for corporate energy market activity and oil market activity which is non-MiFID business?

In relation to non-MiFID business, COBS 18.2.3 provides that only the following COBS provisions will apply to energy market activity or oil market activity:

(a) application (COBS 1);
(b) acting honestly, fairly and professionally (COBS 2.1.1);
(c) agent as client and reliance on others (COBS 2.4);
(d) client categorisation (COBS 3);
(e) communication to clients including financial promotions, but only in relation to communicating or approving a financial promotion (COBS 4);
(f) e-commerce (COBS 6.2);
(g) investment research (COBS 13); and
(h) occasional reporting requirement (COBS 16.1).

The only COBS provisions which apply to energy market activity or oil market activity which is non-MiFID business and which, if the firm were not authorised, would not be regulated activity because of Article 16 (dealing in contractually based investments) or 22 (deals with or through authorised persons etc) of the Regulated Activities Order are as follows:

(a) application (COBS 1);
(b) agent as client and reliance on others (COBS 2.4);
(c) unregulated collective investment schemes (COBS 4.12); and
(d) e-commerce (COBS 5.2).

For non-MiFID business related commodity derivative instruments, all of COBS applies except COBS 11.2 relating to best execution.

Instead there are specific rules on best execution for non-MiFID business related to commodity and exotic derivative instruments set out in COBS 18.2.6–18.2.9. A firm that executes a customer order in the course of carrying out such activities must provide best execution except where the firm has agreed with a professional client that it need not owe such a duty; or the firm relies on another person to whom it passes a customer order for execution to provide best execution (if it has taken reasonable care to ensure that he will do so). In this context, to provide best execution, a firm must:

(a)   take reasonable care to ascertain the price which is the best available for the customer order in the relevant market at the time for transactions of the kind and the size concerned; and

(b)   execute the customer order at a price which is no less advantageous to the customer, unless the firm has taken reasonable steps to ensure that it would be in the customer's best interests not to do so. The evidential provision at COBS 18.2.9 provides an indication of how a firm should ascertain the price which is the best available.

9.21   What rules apply to energy market activity and oil market activity which is MiFID business?

COBS 18.2.1 sets out that the following provisions in COBS do not apply in relation to any energy market activity or oil market activity carried on by a firm which is MiFID business:

(a)   describing the breadth of a firm's advice on investments (COBS 6.2);

(b)   disclosing information about the services, fees and commission – packaged products (COBS 6.3);

(c)   disclosure of charges, remuneration and commission (COBS 6.4);

(d)   suitability report (COBS 9.4);

(e)   special rules for providing basic advice on a stakeholder product (COBS 9.6);

(f)   use of dealing commission (COBS 11.6);

(g)   guidance on contingent liability transaction (COBS 16.3.9);

(h)   quotations for surrender values (COBS 16.5);
(i)   life insurance contracts – communications to clients (COBS 16.6); and
(j)   information to be provided in accordance with COBS 16.2.1R and 16.3 (COBS 16 annex 1R(1)14).

The following provisions in COBS are unlikely to be relevant to such activity:

(a)   distance communications (COBS 5);
(b)   insurance mediation (COBS 7);
(c)   preparing product information (COBS 13);
(d)   providing product information to clients (COBS 14.2);
(e)   cancellation (COBS 15);
(f)   claims handling for long-term care insurance (COBS 17);
(g)   trustee firms regime (COBS 18.1);
(h)   corporate finance business (COBS 18.3);
(i)   stock lending activity (COBS 18.4);
(j)   pensions supplementary provisions (COBS 19); and
(k)   with profits (COBS 20).

This guidance provision states the provisions which are simply unlikely to be relevant to such activity.

9.22   Are there any special provisions for stock lending?

Particular provisions apply for stock lending activity. Stock lending activity is defined in the FSA Handbook Glossary as the activity of undertaking a transaction for the disposal of a designated investment subject to an obligation or right to re-acquire the same or a similar designated investment from the same counterparty.

As explained above in relation to corporate finance business and energy market activity and oil market activity, under COBS there must now be a distinction between MiFID and non-MiFID business (given that the FSA must apply all relevant COBS rules implementing MiFID where they constitute MiFID business of the firms concerned).

COBS 18.4 does however set out the provisions of COBS which do not apply in relation to any stock lending activity which is MiFID business:

(a) describing the breadth of the firm's advice on investments (COBS 6.2);

(b) disclosing information about services fees and commission – packaged products (COBS 6.3);

(c) disclosure of charges, remuneration and commission (COBS 6.4);

(d) suitability report (COBS 9.4);

(e) special rules for providing basic advice on a stakeholder product (COBS 9.6);

(f) use of dealing commission (COBS 11.6);

(g) guidance on contingent liability transaction (COBS 16.3.9);

(h) quotations for surrender values (COBS 16.5);

(i) life insurance contracts – communications to clients (COBS 16.6); and

(j) information to be provided in accordance with COBS 16.2.1 and 16.3 (COBS 16 Annex 1R(1)14).

Further, the following provisions in COBS are unlikely to be relevant in relation to stock lending activity carried on by a firm which is MiFID business:

(a) distance communications except in relation to distance contracts concluded with consumers (COBS 5);

(b) insurance mediation (COBS 7);

(c) preparing product information (COBS 13);

(d) providing product information (COBS 14.2);

(e) cancellation, except cancellation and withdrawal rights in relation to distance contracts concluded with consumers (COBS 15);

(f) claims handling for long-term care insurance (COBS 17);

(g) trustee firms regime (COBS 18.1);

(h) energy market activity and oil market activity (COBS 18.2);

(i) corporate finance business (COBS 18.3);

(j) pensions – supplementary provisions (COBS 19); and

(k) with profits (COBS 20).

Index

All indexing is to paragraph numbers

advising on investments 3.12
activities in connection with sale of
goods or supply of services
3.29.3
activities in course of profession or
non-investment business 3.29.2
appropriateness rule 7.2.3
Business Order 4.3.4
COBS rules 5.2.2
FSA Guidance 3.12.4
groups 3.29.4
joint enterprises 3.29.4
in newspapers etc 3.12.3.1
overseas firms 3.29.7
personal recommendations 7.2.2
Professions Order 4.2.6, 4.2.7
regulated activities 3.12
exclusions 3.12.3, 3.29.2, 3.29.3,
3.29.4, 3.29.5, 3.29.7
sale of body corporate 3.29.5
suitability rule 7.2.2
trustees or personal representatives
3.29.1
affiliates
client money regime 8.5.2.5
custody rules 8.3.1
agent
client categorisation and 6.3
Client Money Trust 8.5.3.2
dealing as *see* dealing as agent
appointed representative (AR)
content of AR contracts 4.4.4
definition 4.4.1
Regulations *see* AR Regulations
appropriateness rule 7.2.3
AR Regulations 4.4.1
activities not requiring authorisation
4.4.3

content of AR contracts 4.4.4
scope 4.4.2
arrangers
custody rules 8.3.1
attorney
managing investments 3.17.3.1
authorised person 2.1
meaning 1.2.1

bailment of tangibles 8.3.2.5
banker's draft 2.5
best execution 7.2.4
all reasonable steps 7.2.4.4
best possible result 7.2.4.3
COBS rules 7.2.4, 9.7.2
eligible counterparties 7.2.4.1
executing orders 7.2.4.2
order execution policy 7.2.4.5
portfolio managers 7.2.4.6
professional clients 7.2.4.1
receivers and transmitters of orders
7.2.4.6
retail clients 7.2.4.1
bills of exchange 2.5
body corporate
activities carried on in connection
with sale 3.29.5
client categorisation 6.3
bonds 2.5
breakdown insurance 3.4.3.2
business, activities in course of
general exclusions 3.29.2
**business angel-led enterprise capital
funds** 3.29.12
Business Order 4.3.1
accepting deposits 4.3.2, 4.3.3
advising on investments 4.3.4
carrying on investment business not
by way of business 4.3.4

collective investment schemes 4.3.4
custody services 4.3.4
dealing as agent 4.3.4
dealing as principal 4.3.4
deals, arranging 4.3.4
deposit taking not by way of business
    4.3.3
e-money activities 4.3.5
insurance mediation 4.3.6
Lloyd's 4.3.4
managing investments 4.3.4
    occupational pension schemes
    4.3.5
mortgages 4.3.7
multilateral trading facility operation
    4.3.4
pension schemes 4.3.4
regulated home purchase plans 4.3.2,
    4.3.7
regulated home reversion plans 4.3.2,
    4.3.7
scope 4.3.2
sending dematerialised instructions
    4.3.4

cancellation rights 7.3.4
certificates
of deposit 2.5
representing investments 2.5.1
representing securities 2.5
cheques 2.5
Child Trust Fund 3.16.2
client categorisation and 6.3
clearing services 2.5.1
client asset regime 8.1
client money regime *see* client money
    regime
collateral 8.4
    full transfer of ownership 8.4, 8.7.1
    rehypothecation 8.4
custody rules *see* custody rules
EEA firms 8.1
mandate rules 8.10
trustees
    client money regime 8.5.2.7
    custody rules 8.3.1
client categorisation 6.1, 6.12

agents 6.3
Child Trust Fund, services relating to
    6.3
COBS rules 6.1, 6.3
    MiFID compared 6.2.1
consequences 6.9
    incorrect categorisation 6.11
eligible counterparty 6.1, 6.2.1, 6.6
    regulatory protections 6.10
incorrect categorisation 6.11
market counterparty 6.8
MiFID 6.1
    changes in criteria and procedures
    6.2.2
    COBS rules compared 6.2.1
    general approach to
        implementation 6.2.4
    implementation 6.2
    more retail clients 6.2.3
notification to client 6.3
policies 6.7
prior history 6.2
procedures 6.7
professional client 6.1, 6.5
qualitative criteria 6.2.2
quantitative requirements 6.2.2
re-categorisation request 6.3
records 6.7
retail clients 6.1, 6.2.3, 6.4
transitional provisions 6.8
client information *see* information for
    clients
client limit orders 7.2.6
client money bank accounts
MiFID rules 8.7.4
non-MiFID rules
    designated accounts 8.5.4.1
    group accounts 8.5.4.3
    non-approved banks 8.5.4.2
    overseas accounts 8.5.4.4
    structure 8.5.4
client money regime
MiFID rules 8.7
    accounts 8.8
    client bank accounts 8.7.4
    delivery versus payment (DVP)
        transactions 8.7.1

distribution of client money on a default 8.9
organisational requirements 8.7.2
passing client money to third parties 8.7.5
reconciliations 8.8
records 8.8
scope 8.7.1
segregation 8.7.3
non-MiFID rules 8.5
  affiliates 8.5.2.5
  bank accounts *see* client money bank accounts
  banks 8.5.2.2
  client money calculation 8.5.5
  Client Money Trust *see* Client Money Trust
  delivery versus payment (DVP) transactions 8.5.2.4
  money due and payable 8.5.2.1
  opting out of regime 8.5.2.3
  Part 30 futures firms 8.5.2.9
  Quistclose trust 8.5.1
  scope 8.5.2
  solicitors 8.5.2.6
  trustee firms 8.5.2.7
  unclaimed client money balances 8.5.2.8
"the broker's advantage" 8.5.1
Client Money Trust 8.5.3
agents 8.5.3.2
client entitlements 8.5.3.3
distribution of client money on a default 8.5.3.6, 8.9
interest on client monies 8.5.3.4
operation 8.5.3.1
passing client money to third parties 8.5.3.5, 8.7.5
representatives 8.5.3.2
segregation 8.5.3.1
COBS rules 1.2.2, 5.1, 5.4
action by private person under 5.1
activities covered 5.2.2
advising on investments 5.2.2
agent as client 5.3.10
application
  all firms 5.3.1

general application rule 5.1, 5.2, 5.2.1
MiFID or equivalent third country business 5.3.1, 5.3.6
specific activities 5.2.5–5.2.7
best execution 7.2.4, 9.7.2, 9.8
breach 5.1
client asset regime *see* client asset regime
client categorisation 6.1, 6.3
  MiFID compared 6.2.1
collective investment schemes *see* collective investment schemes
consumer credit business 5.2.2
consumer protection 5.2.2
corporate finance business 5.2.6
  MiFID business 9.17
  non-MiFID business 9.18
  stock lending activity 5.2.5, 9.22
  see also energy market activity; oil market activity
deals, arranging 5.2.2
depositaries 9.11
disclosures about the firm 5.3.5
EEA
  firms 5.2.1
  territorial scope 5.2.3
eligible counterparties 5.2.2
energy market activity 5.2.7, 9.19
  MiFID business 9.21
  non-MiFID business 9.20
enforcement proceedings 5.1
evidential provisions 5.1
exclusion of liability 5.3.4
financial promotion 1.2.5, 1.2.6
guidance provisions 5.1
"honesty, fairly and professionally" requirement 5.3.2-5.3.3
inducements 5.3.6
  exceptions to rule 5.3.7
  packaged products 5.3.8
  reasonable non-monetary benefits 5.3.8
  record of disclosures 5.3.9
information barriers 5.3.12
Lloyd's, application to 5.2.2
managing investments 5.2.2

MiFID and 5.1, 5.2.2, 5.2.3, 5.3.1
multilateral trading facilities 5.2.2
nature 5.1
oil market activity 5.2.7, 9.19
  MiFID business 9.21
  non-MiFID business 9.20
overreaching provisions 5.1
overseas branches 5.2.3
packaged products, inducements 5.3.8
periodic statements 7.3.5.2, 9.9.2
private person, right of action 5.1
reasonable non-monetary benefits
  5.3.8
record-keeping 1.2.5, 1.2.6, 6.7
  inducement disclosures 5.3.9
reliance on others 5.3.11
scope 5.2.2
service companies 5.2.1
Specialist Regimes 5.2.1, 5.2.4
stock lending activity 5.2.5, 9.22
suitability rule 7.2.2
territorial scope 5.2.3
types of activity covered 5.2.2
UCITS qualifiers 5.2.1
collateral
client asset regime 8.4
full transfer of ownership 8.4, 8.7.1
rehypothecation 8.4
collective investment schemes 2.6,
  2.6.1, 9.1
authorised unit trusts 9.4.1, 9.7.1
best execution 9.7.2
bodies corporate 2.6.1
Business Order 4.3.4
certain employee share schemes 2.6.1
certain funds relating to leasehold
  property 2.6.1
clearing services 2.6.1
COBS rules
  best execution 9.7.2, 9.8
  depositaries 9.11
  disapplication 9.7.2
  effect of rules on existing schemes
    9.9.3
  modifications 9.7
  periodic statements 9.9.2
  scheme management activity 9.6

commercial purposes related to
  existing business 2.6.1
common accounts 2.6.1
corporate finance business *see*
  corporate finance business
custody rules 8.3.1
debt issues 2.6.1
definition 2.6.1, 9.3.1
  exemptions 9.3.3
  FSA guidance 9.3.4
  open-ended investment company
    2.6, 2.6.2, 9.3.2
depositary
  COBS rules 9.11
  definition 9.10
  documents 9.9.1
employee share schemes 2.6.1
enterprise initiative schemes 2.6.1
exemptions 9.3.3
franchise arrangements 2.6.1
FSA guidance 9.3.4
funeral plan contracts 2.6.1
group schemes 2.6.1
ICVCs 9.4.2, 9.5.1, 9.7.1
individual investment management
  arrangements 2.6.1
individual pension accounts 2.6.1
issue of certificates representing
  investments 2.6.1
limited liability partnerships 2.6.1
member-get-members schemes 2.6.1
occupational pension schemes *see*
  occupational pension schemes
open-ended investment company
  2.6.1
  definition 2.6, 2.6.2, 9.3.2
  investment condition 2.6.2
  Professions Order 4.2.5
  property condition 2.6.2
operators 9.5
overseas firms 3.29.7
periodic statements 9.9.2
permitted third parties 9.13
personal pension schemes 2.6.1, 9.15
pooling 2.6.1
Professions Order 4.2.5, 4.2.7
property, use or enjoyment of 2.6.1

pure deposit based schemes 2.6.1
recognised schemes 9.4.2, 9.7.1
regulated activities 3.21
scheme documents 9.9.1
scheme management activity 9.6
schemes not operated by way of
business 2.6.1
specialist regime 9.2
timeshare schemes 2.6.1
trading schemes 2.6.1
transferable securities 2.6
trustee firms *see* trustee firms
UK authorised funds 9.4.1
unit trusts 9.5.1
authorised unit trusts 9.4.1, 9.7.1
unregulated schemes 9.4.3
best execution 9.7.2, 9.8
COBS rules 9.7.2, 9.7.1, 9.8, 9.9
effect of rules on existing schemes
9.9.3
periodic statements 9.9.2
providers 9.5.3
scheme documents 9.9.1
Committee of European Securities
Regulators (CESR) 5.2.3
common accounts 2.6.1
Conduct of Business Sourcebook *see*
COBS rules
consumer credit business
COBS rules 5.2.2
contracts for differences 2.8
controlled investments
financial promotion 1.2.4
list 2.1
corporate finance business 9.16
COBS rules 5.2.6
MiFID business 9.17
non-MiFID business 9.18
stock lending activity 5.2.5, 9.22
see also energy market activity; oil
market activity
CREST
sending dematerialised instructions
3.20, 4.3.4
custody rules
MiFID custody rules 8.6
appointing sub-custodians 8.6.2.3

authorisation requirements 8.6.2.4
exclusions 8.6.1
general approach 8.6.2.1
instruments, using 8.6.2.5
jurisdictional requirements 8.6.2.4
monitoring sub-custodians 8.6.2.3
protecting client's proprietary
interest 8.6.2.2
reconciliations 8.6.2.6
rehypothecation 8.6.2.5
repos 8.6.2.5
scope 8.6.1
specific requirements 8.6.2
stock lending 8.6.2.5
non-MiFID custody rules 8.2, 8.3
account statements 8.3.2.8
affiliates 8.3.1
appointing sub-custodians 8.3.2.6
arrangers 8.3.1
authorised professional firms 8.3.1
bailment of tangibles 8.3.2.5
client agreement 8.3.2.7
delivery versus payment (DVP)
settlement 8.3.1
depositaries 8.3.1
depositories 8.3.1
depository receipts 8.3.1
eligible counterparties 8.3.1
monitoring sub-custodians 8.3.2.6
nominees 8.3.1
occupational pension schemes 8.3.1
protecting client's proprietary
interest 8.3.2.3
recognised collective investment
schemes 8.3.1
reconciliations 8.3.2.11
registration of intangibles 8.3.2.4
safe custody investments 8.3.2.10
scope 8.3.1
segregation 8.3.2.2
specific requirements 8.3.2
stock lending 8.3.2.10
sub-custody agreements 8.3.2.9
temporary custody 8.3.1
trustees 8.3.1
see also client asset regime
custody services 3.19

acceptance of responsibility by third
party 3.19.3.1
activities in connection with sale of
goods or supply of services 3.29.3
activities in course of profession or
non-investment business 3.29.2
activities not constituting
administration 3.19.3.3
Business Order 4.3.4
employee share schemes 3.29.6
groups 3.29.4
introduction to qualifying custodians
3.19.3.2
joint enterprises 3.29.4
overseas firms 3.29.7
Professions Order 4.2.7
regulated activities 3.19
exclusions 3.19.3, 3.29.1, 3.29.2,
3.29.3, 3.29.6, 3.29.7
trustees and personal representatives
3.29.1

dealing as agent 3.6
activities in connection with sale of
goods or supply of services 3.29.3
activities in course of profession or
non-investment business 3.29.2
Business Order 4.3.4
deals with or through authorised
persons 3.6.3.1
employee share schemes 3.29.6
groups 3.29.4
joint enterprises 3.29.4
overseas firms 3.29.7
regulated activities 3.6
exclusions 3.6.3, 3.29.2, 3.29.3,
3.29.4, 3.29.5, 3.29.7
risk management 3.6.3.2
sale of body corporate 3.29.5
dealing with clients 7.1, 7.2
appropriateness rule 7.2.3
best execution *see* best execution
client limit orders 7.2.6
client order handling 7.2.5
credit limit orders 7.2.6
information
about firm 7.2.1

compensation schemes 7.2.1.1
costs and associated charges 7.2.1.1
investment research *see* investment
research
personal account dealing 7.2.7
suitability rule 7.2.2
dealing as principal 3.5
acceptance of instruments creating or
acknowledging indebtedness
3.5.3.3
activities in connection with sale of
goods or supply of services 3.29.3
Business Order 4.3.4
contractually based investments
3.5.3.2
dealing by company in own shares
3.5.3.5
derivative instruments 3.5.3.6
employee share schemes 3.29.6
groups 3.29.4
issue by company of own shares
3.5.3.4
joint enterprises 3.29.4
overseas firms 3.29.7
Professions Order 4.2.5
regulated activities 3.5
exclusions 3.5.3, 3.29.1, 3.29.3,
3.29.7, 3.29.5, 3.29.6, 3.29.7
risk management 3.5.3.6
sale of body corporate 3.29.5
in securities and qualifying contracts,
but not on a professional basis
3.5.3.1
trustees and personal representatives
3.29.1
deals in investments, arranging
acceptance of debentures in
connection with loans 3.7.3.6
activities in course of profession or
non-investment business 3.29.2
arrangements not causing deal 3.7.3.1
Business Order 4.3.4
deals arranged with or through
authorised persons 3.7.3.4
enabling parties to communicate
3.7.3.2
finance provision 3.7.3.7

FSA guidance 3.7.4
groups 3.29.4
international securities self-regulating
    organisations 3.7.3.10
introductions 3.7.3.8
issue of shares etc. 3.7.3.9
joint enterprises 3.29.4
overseas firms 3.29.7
Professions Order 4.2.6, 4.2.7
regulated activities 3.7
    exclusions 3.7.3, 3.29.1, 3.29.2,
    3.29.3, 3.29.4, 3.29.7
transactions in connection with
    lending on security of insurance
    policies 3.7.3.5
transactions to which arranger is
    party 3.7.3.3
trustees 3.29.1
debenture stock 2.5
debentures 2.5
accepted in connection with loans
    3.7.3.6
debt issues 2.6.1
debt securities
sums received in consideration for
    2.2.4
**delivery versus payment settlement
    (DVP) systems**
client money rules
    MiFID 8.7.1
    non-MiFID rules 8.5.2.4
custody rules
    MiFID 8.6.1
    non-MiFID 8.3.1
dematerialised instructions *see* sending
    dematerialised instructions
depositary
COBS rules 9.11
custody rules 8.3.1
definition 9.10
trustee firms 9.11
depository
custody rules 8.3.1
depository receipts
custody rules 8.3.1
deposits
accepting 3.2

Business Order 4.3.2, 4.3.3
COBS rules 5.2.1
Professions Order 4.2.5
definition 2.2
exchange for electronic money 2.2.5
regulated activities 3.2
    exclusions 3.2.3
as specified investments 2.2
    exclusions 2.2.1–2.2.5
sums paid by certain persons 2.2.1
sums received by authorised persons
    2.2.3
sums received in consideration for
    issue of debt securities 2.2.4
sums received by solicitors 2.2.2
taking not by way of business 4.3.3
derivative instruments 2.8
contracts for differences 2.8
dealing as principal 3.5.3.6
futures 2.8
MiFID and 2.8.1
options 2.8
designated investment
activities 3.31
definition 3.31
**Designated Professional Bodies
    (DPBs)** 4.2.3
disclosure
COBS rules 5.3.5
distance contracts
definition 7.3.1
Distance Marketing Directive 7.3.1
information for clients 7.3
key features documents 7.3.2.1
means of distance communication
    7.3.1
preparation of product information
    7.3.2.1
provision of product information
    7.3.2.2

e-money *see* electronic money
Electronic Commerce Directive 5.2.3
electronic money
Business Order 4.3.5
FSA guidance 3.3.4
issuing 3.3, 4.3.5

Professions Order 4.2.5
regulated activities 3.3
  exclusions 3.3.3
specified investments 2.2.5, 2.3
eligible counterparties
best execution 7.2.4.1
client categorisation 6.1, 6.2.1, 6.6
  regulatory protections 6.10
COBS rules 5.2.2
custody rules 8.3.1
employee share schemes 2.6.1, 3.29.6
energy market activity
COBS rules 5.2.7, 9.19
  MiFID business 9.21
  non-MiFID business 9.20
enterprise capital funds
business angel-led 3.29.12
enterprise initiative schemes 2.6.1
equity release
home reversion plans 2.11.2
exclusion of liability
COBS rules 5.3.4
exempt person 2.1
meaning 1.2.1

financial promotion 1.2.4
COBS rules 1.2.5, 1.2.6
communication 1.2.4, 4.2.8
  authorised person 1.2.4
  cold calling 1.2.4
  contents requirements 1.2.5
  EEA territorial scope rule 1.2.6
  exempt 1.2.5
  non-real time 1.2.4, 4.2.8
  originating outside UK 1.2.4, 1.2.6
  real time 1.2.4, 4.2.8
  solicited communication 1.2.4
  unsolicited communication 1.2.4
controlled activity 1.2.4
controlled investment 1.2.4
criminal offence 1.2.4
defences 1.2.4
engaging in investment activity,
  definition 1.2.4
exemptions 1.2.5
FSA Guidance 3.12.4
  effects 4.2.8–4.2.9

identification as 1.2.6
indications 1.2.4
  degree of prominence 1.2.5
Professions Order 4.2.8
prohibition 1.2.4
  exemptions 1.2.5
record-keeping 1.2.5, 1.2.6
systems and controls requirement
  1.2.6
Financial Promotion Order 1.2.5, 4.2.8
exemptions 1.2.5
indications 1.2.5
non-real time communications 1.2.4,
  4.2.8
real time communications 1.2.4, 4.2.8
solicited and unsolicited
  communications distinguished
  1.2.4
franchise arrangements 2.6.1
funeral plan contracts 2.6.1, 2.10
definition 2.10
Professions Order 4.2.5
regulated activities 3.24
futures 2.8
futures firms
client money regime 8.5.2.9

government securities 2.5
groups of companies
regulated activities 3.29.4

head office
identifying 1.3.3.2
home purchase plans *see* regulated
  home purchase plans
home reversion plans *see* regulated
  home reversion plans

inducements
COBS rules 5.3.6–5.3.9
  exceptions 5.3.7
packaged products 5.3.8
reasonable non-monetary benefits
  5.3.8
record of disclosures 5.3.9
information for clients 7.1, 7.3
about firm 7.2.1

cancellation rights 7.3.3
compensation schemes 7.2.1.1
costs and associated charges 7.2.1.1
designated investments 7.3.3
distance contracts *see* distance
    contracts
key features documents 7.3.2.1
occasional reporting 7.3.5.1
packaged products 7.3
periodic reporting 7.3.5.2, 9.9.2
preparation of product information
    7.3.2.1
provision of product information
    7.3.2.2
reporting information to clients 7.3.5
withdrawal rights 7.3.4
information society services 3.29.8
**instruments creating or acknowledging
    indebtedness** 2.5
acceptance of 3.4.3.3
**instruments giving entitlements to
    investments** 2.5
insurance 2.4
acting as principal 3.4.1, 3.4.4
administration 3.18
    exclusions 3.18.3, 3.29.1, 3.29.2
breakdown insurance 3.4.3.2
Business Order 4.3.6
claims management services 3.18.3
Community co-insurers 3.4.3.1
complementary insurance 3.29.9
contract of insurance
    definition 2.4
    as transferable security 2.5
IMD firms, exclusions not available
    3.30, 3.30.2
intermediaries 3.4.4
    Business Order 4.3.6
    "by way of business test" 3.29.4.1
    groups and joint enterprises 3.29.4
    Record of Insurance Intermediaries
        4.2.6
    third-party processors 5.2.2
introducing insurance 3.29.10
large risks situated outside EEA
    3.29.1
long-term contract 2.4

COBS rules 5.2.1
marketing, advice and intermediation
    2.4
Professions Order 4.2.5, 4.2.6
providing 3.4
qualifying contract of insurance,
    definition 2.4
regulated activities
    acting as principal 3.4.1, 3.4.4
    administration 3.18
    exclusions 3.4.3, 3.18.3
    exclusions not available to IMD
        firms 3.30, 3.30.2
    general exclusions 3.29.1, 3.29.2,
        3.29.9, 3.29.10
    providing 3.4
related to supply of goods or services
    3.29.9
as specified investment 2.4
transactions in connection with
    lending on security of insurance
    policies 3.7.3.5
travel agents 3.29.9
trustees and personal representatives
    3.29.1
see also packaged products
Insurance Mediation Directive (IMD)
    3.30, 3.30.2, 4.2.6
territorial scope 5.2.3
**International Capital Market
    Association** 3.7.3.10
**international securities self-regulating
    organisations** 3.7.3.10
introductions
custody services 3.19.3.2
insurance 3.29.10
regulated activities 3.7.3.8, 3.9.3.2,
    3.19.3.2, 3.29.10
**investment company with variable
    capital (ICVC)** 9.4.1, 9.5.2, 9.7.1,
    9.10
investment research 7.2.8
conflicts of interest 7.2.8.1
definition 7.2.8.1
independent research 7.2.8.1
non-independent research 7.2.8.2
research recommendations 7.2.83

Islamic finance 2.11.3
  see also regulated home purchase
    plans

joint enterprises
  regulated activities 3.29.4

leasehold property
  funds relating to 2.6.1
letter of credit 2.5
limited liability partnerships 2.6.1
Lloyd's
  Business Order 4.3.4
  COBS rules 5.2.2
  Professions Order 4.2.5, 4.2.6
  regulated activities 3.23
  underwriting interests 2.9
loan stock 2.5
loans
  debentures accepted in connection
    with 3.7.3.6

managing investments 3.17
  activities in connection with sale of
    goods or supply of services 3.29.3
  attorneys 3.17.3.1
  Business Order 4.3.4
    occupational pension schemes 4.3.5
  COBS rules 5.2.2
  custody rules *see* client asset regime
  groups 3.29.4
  individual investment management
    arrangements 2.6.1
  information about firm 7.2.1
  joint enterprises 3.29.4
  occupational pension schemes 4.3.5
  overseas firms 3.29.7
  periodic statements 7.3.5.2, 9.9.2
  Professions Order 4.2.6, 4.2.7
  regulated activities 3.17
    exclusions 3.17.3, 3.29.1, 3.29.4,
      3.29.7
  suitability rule 7.2.2
  trustees or personal representatives
    3.29.1
market counterparty
  carrying on activities with 5.2.2

client categorisation 6.8
COBS rules 5.2.2
**Markets in Financial Instruments
  Directive (MiFID)** 1.1
  application to non-MiFID business
    5.1
  branches of third-country firms 5.1
  client asset regime *see* client money
    regime; custody rules
  client categorisation *see* client
    categorisation
  COBS rules and 5.1, 5.2.2, 5.2.3, 5.3.1
  country of origin approach 5.2.3
  derivative instruments 2.8.1
  operation of multilateral trading
    facility 3.11
  passporting rights 1.3.1, 8.1
  requirements 5.1
  specialist regimes 9.1.2
  trustee firms 9.13.2–9.13.3
mortgages
  advice 3.13, 3.29.2
    Professions Order 4.2.6
  arranging 3.8, 3.29.2
  Business Order 4.3.7
  lending under and administering
    mortgages 3.29.1
  overseas firms 3.29.7
  regulated activities 3.8, 3.13, 3.25
    exclusions 3.25.3, 3.29.1, 3.29.2,
      3.29.7
  regulated mortgage contracts 2.11.1,
    3.25, 4.2.5
    activities in course of profession
      or non-investment business
      3.29.2
    administration pursuant to
      agreement with authorised
      person 3.25.3.2
    arranging administration by
      authorised person 3.25.3.1
    Business Order 4.3.2, 4.3.7
    definition 2.11.1
multilateral trading facility operation
  Business Order 4.3.4
  COBS rules 5.2.2
  regulated activities 3.11

National Savings Bank 2.5
nominees
general exclusions 3.29.1

occupational pension schemes 2.6.1,
9.15
Business Order 4.3.5
custody rules 8.3.1
firms 9.15.2
regulation 9.15.4
managing investments 4.3.5
position 9.15.1
Professions Order 4.2.6
scheme activity 9.15.3
oil market activity
COBS rules 5.2.7, 9.19
MiFID business 9.21
non-MiFID business 9.20
**open-ended investment company
(OEIC)** 2.6.1, 2.6.2
custody rules 8.3.1
definition 2.6, 2.6.2, 9.3.2
investment condition 2.6.2
Professions Order 4.2.5
property condition 2.6.2
options 2.8
order handling *see* dealing with clients
overseas firms
general exclusions 3.29.7

packaged products
COBS rules 5.3.8
Distance Marketing Directive 7.3.1
inducements 5.3.8
information requirements 7.3
key features documents 7.3.2.1
pension schemes
Business Order 4.3.4
client categorisation 6.3
Professions Order 4.2.7, 4.2.6
see also occupational pension schemes;
personal pension schemes;
stakeholder pension schemes
periodic statements 7.3.5.2, 9.9.2
**permission to carry on regulated
activities** 1.2.2
applications 1.3.1

application pack 1.3.2
consideration process 1.3.2
EEA firms 1.3.1
limitations 1.3.4
procedure 1.3.2
requirements 1.3.4
Threshold Conditions 1.3.3
adequate resources 1.3.3.4
close links 1.3.3.3
fit and proper person 1.3.3.5
head office, identifying 1.3.3.2
legal status 1.3.3.1
location of offices 1.3.3.2
suitability 1.3.3.5
personal account dealing 7.2.7
see also dealing with clients
personal pension schemes
advice 4.2.6
client categorisation 6.3
definition 2.7.2
Professions Order 4.2.6
regulated activities 3.22
rights under, as specified investment
2.7.2
personal representatives
advising on investments 3.29.1
custody services 3.29.1
dealing as principal 3.29.1
insurance 3.29.1
managing investments 3.29.1
regulated activities 3.29.1
general exclusions 3.29.1
sending dematerialised instructions
3.20.3.3
principal
dealing as *see* dealing as principal
profession, activities in course of
general exclusions 3.29.2
Professions Order 4.2
accepting deposits 4.2.5
advising on investments 4.2.6, 4.2.7
collective investment schemes 4.2.5,
4.2.7
custody services 4.2.7
dealing as principal 4.2.5
deals in investments, arranging 4.2.6,
4.2.7

Designated Professional Bodies
(DPBs) 4.2.3, 4.2.7
electronic money issues 4.2.5
financial promotion 4.2.8
funeral plan contracts 4.2.5
insurance 4.2.5, 4.2.6
Lloyd's 4.2.5, 4.2.6
managing investments 4.2.6, 4.2.7
non-exempt activities
completely non-exempt 4.2.5
subject to conditions 4.2.6
open-ended investment company
4.2.5
pension schemes 4.2.7, 4.2.6
retail mortgages 4.2.6
RPB regime compared 4.2.1–4.2.2
simplification 4.2.2
specified activities 4.2.4
stakeholder products 4.2.5
Treasury Order and 4.2.3
trustees 4.2.5
prohibited activities
general prohibition 1.2.1
public securities 2.5

Quistclose trust 8.5.1

Record of Insurance Intermediaries
4.2.6
records
client categorisation 6.7
COBS rules 1.2.5, 1.2.6, 5.3.9, 6.7
financial promotion 1.2.5, 1.2.6
inducement disclosures 5.3.9
regulated activities 1.1, 1.2.2, 1.2.3, 3.1
advising on investments *see* advising
on investments
agreeing to carry on 3.28
authorised person 2.1
meaning 1.2.1
body corporate, activities carried on
in connection with sale 3.29.5
business angel-led enterprise capital
funds 3.29.12
"carried on by way of business" 1.2.3,
3.29.4.1
collective investments, providing 3.21

criminal offence 2.1
custody services *see* custody services
dealing as agent *see* dealing as agent
dealing as principal *see* dealing as
principal
deals in investments *see* deals in
investments
definition 1.2.3, 2.1
deposits, accepting 3.2
exclusions 3.2.3
employee share schemes 3.29.6
exclusions not available to IMD firms
3.30, 3.30.2
exclusions not available to MiFID
firms 3.30, 3.30.1
exempt person 2.1
meaning 1.2.1
FSA guidance 3.7.4
funeral plans 3.24
general exclusions
activities in connection with
employee share schemes 3.29.6
activities in connection with sale of
goods or supply of services
3.29.3
activities in course of profession
or non-investment business
3.29.2
body corporate, activities carried
on in connection with sale 3.29.5
business angel-led enterprise
capital funds 3.29.12
groups 3.29.4
information society services 3.29.8
insurance 3.29.1, 3.29.2, 3.29.9,
3.29.10
introducing insurance 3.29.10
joint enterprises 3.29.4
large risks situated outside EEA
3.29.1
nominees 3.29.1
overseas firms 3.29.7
personal representatives 3.29.1
supply of goods or services and
related insurance 3.29.9
travel agents 3.29.9
trustees 3.29.1

groups 3.29.4
home purchase plans *see* regulated
    home purchase plans
home reversion plans *see* regulated
    home reversion plans
information society services 3.29.8
insurance *see* insurance
introductions 3.7.3.8, 3.9.3.2
    custody services 3.19.3.2
    insurance 3.29.10
investments
joint enterprises 3.29.4
limitations 1.3.4
Lloyd's 3.23
managing investments *see* managing
    investments
mortgages *see* mortgages
multilateral trading facility operation
    3.11
nominees 3.29.1
non-investment business 3.29.2
non-mainstream 5.2.1
overseas firms 3.29.7
pension scheme, providing 3.22
permission requirement *see*
    permission to carry on regulated
    activities
personal pension scheme, providing
    3.22
personal representatives 3.29.1
profession, activities in course of
    3.29.2
requirements 1.3.4
sale of body corporate, activities
    carried on in connection with
    3.29.5
sale of goods 3.29.3
sending dematerialised instructions
    see sending dematerialised
    instructions
specified investments *see* specified
    investments
stakeholder pension, providing 3.22
stakeholder products, basic advice
    3.16
supply of services 3.29.3
trustees 3.29.1

regulated home purchase plans 2.11.3
    advice 3.15
    arrangement 3.10
    Business Order 4.3.2, 4.3.7
    definition 2.11.3
    regulated activities 3.15, 3.27
regulated home reversion plans 2.11.2
    advice 3.14
    arrangement 3.9
    Business Order 4.3.2, 4.3.7
    definition 2.11.2
    regulated activities 3.9, 3.14, 3.26
regulated mortgage contract *see*
    mortgages
reliance on others
    COBS rules 5.3.11
reporting information to clients 7.3.5
    periodic statements 7.3.5.2, 9.9.2
research *see* investment research

**safeguarding and administering
    investments** *see* custody services
sale of goods
    activities in connection with 3.29.3
    related insurance 3.29.9
Second Banking Directive
    passporting rights 1.3.1
securities
    dealing in 3.4.3.1
sending dematerialised instructions
    3.20
    Business Order 4.3.4
    in course of providing a network
        3.20.3.2
    CREST 3.20, 4.3.4
    groups 3.29.4
    investments held by a trustee or
        personal representative 3.20.3.3
    joint enterprises 3.29.4
    offerors 3.20.3.1
    overseas firms 3.29.7
    participating issuers 3.20.3.1
    regulated activities 3.20
        exclusions 3.20.3, 3.29.1, 3.29.4,
            3.29.7
    settlement banks 3.20.3.1
    trustees 3.29.1

share options 2.5
shares
  dealing by company in own shares
    3.5.3.5
  employee share schemes 2.6.1, 3.29.6
  issue of
    arrangements for 3.7.3.9
    own shares by company 3.5.3.4
  sale of body corporate 3.29.5
shares and stock 2.5
solicitors
  client money regime 8.5.2.6
  sums received by 2.2.2
specified investments 2.1
  collective investments schemes 2.5
  contracts for differences 2.8
  contractually based investment,
    definition 2.13
  deposits 2.2
    exclusions 2.2.1–2.2.5
  derivative instruments 2.8
  electronic money 2.2.5, 2.3
  equity release 2.11.2
  funeral plan contracts 2.10
  futures 2.8
  home reversion plans 2.11.2
  insurance 2.4
  Islamic finance 2.11.3
  list 2.1
  Lloyd's underwriting interests 2.9
  open-ended investment company 2.6.2
  options 2.8
  overlap between different types 2.13
  regulated home purchase plans 2.11.3
  relevant investment, definition 2.13
  residential mortgage contracts 2.11.1
  rights to or interests in investments
    2.12
  rights under pension schemes
    personal pensions 2.7.2
    stakeholder pensions 2.7.1, 2.13
  security, definition 2.13
  sums paid by certain persons 2.2.1
  sums received
    authorised persons, by 2.2.3
    issue of debt securities, in
      consideration for 2.2.4

  solicitors, by 2.2.2
  transferable securities 2.5
    see also transferable securities
stakeholder pension schemes
  advice on rights under 3.16.2
  client categorisation 6.3
  definition 2.7.1
  overseas firms 3.29.7
  regulated activities 3.22
  rights under, as specified investment
    2.7.1, 2.13
  see also packaged products
stakeholder products
  basic advice 3.16, 4.2.5
  Child Trust Fund 3.16.2
  Professions Order 4.2.5
stock lending activity
  COBS rules 5.2.5, 9.22
suitability rule 7.2.2
supply of services
  activities in connection with 3.29.3
  related insurance 3.29.9

takeover offer
  meaning 3.20.3.1
timeshare schemes 2.6.1
trading schemes 2.6.1
transferable securities 2.5
  bonds 2.5
  certificates of deposit 2.5
  certificates representing certain
    securities 2.5
  collective investments 2.5
  debenture stock 2.5
  debentures 2.5
  definition of "security" 2.5
  government securities 2.5
  instruments creating or
    acknowledging indebtedness 2.5
  instruments giving entitlements to
    investments 2.5
  loan stock 2.5
  pension rights 2.5
  public securities 2.5
  share options 2.5
  shares and stock 2.5
travel agents 3.29.9

TRAX system 3.7.3.10
Treasury Order 4.2.3
trustee firms
  bare trustees 9.12
  client money regime 8.5.2.7
  depositaries 9.11
  MiFID 9.13.2–9.13.3
  nature 9.12
  non-depositories 9.13
  obtaining proper advice 9.14
  specialist regimes 9.2
trustees
  administration of insurance 3.29.1
  advising on investments 3.29.1
  arranging deals and mortgages 3.29.1
  client asset regime
    client money regime 8.5.2.7
    custody rules 8.3.1
  client categorisation 6.3
  custody services 3.29.1
  dealing as principal 3.29.1

dematerialised instructions 3.20.3.3
general exclusions 3.29.1
managing investments 3.29.1
mortgages
  advising on 3.29.1
  lending under and administrating
    3.29.1
occupational pension schemes 4.3.8
Professions Order 4.2.5
sending dematerialised instructions
  3.29.1
see also Child Trust Fund; Client
  Money Trust

unit trusts 9.5.1
authorised unit trusts 9.4.1, 9.7.1
depositary 9.10
Professions Order 4.2.5
see also packaged products

withdrawal rights 7.3.4

CURRENT TITLES AVAILABLE FROM
CITY & FINANCIAL PUBLISHING

Book Title	Price
Compliance Officer Bulletin – Published 10 times per year	£299 p.a.
A Practitioner's Guide to The FSA Handbook – 5th Edition	£99
A Practitioner's Guide to The FSA Regulation of Designated Investment Business – 3rd Edition	£95
A Practitioner's Guide to The AIM Rules – 5th Edition	£89
A Practitioner's Guide to The City Code on Takeovers and Mergers 2008/2009	£99
U.S. Regulation for Asset Managers Outside the United States	£95
A Practitioner's Guide to Financial Promotion – 2nd Edition	£89
A Practitioner's Guide to Mortgage Regulation	£79
A Practitioner's Guide to Directors' Duties and Responsibilities – 3rd Edition	£95
A Practitioner's Guide to The Financial Services Authority Listing Regime 2007/2008	£95
A Practitioner's Guide to MiFID	£85
A Practitioner's Guide to FSA Investigations and Enforcement – 2nd Edition	£85
U.S. Securities Laws and Foreign Private Issuers	£95
A Practitioner's Guide to The FSA Regulation of Banking – 2nd Edition	£85
A Practitioner's Guide to EU Financial Services Directives – 2nd Edition	£85
A Practitioner's Guide to The FSA Regulation of Investment Banking – 2nd Edition	£85
A Practitioner's Guide to Inside Information	£85
Outsourcing Contracts – A Practical Guide – 2nd Edition	£70
A Practitioner's Guide to Securitisation	£95
Pensions Risk and Strategy	£59
A Practitioner's Guide to Takeovers and Mergers in the European Union – 4th Edition	£130
Consumer Complaints and Compensation: A Guide for the Financial Services Market	£60
A Practitioner's Guide to Alternative Investment Funds	£85
A Practitioner's Guide to The Basel Accord	£85
International Insider Dealing	£130
A Practitioner's Guide to The FSA Regulation of Lloyd's – 2nd Edition	£75
A Practitioner's Guide to The FSA Regulation of Insurance – 2nd Edition	£75
Practical Company Law and Corporate Transactions	£85
A Practitioner's Guide to UK Money Laundering Law and Regulation	£80
A Practitioner's Guide International Money Laundering Law and Regulation	£130

SPECIAL OFFER – Buy any combination of 5 titles and get the lowest priced free of charge

Post and packing

The following amounts should be added up to a maximum of £50
UK:	£5 per copy
Europe:	£8 per copy
Rest of world:	£10 per copy

How to order

By post . . .
Send your order, along with your payment to:
City & Financial Publishing, 8 Westminster Court, Hipley Street
Old Woking, Surrey. GU22 9LG United Kingdom

By fax . . .
If you wish to pay by credit card or BACS, or if you require an invoice,
fax your order to: 00 44 (0)1483 727928

Or order online
www.cityandfinancial.com